Few volumes confront the big questions of how we interpret our place in a rapidly changing world as well as this elegant collection of essays. A major contribution to the emerging field of Anthropocene studies, this volume should be read by anyone interested in how we have come to understand our current predicament and what this means for the future of humanity.

Simon Dalby, *CIGI Chair in the Political Economy of Climate Change, Balsillie School of International Affairs, Wilfrid Laurier University*

In this fascinating new book, scholars from different disciplines provide fresh insights into the concept of globality and its appropriation within an array of political and ideological contexts since 1945. By exposing the inherent ambiguities and contradictory meanings of globality, the authors offer a critical analysis of its contemporary usage from a wide variety of perspectives. It should be read by anyone interested in the contested foundations of globalization and world politics.

Jens Bartelson, *Professor of Political Science, Department of Political Science, Lund University, Sweden*

The Politics of Globality since 1945

This timely, comprehensive and interdisciplinary volume advances an original argument about the complex roots and multiple politics of globality. It shows that technological innovations and decisive developments since 1945 – from the nuclear revolution to anthropogenic climate change and debates about the Anthropocene – have prompted reflections on the global condition of humanity and helped reshape political communities by making the world (appear) small, manageable and interconnected.

The contributors stress how human beings have transformed both their habitat and their view of human-Earth relations since 1945. Such changes have been accompanied by important shifts in political visions, prompted new forms of human association, encouraged legal and institutional reform and spurred ideas about ecological humility. At the same time, the spatially all-encompassing nature of globality has also informed projects of human mastery and a range of practices historically associated with militarization and a strongly statist conception of national security. This volume reflects on these paradoxical relationships, their history and contemporary relevance.

Contributing to the overlapping concerns of four burgeoning fields of study across the humanities and the social sciences – globality and globalization studies; geopolitics and political geography; Anthropocene studies; global governance and political theory – the book will be of great use to scholars and graduates working in these areas.

Rens van Munster is senior researcher at the Danish Institute for International Studies (DIIS). Located at the intersection of IR theory and critical security studies, his research critically interrogates practices of security and risk management, with a particular focus on the politics and governance of catastrophes.

Casper Sylvest is associate professor at the Department of History, University of Southern Denmark. Combining the study of politics, history, law and technology, most of his work has examined realist and liberal visions of international and global politics during the nineteenth and twentieth centuries.

New International Relations

Edited by Richard Little, University of Bristol, Iver B. Neumann, Norwegian Institute of International Affairs (NUPI), Norway and Jutta Weldes, University of Bristol.

The field of international relations has changed dramatically in recent years. This new series will cover the major issues that have emerged and reflect the latest academic thinking in this particular dynamic area.

The Politics of Globality since 1945

Assembling the planet

Edited by
Rens van Munster and Casper Sylvest

Routledge
Taylor & Francis Group

LONDON AND NEW YORK

First published 2016
by Routledge
2 Park Square, Milton Park, Abingdon, Oxon OX14 4RN

and by Routledge
711 Third Avenue, New York, NY 10017

Routledge is an imprint of the Taylor & Francis Group, an informa business

British Library Cataloguing in Publication Data
A catalogue record for this book is available from the British Library

Library of Congress Cataloging in Publication Data
Names: Munster, Rens van, 1977- editor. | Sylvest, Casper, editor.
   Title: The politics of globality since 1945 : assembling the planet / edited by Rens van Munster & Casper Sylvest.
   Description: New York, NY : Routledge, 2016. | Series: New international relations | Includes bibliographical references and index.
   Identifiers: LCCN 2016002119| ISBN 9781138645622 (hardback) | ISBN 9781315628059 (ebook)
   Subjects: LCSH: Globalization. | International relations. | World politics–1945-1989. | World politics–1989-
   Classification: LCC JZ1320 .P66 2016 | DDC 327.09/045–dc23
LC record available at http://lccn.loc.gov/2016002119

ISBN: 978-1-138-64562-2 (hbk)
ISBN: 978-1-31562-805-9 (ebk)

Typeset in Times New Roman
by Taylor & Francis Books

Contents

List of figures

Contributors

Tanja E. Aalberts is Senior Researcher in the Department of Transnational Legal Studies, VU Amsterdam. Her research and publications focus on the interplay of law and politics in practices of global governance. She has recently co-edited *Power of Legality. Practices of International Law and their Politics* (Cambridge University Press, 2016), and is series editor of the Routledge bookseries on Politics of Transnational Law.

Jenny Andersson is CNRS Research Professor at the Center for European Studies at Sciences Po, Paris and Director for the ERC-funded project 'Futurepol' on knowledge production and future governance in the post-war period. She is the author of *Between Growth and Security: Swedish Social Democracy from a Strong Society to a Third Way* (Manchester University Press, 2006) and *The Library and the Workshop: Social Democracy and Capitalism in an Age of Knowledge* (Stanford University Press, 2009). Her latest work on 'the future' as a category of action appeared in the *American Historical Review*.

Nigel Clark is Professor of Human Geography at the Lancaster Environment Centre, Lancaster University, UK. He is the author of *Inhuman Nature: Sociable Life on a Dynamic Planet* (Sage, 2011), co-editor of *Material Geographies* (Sage, 2008), *Extending Hospitality: Giving Space, Taking Time* (Edinburgh University Press, 2009) and *Atlas: Geography, Architecture and Change in an Interdependent World* (Black Dog, 2012). He is currently co-editing a special issue of *Theory, Culture & Society* on 'Geosocial Formations and the Anthropocene' and researching a book on 'human geology'.

Campbell Craig is Professor of International Politics at Cardiff University and has been a Senior Research Fellow at the Nobel Institute (2009), the European University Institute in Florence (2013) and University of Bristol (2015). He is the author of numerous books and articles, including *Glimmer of a New Leviathan. Total War in the Realism of Niebuhr, Morgenthau, and Waltz* (Columbia University Press, 2003), *The Atomic Bomb and the Origins of the Cold War* (Yale University Press, 2008, with Sergey Radchenko) and

America's Cold War. The Politics of Insecurity (Harvard University Press, 2009, with Fredrik Logevall).

Daniel Deudney is Associate Professor in Political Science at Johns Hopkins University, Baltimore. He has published widely on matters related to international relations and political theory, including nuclear weapons, security and American foreign policy. He is the author of *Bounding Power: Republican Security Theory from the Polis to the Global Village* (Princeton University Press, 2007), which received the International Studies Association's Book of the Decade Award in 2010.

Sibylle Duhautois is a PhD student at the Centre d'histoire at Sciences Po, Paris and is affiliated with the ERC-funded project Futurepol on knowledge production and future governance in the post-war period. Her PhD project focuses on the notion of 'long-term world problems'. It examines how, after the Second World War, the future was constructed as a global issue that needed specific forms of expertise and international governance.

Paul N. Edwards is Professor in the School of Information and the Department of History at the University of Michigan. He is the author of *A Vast Machine: Computer Models, Climate Data, and the Politics of Global Warming* (MIT Press, 2010) – named a 'Book of the Year' by *The Economist* magazine and awarded two prizes by the American Meteorological Society – and *The Closed World: Computers and the Politics of Discourse in Cold War America* (MIT Press, 1996). His current research concerns knowledge infrastructures for the Anthropocene.

Joseph Masco is Professor of Anthropology at the University of Chicago. He is the author of *The Nuclear Borderlands: The Manhattan Project in Post-Cold War New Mexico* (Princeton University Press, 2006), which won the 2014 J.I. Staley Prize from the School of Advanced Research and the 2008 Rachel Carson Prize from the Society for Social Studies of Science, and *The Theater of Operations: National Security Affect from the Cold War to the War on Terror* (Duke University Press, 2014). He is currently researching a book on the environmental crisis and the evolution of planetary thinking.

Elizabeth Mendenhall is a PhD candidate in International Relations at Johns Hopkins University, Baltimore. In 2011 she graduated from Kansas State University with a BA in Political Science and Philosophy and won the 2011 Cross Examination Debate Association national championship in policy debate. Her research interests include ocean governance, grand strategy and the relationships between science, technology and politics.

Rens van Munster is Senior Researcher at the Danish Institute for International Studies (DIIS). His research critically interrogates practices of security and risk management, with a particular focus on the politics and governance of catastrophes. His most recent book is *Nuclear Realism:*

Global Political Thought during the Thermonuclear Revolution (Routledge, 2016, with Casper Sylvest).

Columba Peoples is Senior Lecturer in International Relations in the School of Sociology, Politics and International Studies (SPAIS) at the University of Bristol. He is the author of *Justifying Ballistic Missile Defence: Technology, Security and Culture* (Cambridge University Press, 2010) and has published articles in *Review of International Studies, Contemporary Security Policy, Cold War History* and *Cambridge Review of International Affairs.*

Samuel Randalls is Lecturer at the Department of Geography, University College London. Prior to that he was a James Martin Fellow at the University of Oxford. He is the co-editor of the Routledge four-volume project on *Future Climate Change* and has published widely on the relationship between weather and economy, including weather futures trading, histories of climate change economics, and Victorian weather insurance. His work has appeared in *Environment and Planning A, Environment and Planning D, Geoforum* and *Social Studies of Science.*

Casper Sylvest is Associate Professor at the Department of History, University of Southern Denmark. He is the author of *British Liberal Internationalism, 1880–1930: Making Progress?* (Manchester University Press, 2009) and a series of articles on visions of international and global politics during the during the nineteenth and twentieth centuries that have appeared in *Review of International Studies, Modern Intellectual History, International Studies Quarterly, International Theory, International History Review* and *Security Dialogue*. His latest book, with Rens van Munster, is *Nuclear Realism: Global Political Thought during the Thermonuclear Revolution* (Routledge, 2016).

Wouter G. Werner is Professor in Public International Law at the Department of Transnational Legal Studies, VU University Amsterdam. His research focuses on international legal theory, the role of experts in international law and visual representations of international criminal law. Together with Tanja Aalberts he is series editor of the Routledge book series on Politics of Transnational Law.

Foreword

Looking back on the early years of the Cold War when it has been argued that the formal study of international relations was first established, or at least institutionalized, it is often argued that the newly emerging discipline was beset by what later came to be seen as the putative sin of state-centrism. International Relations was ubiquitously defined as the study of the behaviour of states interacting in an international system. The prevailing metaphors, it is argued, helped to consolidate this approach. States were envisaged as chess pieces locked in combat in an international system portrayed as a chess board or in John Herz's well-worn image in *International Politics in the Atomic Age* states are depicted as billiard balls banging in to each other on a billiard table which serves as the international system. Often, it is argued that it was the Cold War itself that helped to generate such images. The United States and the Soviet Union were depicted as rational actors engaged in strategic interaction such that the outcome of any encounter was determined by the intersection of the two independent decisions made by these superpowers. Such encounters could very easily be modeled by drawing on the matrices established by mathematical game theorists. Although most analysis at this time did not explicitly draw on formal game theory, the basic idea of treating states as rational actors was pervasive.

But the depiction of international relation as a kind of game played by impermeable and rational actors was always contestable and contested and as the Cold War wore on, more ominous metaphors began to emerge. The revisionist historian, Louis Halle, for example, in *The Cold War as History* described the Soviet Union and the United States as two scorpions in a bottle. Here the ludic associations of the earlier metaphors gave way to an altogether more existential image. Moreover with the development of thermonuclear weapons by both the United States and the Soviet Union, it was extraordinarily difficult not to be aware of the danger and real possibility of what sometimes came to be called a nuclear holocaust. Yet curiously with the end of the Cold War, despite the continued existence and indeed proliferation of nuclear weapons, for many the threat appears to have receded into the background. One of the central aims of this book is to reassert the continuing importance of nuclear weapons and to recognize that with the development of nuclear weapons the world entered a completely new era.

Although most scholars in International Relations acknowledged that the emergence of nuclear weapons had transformed the international arena in a fundamental way, they nevertheless continued to rely on a vocabulary that continued to reflect an earlier era. This orientation persisted despite the fact that in other disciplines there was a growing recognition that there was a need to take account of globality which acknowledged that a transformation had taken place in the world. Globality is sometimes seen as the hypothetical end point of globalization – a process that has been going on for centuries – indeed millennia in some accounts. But this is not how globality is treated in this fascinating book. In the first place, it is not an end point but an ongoing process and, second, globality is best seen as a process that has only came into its own in the second half of the twentieth century. The approach adopted in the book is inherently inter-disciplinary and transcends the divide between the natural and social sciences but it also shows that the approach has particularly important implications for International Relations. Although the idea of globality is highly contested, as this book clearly shows, at the very least globality denotes the idea of the world as a single space. Astronauts have noted that when they first view the Earth from space they tend to focus on where they live and then their own country and continent but very soon they are mainly aware of the Earth as a single entity. Of course, planet Earth has been represented as a globe since the fifteenth century when globes representing the Earth began to be given to rulers as gifts. But at that time it was not the singularity of the Earth that drew attention but rather it was the vast areas of territory available for conquest that came into focus.

From space, by contrast, astronauts have been struck by how beautiful, delicate and potentially vulnerable the planet appears to be. Globality operates from this perspective and draws attention to how briefly humans have inhabited planet Earth and by the same token how powerful the geological forces are that can affect the course of the Earth's history and over which humans have absolutely no control. But, at the same time, globality draws attention to the fact that humans can now also affect the Earth, as a whole, in potentially devastating ways. This kind of perspective has huge implications for the study of international relations and it is to be hoped that this book will help to nudge the discipline in a direction where such a perspective will be more fully taken into account. In the orthodox study of international relations, the international system is treated as an arena that shapes and moulds the behaviour of states. And in terms of the ludic metaphors that have been generated within the discipline, the international system has no meaning outside of the game being played by the states. There is nothing intrinsically wrong with this perspective but it is very circumscribed and potentially very dangerous. It is possible to view climate talks or arms control meetings as a kind of game where each state wishes to come off best. But a globality perspective forces us to step back and widen our focus and recognize that there are more far-reaching consequences for the games that states play.

Richard Little, University of Bristol

Preface

Most of the chapters collected in this volume were originally presented at a conference on 'Constructions of Globality: Ideas, Artefacts and Images' in Copenhagen, 17–18 June 2013. We are greatly indebted to several colleagues who participated in this conference and extended and challenged our early ideas about the politics of globality: Claudia Aradau, Duncan Bell, Myra Hird, Charles Jones, Robert Poole, Bill Scheuerman, Robin May Schott, Jeppe Strandsbjerg and Ole Wæver. Several papers on the multiple dimensions of globality before 1945 inspired lively discussions about how to study the politics of globality and helped us enormously in clarifying our original ambition for the book. At this stage conversations with Jens Bartelson, Simon Dalby and Ole Jacob Sending were also immensely helpful. Having decided to focus on the post-1945 period and bring in new themes, we organized a workshop at the National Museum in Copenhagen, 24–25 April 2014. It was at this stage that the book took shape. Again, we and the authors benefited from the comments and interventions by other participants, including Signe Blaabjerg Christoffersen, Steven Jensen, Johannes Lang and (again) Robin May Schott. As editors, we gratefully acknowledge the support of the Danish Research Council for Independent Research and the COST Action on the Constitutionalization and Fragmentation of International Law without which the conference and the workshop would not have been possible. We would also like to thank the contributing authors for their patience and for their willingness to engage in a dialogue about globality and its politics. Finally, we thank everyone at Routledge, including the series editors, for their interest in and commitment to the project.

Copenhagen, November 2015
Rens van Munster and Casper Sylvest

Introduction

Rens van Munster and Casper Sylvest

The fundamental event of modernity is the conquest of the world as picture.
Martin Heidegger (2002 [1938])

The most dramatic impact of the Apollo missions, journalist and writer Norman Cousins said in 1975, 'was not that men set foot on the Moon, but set eye on the Earth'. In this brief sentence, Cousins astutely captured that alongside the vast political, cultural and ideological conflicts of the twentieth century, a pervasive sense of globality or oneness had emerged. This oneness is still with us. It is reflected in a range of ideas and practices, including the ubiquitous use of global maps and iconography and the proclamation of planetary problems of security or ecology, as well as in omnipresent invocations of a common humanity. Globality, however, is the harbinger of multi-directional change. Imaginaries of globality draw on different popular and scientific metaphors and can take many different institutional forms, ranging from a (republican or federal) world state and global functional regimes to more shady forms of governance and empire. They may prompt new forms of human association and encourage ecological humility but have just as often informed projects of imperial violence and military power projection. The politics of globality is not a one-way street.

The aim of this interdisciplinary volume is to examine the politics of globality since 1945. By approaching this theme from a variety of perspectives, the book pushes a common concern with the production and implications of the global into new territory. This is done by placing the concept of globality (rather than globalization) centre stage, by pointing to the distinctive qualities of a post-war planetary perspective and by examining some of the most prominent ideas, artefacts and images through which globe-making has taken place. Our aim is not to provide an exhaustive treatment but to stake out an alternative trajectory that can inspire scholars in several fields, not least International Relations (IR), and facilitate more robust interdisciplinary exchanges in the study of globality and its politics.[1] Our focus on the late twentieth and early twenty-first century is deliberate and adds a fresh perspective to a huge field that often sees globalization as a process to be studied over centuries or through the prism of recent, often post-Cold War, events. In retrospect, at least, it appears that the post-war decades – characterized by a massive spread and growth in industrial output, space travel, nuclear weapons, human rights discourse and the rise of global problems such as climate change – were essential for the ways in which humans transformed both their habitat *and* their view of human–Earth relations. These changes in turn were accompanied by important shifts in political ambition and vision. The metaphor of assemblage, which usefully draws attention to how things are put together to form fragile wholes made up of textual, visual and material elements, nicely captures the aspiration of this volume.[2] On the one hand it assembles an alternative story of some of the ideas, images and artefacts through which the world has been rendered as one. On the other, the emphasis on assemblages is particularly useful in highlighting the role of different technologies in mediating planetary processes as well as the function of visual imagery in producing and gaining access to the globe as a single and *sui generis* realm. Indeed, the chapters in this book show how crucial developments since 1945 – the nuclear revolution, the space race and the rise of global environmentalism – have produced a politics of globality that draws upon an intimately linked repertoire of ideas, images and artifacts.

This introduction provides the context for the chapters that follow. The next section begins with an examination of current understandings of globality as a singular condition or as the end-state of globalization and suggests an alternative interpretation that stresses the multiple, even conflicting, ways in which planet Earth has been imagined, realized and visualized or has achieved concrete material expression. Upon this reworked understanding, the study of globality is bound up with the historical and cultural practices through which this 'wholeness' arises. The third section zooms in on globality after 1945. Although planet Earth had been imagined as a unified spherical body long before the Apollo missions allowed us to actually set eye on it, post-1945 globality nonetheless stands out from earlier imageries in terms of three distinct qualities: verticality, materiality and temporality. Understanding these dimensions is essential for being able to grasp the various kinds of politics that have been invested (and continue to be invested) in claims about globality. The introduction closes with a brief overview of the individual chapters in this volume.

What is globality?

In the *Oxford English Dictionary*, globality is defined as '[t]he quality of being global; universality, totality, *spec.* the quality of having worldwide inclusiveness, reach or relevance; (the potential for) global integration, operation, or influence (esp. in business and financial contexts)'. In the academic literature, sociologists and political theorists have used the term in a similar sense, often to distinguish globality from globalization, which for decades now has been (accused of being) trite and lacking analytical clarity. As Wolf Schäfer (2007) argues, the condition of globality should be contrasted to the process of globalization, and to globalism, a term that represents an ideology. Despite a considerable variety in definitional scope and emphasis, most definitions share the minimum requirement that globality refers to 'the circumstance in which the entire world is regarded as "a single place"' (Shaw 2000: 25).[3]

These careful attempts to differentiate globality from globalization raise, however, a whole range of other thorny issues. Most obviously there is the risk of investing globality with a teleology, installing it as the more or less automated end-product of globalization. This danger is particularly evident in analyses of economic globalization and its impacts on the scale and condition of businesses. In such literature, the term globality is often employed to underline the momentous fact that the world has now entered a new reality of omnipresent competition, where businesses compete with everyone from everywhere for everything (Yergin 1998; Sirkin et al. 2008). Such references to a global condition are more than supposedly objective markers of reality; they serve to endow certain modes of production, trade, lifestyles and political arrangements with a sense of legitimacy – if not necessity – and imprint upon individuals, institutions, economies and political systems the idea that they have no choice but to adapt to the economic commandments of a globalized world (Roy 2001; Radhakrishnan 2005).

Even when globality is not identified as the natural end-state of economic globalization, the idea that globality (only) exists in the singular can easily be taken as an indication that it is the unique, defining feature of our age. For example, in their programmatic statement for 'world history', Geyer and Bright explicitly argue that the writing of history should take point of departure in today's globalized world: 'The central challenge of a renewed world history at the end of the twentieth century is to narrate the world's past in an age of globality' (Geyer and Bright 1995: 1041). Statements like this clearly show that, as a field, global (or world) history has a tendency to see the globe as always already present and often appears unconcerned with the history and practices of globe-making.[4] A related universalizing tendency is to see globality as originating in a process of Western globalization while neglecting the systematic inequalities conditioning both the origins and effects of this process.

It would be more accurate (if perhaps grammatically incorrect) to speak of *globalities* in the plural: there is not one, single globality but multiple, at times even competing, visions of globality across time and space. Several of the central ideas of globality expressed during the second half of the twentieth century have long lineages that clearly predate this period. They can be detected in the cosmological tendency of cartography and persistent attempts to grasp and plot the whole Earth, in the political visions invested in new technologies during the nineteenth century, or in the fundamentally universalist worldview that has coloured much social, political and legal thinking since the late eighteenth century (e.g. Cosgrove 2001).

In line with our focus on practices of assembling, this volume adopts the view that any invocation of globality has to be placed in the context of the mood, orientation or viewpoint through which it has become possible to see the world as a globe or sphere: 'Globality is neither a timeless condition nor a recent invention, but rather a social fact whose basic structure, genesis, dissemination and subsequent functions can be opened to historical and sociological inquiry' (Bartelson 2010: 231).[5] Seeing the world as globe thus directs our attention both to a planetary condition and the various attempts to tame this condition by incorporating it within longstanding notions of human mastery of nature through technology and military power. Indeed, Cosgrove (2001) associates the aspiration to know and master the globe with the cosmic perspective of Apollo, the Greek and Roman god of light and the sun, truth and harmony. In particular since the fifteenth century, when a muscular European imperialism began to spread around the globe, visions of the globe have shored up Western aspirations of colonial rule (Deloughrey 2014: 261), but globality also undermines and challenges the very Euro-centric vision out of which it emerges; as spherical objects have no privileged midpoint, globe-making is a profoundly decentralizing experience (Woodward 1989: 7).[6]

At the same time, there are good reasons for distinguishing post-1945 assemblages of globality from earlier invocations of the world as globe, most notably because a decidedly planetary perspective was epitomized in the invention of atomic and thermonuclear weapons, scientific discoveries of the workings of the Earth, the cultural repercussions of the space race and lunar voyages, the growth of environmentalist thinking, as well as in various cultural trends towards holist thinking in the postwar decades.[7]

Indeed, the concept of globality is itself a relatively recent invention that only became an actual feature of public and scholarly debate in the post-1945 period.[8] Thus, the realist scholar of international relations, John H. Herz (1908–2005), explicitly used globality to depict the condition of intense (security) interdependence brought about by nuclear weapons and intercontinental ballistic missiles.[9] In sketching the contours and prospects of 'a new universalism' based on a common human 'ethics of survival', he argued that 'the underlying facts of "globality" must, and do, have their impacts on minds and attitudes' (Herz 1959: 319). Hence, Herz discussed the possibilities of developing 'a "planetary mind"' and of obtaining '"a comprehensive view," a "world's-eye view," a *Gesamtschau*' for 'the world and mankind as a whole' (Herz 1959: 317). Herz's contemporary Hannah Arendt hinted at something similar when she declared in the context of space exploration that 'the search for a point outside the earth from which it would be possible to move, unhinge, as it were, the planet itself, is no accidental result of the modern age's science' (Arendt 1963: 53–54). This quest could potentially transform the 'geocentric' and 'anthropomorphic' elements of the human scientific worldview so as to install a more holistic perspective with greater sense of humility. More likely, she feared, the abstract point of view would lower the stature of humankind and bring it closer to destruction.[10] Despite such differences in gauging the politics of globality, post-1945 invocations of globality have important commonalities in terms of their origin and characteristics.

The characteristics of post-1945 globality

The post-war planetary perspective was driven primarily by large-scale technological innovations, which made it both possible and, many would argue, necessary to reflect on the new global condition. While most of these developments, such as nuclear weapons or the space race, have been associated with a strongly statist conception of national security, the Cold War also enabled a vision of the globe as an integrated ecological system – a political vision that today exists in intense competition for political attention with the national security state that helped bring it about (Masco 2010).[11] Ideas, artefacts and images have made it possible to assemble and conceive globality in more ways than one. Although the Cold War has come to an end, many contemporary invocations of globality share assumptions, imagery and a common language with forms of globality that emerged in the immediate post-war decades. Three characteristics stand out: a perspective of verticality that complements and transcends horizontal relations between states, a decidedly materialist focus that brings together human agency with planetary geophysical processes and, finally, an understanding of time as abrupt rupture.

Verticality

Perhaps the most striking characteristic of the post-1945 period is an emerging verticality that challenges understandings of the Earth as the mere surface or background stage for horizontal relations between states or other units. Until the twentieth century, the politics of globality involved the spatial circumvention or enclosure of the globe. One could here think of Columbus's discovery of the New World, Cook's circumnavigation of the globe or simply consider Alfred Thayer Mahan's (1890) late nineteenth-century description of the oceans as highways of the world. This was a proclamation intimately related to the age of empire, ideas about the nature and benefits of global maritime trade, the power associated with the transport and communication technologies that helped shrink the world, and a particular way of imagining, reducing and domesticating global space.[12]

Even though the encirclement of the globe was largely a process of horizontal expansion, it was anticipated, assisted and contemplated by the vertical imagination of cartography ('the view from above'). Still, verticality only became a concrete achievement in the early twentieth century, when air power and aerial photography opened up for a 'reconfigured reality, augmented and abstracted, yet heightened at the same time' (Adey et al. 2011: 179). Embraced for its ability to add geographical depth to surface views, the aerial perspective has also been condemned for its distance to social activities on the ground and for enabling a view of the Earth as a target.[13] As a result of advances in rocketry, radar and computing, which were all critically linked to Cold War militarism and the new vertical regime enabled by space exploration, both the hopes and the fears invested in the vertical perspective were further augmented. Indeed, the ascent into outer space was shrouded in ambivalence. It gave rise to wild and remarkably persistent expectations about the extension of Earthly activities and human life into a vast, new territory. But scepticism was widespread, particularly among intellectuals such as Hannah Arendt (1963) and Martin Heidegger (1966). They worried that space travel would uproot the terrestrial worldliness (*Dasein*) of humankind and heralded the final victory of technological artefacts over organic life. Lewis Mumford's (1958: 3) call to 'reclaim this planet for humanity' instead of 'planting our flag on the moon' expressed this sentiment very directly. These differences notwithstanding, space exploration and space travel raised the stakes of the geopolitical struggle between the United States and the Soviet Union. Just as the control of the seas had been linked to global dominance, now control of outer space was considered a prerequisite for political control on Earth.[14]

At the same time, the vertical perspective also enabled a form of globality that transcended geopolitics and instead appealed 'to the organic and spiritual unity of terrestrial life' (Cosgrove 1994: 290). Most potently, such unitary sentiments were provoked by photographs of Earth taken from outer space. In the literature, most attention has been devoted to analysing the reactions to some of the first pictures – *Earthrise* (1968) and *Blue Marble* (1972) – which vividly contrast the green, blue and brown colours of Earth to the immense, dark and lifeless void in which the colourful planet dwells.[15] Many of the aspirations and assumptions of environmentalism – robustly tied to a sense of humility and vulnerability – were manifest in responses to space photography. When Earth Day was celebrated for the first time in 1970, it naturally involved the reproduction of the perfect spherical form of a fragile globe. Later photographs have solicited similar responses of unity and oneness. In his famous reaction to the publication of the photograph *Pale Blue Dot*, taken in 1990 by the *Voyager 1* space probe from a distance of about 3.7 billion miles from Earth, the astronomer Carl Sagan argued:

> The Earth is a very small stage in a vast cosmic arena. Think of the endless cruelties visited by the inhabitants of one corner of this pixel on the scarcely distinguishable inhabitants of some other corner, how frequent their misunderstandings, how eager they are to kill one another, how fervent their hatreds. Think of the rivers of blood spilled by all those generals and emperors so that, in glory and triumph, they could become the momentary masters of a fraction of a dot ... . There is perhaps no better demonstration of the folly of human conceits than this distant image of our tiny world. To me, it underscores our responsibility to deal more kindly with one another, and to preserve and cherish the pale blue dot, the only home we've ever known.
>
> (Sagan 1994: 6)

To be sure, such cosmopolitan proclamations of unity are not new. Post-war invocations of 'whole Earth globality' continued to draw on a well-established historical repertoire of ideas, traditions, tropes and symbols, not least those linked to the Christian theme of the birth of the world and the creation of life. For example, on Christmas morning, in a live radio transmission from *Apollo 8*, the three astronauts read out from the *Book of Genesis*. Similarly, the image on the United States International Geophysical Year (IGY) commemorating stamp features part of Michelangelo's famous fresco *The Creation of Adam* pitched against an orange background of solar flare. Ervin Metzl, the designer, explains that the image represents 'man's wonder at the unknown, together with his determination to understand it and his spiritual inspiration to further his knowledge'.[16]

Yet, political, technological and scientific developments during the Cold War combined to produce a new technology mediated verticality that issued in distinctive forms of globality: impossible to experience from the Earth's surface though equally impossible to avoid in representation. In contrast to earlier practices of globe-making, the Cold War firmly put the planetary perspective first in the far-reaching sense that often 'modern technology, wherever it happens locally to be deployed, already presupposes a global or planetary scope' (Lazier 2011: 610; see also Kurgan 2013). Sloterdijk appropriately speaks of an 'inverted astronomy' (cited in Sachs 1994: 170): rather than looking upon the stars from Earth's surface, humankind now gazes upon the Earth from a position far removed from the planet's gravitational grip.[17]

Materiality

Verticality and the new vision of 'whole Earth globality' cannot be seen in isolation from questions about materiality, in particular those pertaining to technology and the vulnerability or resilience of the human and non-human. Sentiments of global unity did not only emerge from the idea of a common humanity with a shared destiny but were also rooted in scientific understandings and technologies through which the materiality of the planet was mediated.[18] The Earth Sciences in particular played an important role in making the Earth appear as one. The study of planetary phenomena was boosted significantly during the early Cold War years (Masco 2010; Agar 2012; Hamblin 2013), a development symbolized by the organization of the 1957/8 IGY when 4,000 scientific stations across the world were engaged in the collection and processing of large sets of data about Earth geophysical processes. The IGY counts among its most impressive immediate achievements the detection of radiation belts surrounding Earth, the discovery of mid-ocean submarine ridges (an important link in the development of plate tectonics theory in the late 1950s and early 1960s) and the launching of artificial satellites for outer space Earth-monitoring.[19] In subsequent years – relying upon the view from outer space, remote sensing technology as well as complex computer modelling – the Earth Sciences have been prominent in rendering Earth intelligible as a planetary system in which all human and non-human processes are interlinked (Edwards 2012a: xiii).

Today, the idea of Earth as a living organism or interconnected system of natural forces figures most prominently in debates about anthropogenic climate change.[20] It is also at the heart of current claims that Earth has now entered a new geological epoch, the Anthropocene, defined by the central role of humankind in shaping Earth's geological and ecological processes.[21] The beginning of the Anthropocene is typically seen to coincide with the onset of the industrial revolution around the turn of the eighteenth century, but scientists argue that a decisive intensification took place with 'The Great Acceleration' following the end of World War II (Steffen et al. 2007: 617–18; Steffen et al. 2015). Most prominently, the development and testing of nuclear weapons have been linked to the arrival of the Anthropocene, as radioactive fallout produced an everlasting effect on the atmosphere as well as the biosphere. Scientists involved in American nuclear testing were able to discover atmospheric patterns by tracing radioactive fallout, making possible more complex understandings of the climate and climate change, leading for example to the discovery of the hole in the ozone layer (Masco 2010; Edwards 2012b; Hamblin 2013). Hence, the image of the mushroom cloud is as iconic for post-1945 globality as the 'whole Earth' images beamed back from outer space.[22]

The idea that human and ecological systems are tightly coupled together has both emboldened and discouraged the centrality accorded to humankind. By suggesting that humankind has become a dominant geological force, the Anthropocene automatically puts humans at the centre of planetary processes. This central position has inspired a wide range of geoengineering projects concerned with the management of planetary boundaries, limits and thresholds, which are now a growing political concern.[23] Over the last few decades, some thinkers have been drawn to the utopian aspirations invested in an integrated (cybernetic) whole between humans, Earth and machine, while others have pointed out that the Avatar-like dream of a full symbiosis between the human and non-human is more likely to end up in a dystopian, totalitarian nightmare of a 'Green Leviathan' slowly enveloping the globe and reducing humanity to little more than its biogenetic code.[24]

At the same time, the Anthropocene tempers the significance of humans by stressing that the planet is a vast interconnected system of which humans make up a small part and which in the course of planetary history illustrates the very limits, rather than the potential, of the political (Clark, this volume). Moreover, the immense complexity of other-than-human forms of activity and regulation through which planetary processes are enacted, including bacterial symbiosis or astronomic events such as meteorite showers, are beyond human knowledge and control (Clark 2005). The downplaying of the role and significance of humans could be interpreted in a fatalist, perhaps even defeatist, sense that the state of the planet is beyond human repair, but also beckons us to reflect upon the ways in which humans respond to the alterity and other-worldliness of the non-human.[25]

Temporality

In modern Western understandings of temporality, time is generally understood in terms of progress. Progressive time dates back to the age of Enlightenment and the widespread expectation that science and intellectual activity would ultimately work to improve human life.[26] The expectation of salvation in the future 'demands a memory of qualitative social change, a concrete vision of the past which we may expect to find completed by that far more abstract and empty conception of some future terminus which we sometimes call "progress"' (Jameson 2005: 284).

Post-1945 globality both complicates and contributes to this progressive understanding. First, mid-twentieth century events of total war, totalitarianism, the Holocaust and the development of nuclear weapons led many to argue that a progressive arc seamlessly connecting past, present and future was rapidly crumbling (Katznelson 2003; Gumbrecht 2013). A profound sense of global crises – that has since been extended to debates on environmental degradation and climate change – suggested instead a radical break between the present and an increasingly bleak future. Chakrabarty calls this temporality of rupture for 'negative universal history' in which universality 'arises from a shared sense of catastrophe' rather than from the progressive expansion of Enlightenment values (Chakrabarty 2009: 222). For the German philosopher Günther Anders, the atomic destruction of Hiroshima and Nagasaki symbolized this shift more than anything else:

> On August 6, 1945, the Day of Hiroshima, a New Age began: the age in which at any given moment we have the power to transform any given place on our planet, and even our planet itself, into a Hiroshima ... . However long this age may last, even if it should last forever, it is 'The Last Age': for there is no possibility that its '*differentia specifica*', the possibility of our self-extinction, can ever end – but by the end itself.
>
> (Anders 1962: 493; see also Anders 1972)[27]

Whether or not one agrees with the exact dating, Anders' idea of the present as the final age nonetheless captures an important tendency of post-1945 invocations of globality: an understanding of the present as an intensification of past events that can no longer be transcended by the future.

The political implications of viewing the present through the prism of urgency and impending disaster are, it must be stressed, multifarious. On the one hand it has been argued that such views of the present stand in the way of more progressive change and political reform. Sometimes claims to pre-empt the worst from happening have been used to justify emergency measures such as widespread surveillance, war and the curbing of political freedoms (Aradau and van Munster 2011; de Goede 2012). On the other, the temporal figure of disaster has also been inherently linked to efforts to increase the horizons of hope, expand the imagination, produce greater equity and develop new models of global citizenship. Moving away from the archetypical modern view that the present necessarily is better than the past has led some to revalue the past as providing realistic alternatives for present political solutions to global problems: '[T]he long-term perspective opens up doors and windows, allowing us to look around at other ways of organising our society. A longer history of international government can even demonstrate that alternatives exist to our own political system' (Guldi and Armitage 2014: 75–6; see also Craig, this volume). In its most radical form, the long-term perspective also brings human history in dialogue with the deep time of geophysical events and planetary tipping points. The current popularity of 'Big History', in which the past is studied as a as a series of planetary thresholds ranging from the Big Bang to the rise of agriculture, shows how the current focus on climate change actively forges the past as a globally shared *planetary* past.[28]

The future, too, has been appropriated as a site for forging a global consciousness (see e.g. Appadurai 2013). Despite Anders' characterization of our time as the final age, he strongly resisted tendencies to 'defuturize' the future (*defuturisieren*) and instead sought to attune human beings to the very real possibility of future catastrophe (Anders 1956: 282–3).[29] In a world divided by the Cold War, imaginaries of a global future increasingly appeared as a universal antidote to the crisis-ridden present. The active cultivation of imaginaries of anthropogenic destruction served to craft a universal, global future. In *Mankind 2000* (1969), two central figures in the quest to reclaim the future argued:

> If we tamper with the time ahead of us, as we have already done with the space around us, in an egocentric, power-directed, narrow-minded spirit, if we spoil the future as we have spoiled our environment, then we are in for an epoch of despotism and desperation – a tyranny of a new modernistic type … . This must not happen. The future belongs to all of us.
>
> (Jungk and Galtung 1969: 368)

In a world where spatial boundaries continue to exist but acquire a new political character, this injunction to invent, see and take responsibility for the future meant first and foremost developing the capacity of political and moral imagination.[30]

Plan of the book

What we have introduced here and what unites the chapters in this book is an approach to globality that stresses the multifarious, contradictory and deeply political ways in which the world and planet Earth have been rendered whole in the period since 1945. Globality in this sense is not a new phenomenon, yet the post-war period is distinctive by virtue of significant shifts in three qualities – verticality, materiality and temporality – that have shaped its politics. The eight chapters that follow are situated in various moments stretching back to the end of World War II. Together they unpack some of the complex roots and interlacing trajectories of post-war invocations of globality and provide access to important elements through which the planet has been assembled as 'one' since 1945. They have been arranged in a roughly chronological order to set out a rich, layered analysis that productively juxtaposes the interlocking terrains on which multiple forms of globality have manifested themselves.

The growing recognition that the human situation is 'global' or 'planetary' has stimulated extensive efforts to capture this novel situation in simple metaphors and images that all carry heavy spatial and material connotations. By combining mappings of planetary space and place with claims about the appropriateness of particular political arrangements, the first chapter examines the history and politics of some of the most prominent representations of post-1945 globality. Here, Daniel Deudney and Elizabeth Mendenhall examine the geopolitics of various metaphoric imageries and ask what these mappings capture or fail to capture about the planetary situation and which political implications can be derived, explicitly or implicitly, from these mappings.

The three following chapters find their points of departure in political and legal articulations of globality during the late 1950s and 1960s, a period defined by the invention of nuclear weapons, rocket and satellite technologies as well as a strong commitment to military spending on the Earth Sciences. Chapter 2, by Joseph Masco, interrogates the foundations of planetary thinking in Cold War nuclear weapons programmes. Examining the linkages between atmospheres, territoriality and experimental nuclear science, the chapter lays bare the military origins of current understandings of globality and argues that post-1945 globality is best understood as the 'Age of Fallout': a period in which cumulative form of planetary engineering and the remaking of Earth systems have produced an atmosphere that is increasingly hostile to human life. In Chapter 3, Campbell Craig also takes nuclear weapons as his point of departure by returning to the ideas of the central realist thinker of the time: Hans J. Morgenthau. Craig argues that Morgenthau's thinking placed technological developments at the core of ideas about globality and saw nuclear weapons as necessitating supranational government. Although the Cold War made this political structure impossible to attain, Craig extrapolates from Morgenthau's insights and applies them to our present time. Tanja Aalberts and Wouter Werner go on to explore, in Chapter 4, how in a legal idiom 'mankind' and 'sovereignty' became central, competing components in the contemporary politics of globality. Whereas references to mankind originally served to justify the right to free movement across the seas, the human exploration of the Antarctic and space travel in the mid-twentieth century have promoted a 'whole Earth globality' in legal discourse through which the so-called commons of mankind are invested with a new significance – as spaces to be nourished, protected and exploited for the benefit of all states, including future generations.

Developments in the 1950s set the tone for much critical thinking in the 1960s and 1970s, when looming global catastrophes such as population growth, resource depletion and environmental degradation gradually replaced nuclear war as the main harbingers of sudden change. In the countercultural climate of these two decades, the politics of globality increasingly played itself out as a struggle for the future. In Chapter 5, Jenny Andersson and Sibylle Duhautois propose that a key element of emerging forms of globality was the reconceptualization, towards the late 1960s, of the future as a common problem to all mankind and – despite its gendered bias – as a universal category of the world. They examine the history and emergence of global futures across various institutional fora – from the UN and UNESCO to the World Futures Studies Federation and the Club of Rome – and claim that the future was both a site in which the unity of mankind could be contemplated and a catalogue of concrete problems for which world solutions had to be found.

Chapters 6 to 8 consider current framings of globality in debates about climate change, environmental security and global security. In Chapter 6, Nigel Clark argues that the idea of the Anthropocene signifies a geological turn that puts an end to any lingering sense of human exceptionalism. Contrasting the Anthropocene to constructions of planetary wholeness during the early post-war period, he stresses that the Anthropocene produces a planetary vision that is more fractured. The space-time of the Earth is linked to but also exceeds human geologic agency. Indeed, the planet's inherent agential capacities for system change should urge us to think about the politics of globality as an on-going experiment with planetary rifts. Chapter 7, by Samuel Randalls, examines the Anthropocene in relation to the debate on climate change and argues that as an indicator of globality the Anthropocene is overly narrow and inattentive to the multiple 'climatic globalities' that are assembled through different forms of expertise, models, imaginations, concerns and idealized solutions. Finally, in Chapter 8, Columba Peoples turns to contemporary remote-sensing technologies, most notably satellite systems, and argues that different, even contending, understandings of globality emerge from these modern mapping techniques and global communication infrastructures. By politicizing the practice of viewing Earth from outer space, the chapter investigates how we might come to see globality differently.

The volume ends with an afterword by Paul Edwards that reflects on 'globalities' and ponders our current planetary predicament.

Notes

1 Globe-making has taken many forms across both time and space – from non-Western ideas of globality to countercultural movements such as Afrofuturism – and no single volume can aspire to cover them all. The studies in this volume could be complemented not only by studies of globe-making across time and space but also by approaches (e.g. the study of movements) and themes (e.g. the internet). See also the discussion below.

2 The concept of assemblage has become invested with heavy theoretical loads, as it has been installed at the heart of various ambitious theoretical programs across the humanities and social sciences (see e.g. Bennett 2005; Latour 2005; DeLanda 2006;

Li 2007; Anderson and McFarlane 2011; Acuto and Curtis 2014). Here, the concept is used in heuristic fashion to draw attention to the multiplicity of ideas, images and artefacts that are combined in various ways to produce various socio-technical compositions of globality.

3 Shaw goes on to clarify and expand his definition, which, he argues, must now encompass 'the developing social unity of mankind' (Shaw 2000: 25). Martin Albrow in turn argues that '[g]lobality is to the global, the Global Age and globalism as modernity is to the modern, the Modern Age and modernism' (Albrow 1996: 82). See also Robertson (1991, 2007).

4 The field of 'global history' also remains strongly tied to the study of imperial dynamics of expansion and contraction between a 'centre' and 'periphery' or civilizational encounters between 'self' and 'other'. See e.g. Pomper (1995), Mazlish (1998, 2006), O'Brien (2006) and Crossley (2008).

5 Historicizations of contemporary trends of globalization go some way in this direction, as these will typically also involve an analysis of how such processes reshaped the globe as a physical or socio-political entity. This is, broadly speaking, what C. A. Bayly (2004) does in *The Birth of the Modern World*, in which a discussion of elements and aspects of 'archaic globalization' performs a crucial role in re-opening and redefining global history. One can also look at signature shifts in philosophy, cultural history or the history of science, be it at specific moments (the discovery of the New World, the Copernican revolution, etc.) or approach the subject more thematically. This can be done by focusing on the *longue durée* (Elden 2011) or, alternatively, by examining how specific technologies or technological shifts helped reshape political opportunities and communities in specific periods, for example by making the world (appear) 'small, manageable, tame' and, hence, ripe for new types of polities (Bell 2005: 559).

6 Breaking with the dominant Apollonian perspective of global mastery, Stephen Jay Gould suggests that current accounts of globality rather summon the dancing Hindu God Shiva, who, carrying a flame in the one hand and a drum in the other, captures the cosmic beat of astrogeological creation and destruction (Gould 1984; see also Davis 1996).

7 For a discussion of some of these trends, see Cosgrove (1994), Craig (2003), Katznelson (2003), Poole (2008), Wood (2010), Lazier (2011), Hamblin (2013) and van Munster and Sylvest (2016).

8 The *OED* records the first use of the term in 1931 (in *The Times*). In the 1950s, globality was also invoked in discussions on the spatial expansion of total warfare (e.g. Wermuth 1955). A Google Ngram search shows that 'globality' has been used as far back as 1900 as a psychoanalytical term related to, e.g., schizophrenia. On the use of 'culturomics' as a supplement to the study of cultural meaning, its possibilities and limitations, see Michel et al. (2011).

9 There are strong affinities between this argument and Deudney's (2007: 33–41) discussion of violence interdependence. See also Craig (2003), Wendt (2003) and van Munster and Sylvest (2016).

10 Arendt's attempt to formulate a theory of freedom as intimately connected with the public performance of plurality might have originated in her analysis of totalitarianism but faced new challenges under conditions of globality (Axtmann 2006). In 1958 Arendt described this condition (without using the term globality) as arising '[p]recisely when the immensity of available space on Earth was discovered'. As a result, 'in our world [1958] ... each man is as much an inhabitant of the Earth as an inhabitant of his country' (Arendt 1958: 250, 1–6).

11 In his examination of meteorology, which in the second half of the twentieth century was tied to military priorities and nuclear weapons, Paul Edwards shows that meteorological data, simulations and models have become indispensable for our understanding of anthropogenic climate change. While the conception of 'weather

and climate as global phenomena helped promote an understanding of the world as a single physical system', this synergistically modelled totality was partly a product of nuclear weapons research and its central institutions (Edwards 2012a: xiv; Edwards 2012b).

12 Mahan's arguments continue to be referred to in contemporary security politics. See Aalberts and Werner (this volume).

13 The invention of the airborne camera during World War I helped produce a new kinetic military cartography, which culminated in World War II, when 'the bomb sight eye' of strategic bombing took centre stage in total warfare (Galison 2001). A combination of improved mapping and drone technology has recently intensified and expanded this ocular rendition of globe surface as battlefield.

14 In a Senate debate on the establishment of NASA, Lyndon B. Johnson described the successful launch of *Sputnik 1* by the Soviet Union in 1957 as an imperial technology of global control: 'The Roman Empire controlled the world because it could build roads … the British Empire was dominant because it had ships. In the air age we were powerful because we had airplanes. Now the Communists have established a foothold in outer space' (cited in Cosgrove 2001: 256). See also Aalberts and Werner (this volume).

15 See particularly Poole (2008), who details the cultural significance of space photography by referring to Archibald MacLeish's famous 1968 essay 'Riders on the Earth'. See also Sachs (1994), Kelsey (2011), Lazier (2011) and Peoples (this volume).

16 Office of the Special Assistant to the Postmaster General, 'International Geophysical Year Commemorative Postage Stamp', *Postal Bulletin*, LXXIX, April 24 (1958), p. 1.

17 On the political implications of remote sensing and the practice of zooming in and out, see also Peoples (this volume).

18 Even the photographic images which appeared to disclose Earth in its natural dress were – realist appeals to the objectivity and truthfulness of photography notwithstanding – a highly complex outcome of a dispersed process involving camera technology, space craft design, rocket science and the possibility of colour pictures, as well as a range of implicit and explicit editorial decisions on how to frame and cut the pictures (see also Lazier 2011).

19 The IGY was strongly coloured by the Cold War context and crucial scientific breakthroughs – such as plate tectonics theory – were in part the byproduct of practical military problems: submarine navigation required detailed knowledge of the contours and consistency of the ocean floors, while nuclear fallout required knowledge about atmospheric movement. In 1958, the Eisenhower administration used the IGY to conceal the testing of a low-yield nuclear weapon in the higher atmosphere (Operation ARGUS) (see also Mundey 2012).

20 See Randalls (this volume) for a discussion of how this subsumes rich political conflict.

21 See also Clark (this volume) for a discussion of the Anthropocene.

22 Jacobs (2011) has traced the juxtaposition of 'whole Earth' images to 'no Earth' images in editorial cartoons in the US that were published in response to the atomic bombing of Hiroshima and Nagasaki. On the importance of nuclear weapons for the politics of globality, see also Deudney and Mendenhall (this volume), Masco (this volume) and Craig (this volume).

23 Unfortunately, Walker's (2010) otherwise fascinating study of boundaries and limits in political articulations of the state–world relationship – including those forms of politics that take the globe or planet as their privileged reference point – pays little attention to the materiality of geophysical processes expressed in the notion of planetary boundaries or thresholds. Concerns with such boundaries are expressed in ideas of 'planetary stewardship' (Steffen et al. 2011), 'Earth System

governance' (Biermann 2012) and 'Anthropocene security' (Dalby 2009). On the Cold War history of geoengineering and terra-forming, see Masco (this volume).

24 These different views can be traced in scientific and popular references to 'global village' (McLuhan 1962), 'Spaceship Earth' (Boulding 1966; Buckminster-Fuller 1968), 'Gaia' (Lovelock 2007) or 'the noösphere' (Teilhard de Chardin 1961). For a discussion of the history and politics of such one Earth metaphors, see Deudney and Mendenhall (this volume).

25 See also Clark (this volume), Edwards (this volume) and Hamilton et al. (2015).

26 This belief in progress manifests itself in different ways, e.g. in Darwin's evolutionism, Marx' historical materialism or in Kant's belief that philosophy worked to produce a cosmopolitan perpetual peace.

27 Chakrabarty explicitly denies that nuclear weapons are a catastrophe on par with global warming. It is important to note, however, that the similarity in reactions to these problems as well as the multifarious ways in which the language ('nuclear winter') and knowledge (geophysics) of climate change and nuclear weapons have been entangled. See also Masco, (2010); Edwards (2012b) and Hamblin (2013). See also Masco (this volume), Clark (this volume) and Craig (this volume).

28 See also Guldi and Armitage (2014: Ch. 3). Arguably, the concern with deep time also changes our view of history, which is increasingly examined as a set of qualitative ruptures and turning points (e.g. Dupuy 2005).

29 The human-made catastrophic future is a pressing concern in post-war scholarship, including the 1946 *One World or None* report by the Federation of American Scientists, Robert Jungk's *Die Zukunft hat schon begonnen* (1952), Karl Jaspers' *The Future of Mankind* (1958), Bertrand Russell's *Has Man a Future?* (1961), Johan Galtung and Robert Jungk's *Mankind 2000* (1969), Ossip Flechtheim's *Futurologie: Der Kampf um die Zukunft* (1972), Donella Meadows et al.'s *The Limits to Growth: A Report for the Club of Rome's Project on the Predicament of Mankind* (1972), the Brundtland report *Our Common Future* (1987), Günther Anders' *Die Zerstörung unserer Zukunft* (1984), Ulrich Beck's *World Risk Society* (1999) and Jean-Pierre Dupuy's *Pour un catastrophisme éclaré* (2002).

30 See also Andersson and Duhautois (this volume).

References

Acuto, Michele and Simon Curtis (eds) (2014) *Reassembling International Theory. Assemblage Thinking and International Relations*. Basingstoke: Palgrave MacMillan.

Adey, Peter, Mark Whitehead and Alison J. Williams (2011) 'Introduction – Air-target: Distance, Reach and the Politics of Verticality', *Theory, Culture and Society*, 28(7–8): 173–187.

Agar, Jon (2012) *Science in the Twentieth Century and Beyond*. Cambridge: Polity.

Albrow, Martin (1996) *The Global Age*. Stanford, CA: Stanford University Press.

Anders, Günther (1956) *Die Antiquiertheit des Menschen. Über die Seele im Zeitalter der zweiten industriellen Revolution*. Munich: C. H. Beck.

Anders, Günther (1961) *Burning Conscience*. New York: Monthly Review Press.

Anders, Günther (1962) 'Theses for The Atomic Age', *Massachusetts Review*, 3(3): 493–505.

Anders, Günther (1972) *Endzeit und Zeitende. Gedanken über die atomare Situation*. Munich: C. H. Beck.

Anderson, Ben and Colin McFarlane (2011) 'Assemblage and Geography', *Area*, 43(2): 124–127.

Andersson, Jenny (2012) 'The Great Future Debate and the Struggle for the World', *American Historical Review*, 117(5): 1411–1430.

Appadurai, Arjun (2013) *The Future as a Cultural Fact: Essays on the Global Condition.* London: Verso.

Aradau, Claudia and Rens van Munster (2011) *Politics of Catastrophe: Genealogies of the Unknown.* Abingdon: Routledge.

Arendt, Hannah (1973 [1958]) 'Karl Jaspers: Citizens of the World?', in Hannah Arendt, *Men in Dark Times.* London: Penguin, pp. 84–96.

Arendt, Hannah (2007 [1963]) 'The Conquest of Space and the Stature of Man', *New Atlantis*, 18 (Fall): 43–55.

Axtmann, Roland (2006) 'Globality, Plurality and Freedom: The Arendtian Perspective', *Review of International Studies*, 32(1): 93–117.

Bartelson, Jens (2010) 'The Social Construction of Globality', *International Political Sociology*, 4(3): 219–235.

Bayly, C. A. (2004) *The Birth of the Modern World, 1780–1914.* Oxford: Blackwell.

Bell, Duncan (2005) 'Dissolving Distance: Technology, Space and Empire in British Political Thought, 1770–1900', *Journal of Modern History*, 77 (September): 523–562.

Bell, Wendell (1997) *Foundations of Future Studies: Human Science for a New Era*, vol. 1. New Brunswick, NJ: Transaction Publishers.

Bennett, Jennifer (2005) 'The Agency of Assemblages and the North American Blackout', *Public Culture*, 17(3): 445–465.

Bentley, Jerry H. (1993) *Old World Encounters: Cross-Cultural Contacts and Exchanges in Pre-Modern Times.* Oxford: Oxford University Press.

Biermann, Frank (2012) *Earth System Governance: World Politics in the Anthropocene.* Cambridge, MA: MIT Press.

Booth, Ken (2007) *Theory of World Security.* Cambridge: Cambridge University Press.

Boulding, Elise (1978) 'Futuristics and the Imaging Capacity of the West', in Magoroh Maruyama (ed.) *Cultures of the Future.* The Hague: Mouton Publishers, pp. 7–32.

Boulding, Kenneth F. (1993 [1966]) 'The Economics of the Coming Spaceship Earth', in Herman E. Daley and Kenneth N. Townsend (eds), *Valuing the Earth: Economy, Ecology, Ethics.* Cambridge, MA: MIT Press, pp. 297–310.

Buckminster-Fuller, Richard (1968) *Operating Manual for Space Ship Earth.* Carbondale, IL: Southern Illinois University Press.

Carver, Terrell and Jens Bartelson (eds) (2011) *Globality, Democracy and Civil Society.* London: Routledge.

Chakrabarty, Dipesh (2009) 'The Climate of History: Four Theses', *Critical Inquiry*, 35(2): 197–222.

Christian, David and Cynthia Brown (2013) *Big History: Between Nothing and Everything.* New York: McGraw-Hill.

Clark, Nigel (2005) 'Ex-orbitant Globality', *Theory, Culture & Society*, 22(5): 165–185.

Clark, Nigel (2014) 'Geo-politics and the Disaster of the Anthropocene', *The Sociological Review*, 62(S1): 19–37.

Connolly, William E. (2013) 'The "New Materialism" and the Fragility of Things', *Millennium – Journal of International Studies*, 41(3): 399–412.

Cosgrove, Denis (1994) 'Contested Global Visions: One-World, Whole-Earth, and the Apollo Space Photographs', *Annals of the Association of American Geographers*, 84 (2): 270–294.

Cosgrove, Denis (2001) *Apollo's Eye: A Cartographic Genealogy of the Earth in the Western Imagination.* Baltimore, MD: Johns Hopkins University Press.

Cosgrove, Denis (2005) 'Apollo's Eye: A Cultural Geography of the Globe', June. Available at www.sscnet.ucla.edu/geog/downloads/418/45.pdf (accessed 2 January 2016).

Craig, Campbell (2003) *Glimmer of a New Leviathan. Total War in the Realism of Niebuhr, Morgenthau and Waltz*. New York: Columbia University Press.

Crossley, Pamela Kyle (2008) *What Is Global History?* Cambridge: Polity.

Dalby, Simon (2009) *Security and Environmental Change*. Cambridge: Polity.

Davis, Mike (1996) 'Cosmic Dancers on History's Stage. The Permanent Revolution in the Earth Sciences', *New Left Review*, 217 (May/June): 48–84.

de Goede, Marieke (2012) *Speculative Security: The Politics of Pursuing Terrorist Monies*. Minneapolis, MN: University of Minnesota Press.

DeLanda, Manuel (2006) *A New Philosophy of Society: Assemblage Theory and Social Complexity*. London: Continuum.

DeLoughrey, Elizabeth (2014) 'Satellite Planetarity and the Ends of the Earth', *Public Culture*, 26(2): 257–280.

Deudney, Daniel (2007) *Bounding Power: Republican Security Theory from the Polis to the Global Village*. Princeton, NJ: Princeton University Press.

Dupuy, Jean-Pierre (2005) *Petite métaphysique des tsunamis*. Paris: Seuil.

Edwards, Paul (2012a) *A Vast Machine: Computer Models, Climate Data and the Politics of Global Warming*. Cambridge, MA: MIT Press.

Edwards, Paul (2012b) 'Entangled Histories: Climate Science and Nuclear Weapons Research', *Bulletin of the Atomic Scientists*, 68(4): 28–40.

Elden, Stuart (2011) 'The Space of the World', in El Hadi Jazairy (ed.), *Scales of the Earth*, vol. 4: *New Geographies*. Cambridge, MA: Harvard University Press, pp. 26–31.

Galison, Peter (2001) 'War Against the Center', *Grey Room*, 4 (Summer): 5–33.

Geyer, Michael and Charles Bright (1995) 'World History in a Global Age', *The American Historical Review*, 100(4): 1034–1060.

Gould, Stephen Jay (1984) 'The Cosmic Dance of Siva', *Natural History*, 93(8): 14.

Guldi, Jo and David Armitage (2014) *The History Manifesto*. Cambridge: Cambridge University Press.

Gumbrecht, Hans Ulrich (2013) *After 1945. Latency as Origin of the Present*. Stanford, CA: Stanford University Press.

Haffner, Jeanne (2013) *The View from Above. The Science of Social Space*. Cambridge, MA: MIT Press.

Hamblin, Jacob Darwin (2013) *Arming Mother Nature. The Birth of Catastrophic Environmentalism*. Oxford: Oxford University Press.

Hamilton, Clive, François Gemenne and Christophe Bonneuil (eds) (2015) *The Anthropocene and the Global Environmental Crisis: Rethinking Modernity in a New Epoch*. Abingdon: Routledge.

Hardin, Garett (1968) 'The Tragedy of the Commons', *Science*, 162(3859): 1243–1248.

Heidegger, Martin (2002 [1938]) 'The Age of the World Picture', in Martin Heidegger, *Off the Beaten Track*, ed. and trans. J. Young and K. Haynes. Cambridge: Cambridge University Press, pp. 57–85.

Heidegger, Martin (1976 [1966]), 'Only a God Can Save Us: *Der Spiegel's* Interview with Martin Heidegger', *Philosophy Today*, 20(4): 267–284.

Herz, John H. (1959) *International Politics in the Atomic Age*. New York: Columbia University Press.

Huntington, Samuel P. (1996) *The Clash of Civilizations and the Remaking of World Order*. New York: Simon and Schuster.

Jacobs, Robert (2011) 'Whole Earth or No Earth: The Origin of the Whole Earth Icon in the Ashes of Hiroshima and Nagasaki', *The Asia-Pacific Journal*, 9(13). Available at www.japanfocus.org/-Robert-Jacobs/3505 (accessed 29 October 2014).

Jameson, Frederic (2005) *Archaeologies of the Future: The Desire Called Utopia and Other Science Fictions.* London: Verso.

Jungk, Robert and Johan Galtung (eds) (1969) *Mankind 2000.* Oslo and London: Universitetsforlaget/Allen & Unwin.

Katznelson, Ira (2003) *Desolation and Enlightenment; Political Knowledge after Total War, Totalitarianism, and the Holocaust.* New York: Columbia University Press.

Kelsey, Robin (2011) 'Reverse Shot: Earthrise and Blue Marble in the American Imagination', in El Hadi Jazairy (ed.), *New Geographies, vol. 4: Scales of the Earth.* Cambridge, MA: Harvard University Press, pp. 10–16.

Kurgan, Laura (2013) *Close Up at a Distance. Mapping Technology and Politics.* New York: Zone Books.

Latour, Bruno (2005) *Reassembling the Social: An Introduction to Actor-Network Theory.* Oxford: Oxford University Press.

Lazier, Benjamin (2011) 'Earthrise; or, The Globalization of the World Picture', *American Historical Review*: 602–630.

Li, Tania Murray (2007) 'Practices of Assemblage and Community Forest Management', *Economy and Society*, 36(2): 263–293.

Lovelock, James (2007) *The Revenge of Gaia: Earth's Climate in Crisis and the Fate of Humanity.* New York: Basic Books.

Mahan, Alfred Thayer (1890) *The Influence of Sea Power Upon History, 1660–1783.* London: Sampson Low & Co.

Masco, Joseph (2010) 'Bad Weather: On Planetary Crisis', *Social Studies of Science*, 40(1): 7–40.

Mazlish, Bruce (1998) 'Comparing Global History to World History', *Journal of Interdisciplinary History*, 28(3): 385–395.

Mazlish, Bruce (2006) *The New Global History.* London: Routledge.

Mazlish, Bruce and Akira Iriye (eds) (2005) *The Global History Reader.* London: Routledge.

McNeill, William H. (1976) *Plagues and Peoples.* New York: Anchor Books.

McLuhan, Marshall (1962) *The Gutenberg Galaxy.* London: Routledge & Kegan Paul.

Michel, Jean-Baptiste et al. (2011) 'Quantitative Analysis of Culture Using Millions of Digitized Books', *Science*, 331(6014): 176–182.

Mumford, Lewis (2006 [1958]) *The Human Way Out.* Wallingford, PA: Pendle Hill.

Mundey, Lisa M. (2012) 'The Civilianization of a Nuclear Weapon Effects Test: The ARGUS Operation', *Historical Studies in the Natural Sciences*, 42(4): 283–321.

van Munster, Rens and Casper Sylvest (2016) *Nuclear Realism: Global Political Thought during the Thermonuclear Revolution.* Abingdon: Routledge.

O'Brien, Patrick (2006) 'Historical Traditions and Modern Imperatives for the Restoration of Global History', *Journal of Global History*, 1(1): 3–39.

Pomper, Philip (1995) 'World History and Its Critics', *History and Theory*, 34(2): 1–7.

Poole, Robert (2008) *Earthrise: How Man First Saw the Earth.* New Haven, CT: Yale University Press, 2008.

Radhakrishnan, R. (2005) 'Globality Is Not Worldliness', *Gramma: periodiko theẽorias kai kritikeẽs*, 13: 183–198.

Robertson, Roland (1991) 'Globality, Global Culture and Images of World Order', in H. Haferkampf and N. Smelser (eds), *Social Change and Modernity.* Berkeley, CA: University of California Press, pp. 395–411.

Robertson, Roland (2007) 'Globality', in R. Robertson and J. A. Scholte, *Encyclopedia of Globalization*, vol. 2. London: Routledge, pp. 524–526.

Roy, Parama (2001) 'At Home in the World? The Gendered Cartography of Globality', *Feminist Studies*, 27(3): 709–731.

Sachs, Wolfgang (1994) 'The Blue Planet: An Ambiguous Modern Icon', *The Ecologist*, 24(5): 170–175.

Sagan, Carl (1994) *Pale Blue Dot: A Vision of the Human Future in Space*. New York: Ballantine Books.

Safire, William (2003) *No Uncertain Terms: More Writing from the Popular On Language Column in the New York Times Magazine*. New York: Simon & Schuster.

Schäfer, Wolf (2007) 'Lean Globality Studies', *Globality Studies Journal*, 7, unpaginated.

Scheuerman, William E. (2011) *The Realist Case for Global Reform*. Cambridge: Polity.

Shaw, Martin (2000) *Theory of the Global State: Globality as an Unfinished Revolution*. Cambridge: Cambridge University Press.

Sirkin, Harold L., James W. Hemerling and Arindam K. Bhattacharya (2008) *Globality: Competing with Everyone from Everywhere for Everything*. Boston, MA: Business Plus.

Sloterdijk, Peter (2004) 'Foreword to the Theory of Spheres' (interview with Jean Christophe Royoux), in Melik Ohanian and Jean Christophe Royoux (eds) *Cosmograms*. New York: Lukas & Sternberg.

Sloterdijk, Peter (2009) 'Geometry in the Colossal: The Project of Metaphysical Globalization', *Environment and Planning D: Society and Space*, 27 (1): 29–40.

Spengler, Oswald (2006 [1922]) *The Decline of the West* (abridged edition by Helmut Werner). New York: Oxford University Press.

Steffen, Will et al. (2011) 'The Anthropocene: From Global Change to Planetary Stewardship', *Ambio*, 40(7): 739–761.

Steffen, Will, Jacques Grinevald, Paul Crutzen and John McNeill (2007) 'The Anthropocene: Conceptual and Historical Perspectives', *Philosophical Transactions of the Royal Society A*, 369(1938): 842–867.

Steffen, Will, Wendy Broadgate, Lisa Deutsch, Owen Gaffney and Cornelia Ludwig (2015) 'The Trajectory of the Anthropocene: The Great Acceleration', *The Anthropocene Review*, 21(1): 81–89.

Teilhard de Chardin, P. (1961) *The Phenomenon of Man*. New York: Harper & Row.

Toynbee, Arnold J. (1934–1961) *A Study of History*, vols 1–12. Oxford: Oxford University Press.

Walker, R. B. J. (2010) *After the Globe, Before the World*. Abingdon: Routledge.

Wallerstein, Immanuel (2004) *World-Systems Analysis. An Introduction*. Durham, NC: Duke University Press.

Wells, Herbert G. (1920) *The Outline of History: Being a Plain History of Life and Mankind*. New York: Garden City Publishing.

Wendt, Alexander (2003) 'Why a World State is Inevitable', *European Journal of International Relations*, 9(4): 491–542.

Wermuth, Anthony L. (1955) 'Globality and Land Forces', *Military Review*, 35(7), 3–11.

Wood, Linda Sargent (2010) *A More Perfect Union: Holistic Worldviews and the Transformation of American Culture after World War II*. Oxford: Oxford University Press.

Woodward, David (1989) 'The Image of the Spherical Earth', *Perspecta*, 25: 2–15.

Yergin, D. (1998), 'The Age of "Globality"', *Newsweek*, 131(20): 24–27.

1 New Earths

Assessing planetary geographic constructs

Daniel Deudney and Elizabeth Mendenhall

Introduction

Humans have always sought to accurately understand and map where they are, their places and spaces. Narratives about space and place legitimated some behaviors and activities over others. For most of human history, people lived in spatially very confined places. But over the last several centuries humans have increasingly acted in, and mapped, much larger, and increasingly global spatial scales. While humans have always lived on the globe-shaped planet Earth, this fact has become practically relevant for human activities only recently. In antiquity, a small handful of astronomers and geographers realized that the overall shape of the world humans inhabited was spherical. This global shape took on practical significance with the first circumnavigation of the oceans, which generated a realization of finitude and closure – if you traveled far enough in one direction you would end up where you started. The new geographic knowledge about the Earth produced by oceanic navigation had disorienting effects, by challenging and even unraveling the spatial dimensions of the many civilizational and cosmological narratives, thus disrupting and subverting long established ways of doing things.

Over the course of the nineteenth and twentieth centuries, as modernization and globalization accelerated due to the spread of science-based technological amplifications of human capabilities, the fact that the human habitat was global began to take on rapidly increasing importance (Pemberton 2001). New technologies of communication and transportation expanded the ability of humans to explore and interact on vast spatial scales. Overall, this globalization of technological civilization produced high levels of interdependency, interaction, and complexity at global scales. These developments were amplified and took new directions during the Cold War, with nuclear, space, and computing technological developments, as well as growing environmental awareness. The Cold War also created new technological vulnerabilities and possibilities for secular catastrophes of unprecedented magnitude and scope, thus raising the stakes of political and technological choices to a level never previously experienced.

These changes produced great disorientations about space and place, as the previously far became near and as human activities expanded in their scope, and direction, both 'up' into 'outer space' and 'down' into the micro-world (Hall 1992). At the same time that these disintegrative and disorienting tendencies were so pronounced, space technology also provided for the first time a 'bird's eye view' of the entire Earth. These images triggered new spatial reinvisionings and mappings, as well as new contestations about globality and planetarity.

The realization of the novel, emergent global and planetary experience of globality stimulated a search for new Earth metaphors. This search has also been propelled by awareness that older over-arching spatial metaphors and frames underpinning and orienting human activity had been rendered obsolete. In a burst of creative activity over the last two centuries, and particularly during the Cold War decades, many self-described global thinkers have advanced a variety of alternative Earth metaphors, analogies, and images. Each attempts to summarize the new human planetary situation. Sometimes they compete and sometimes they overlap. Some of these, such as 'one world', 'whole Earth', 'spaceship Earth', 'mother Earth', 'Gaian Earth', 'global village', and the 'Anthropocene' are widely known. But others, such as 'cradle Earth', 'World Brain', 'laboratory Earth' and 'rare Earth' have less extensive currency. This search for new spatial metaphors has also been accompanied by a similarly motivated effort to recast temporal frames, most notably in the recent 'Big History' movement (Christian, Brown, and Benjamin 2014).

These formulations are architectonic in their ambition to provide a new view of the overall human situation as global. In short, they are advanced as new but simple answers to the basic question of place, of 'where we live'. These new Earths are designed to provide an overarching unity, to put various parts in their proper place as solutions to the fragmentation and acceleration associated with modernization and globalization. These competing summations are intended to have far-reaching implications for human practical activity by making some activities seem 'suitable to the situation'. They seek a new global vernacular consciousness, a new sense of 'common place'. They also combine summary encapsulations of the new situation with legitimate and unified practical political agendas. They combine the descriptive and prescriptive in varying degrees.

Each new Earth formulation contains tensions, even contradictions, between their goals of accurately mapping what is, rhetorically evoking emotions, and advancing political agendas. They are not just simplified maps, they are also carefully chosen words, selected not just for their accuracy but also for their rhetorical persuasiveness and their metaphoric and analogic links to familiar small-scale spaces, places, and entities and relations. As rhetoric, the terms of these formulations succeed or fail in their emotive persuasion depending on the associations they make, or fail to make, with their audiences. They have different resonance with different audiences. And rhetorics, metaphors, and analogies are notoriously 'double edged swords' in that they not only say what is meant to be said but also make points that are quite different, even subversive or contradictory, from their intended associations (Lakoff and Johnson 1980).

Assessing the new Earth representations

Critically examining and evaluating several of the leading new Earth formulations – the aim of this chapter – is complicated because the 'objects' of analysis are unsettled amalgams of (1) visual representations and photographic images of the Earth, (2) everyday, ancient, and emotionally charged words (such as 'mother', 'home', 'cradle'), (3) familiar local spatial forms (such as 'village'), and (4) familiar objects and machines (such as 'ships' and 'laboratories'). They also interchangeably employ the spatial terms of 'world', 'global', and 'planetary', sometimes as loose synonyms, but sometimes to denote very different spatial forms. And many have evolved over time, changing in complex ways, sometimes to reflect new knowledge about the Earth, but sometimes due to their political connotations and the oppositions they arouse.

Given the multi-dimensional nature of the objects examined here, a complete assessment is beyond the scope of this chapter. Our limited focus here is on the 'geo' dimensions of these new Earth formulations. This is a potentially fruitful focus because these new Earths are always in significant part geographical in that they contain images, terms, metaphors, and representations of space and place and because they aim to provide more accurate and up-to-date understandings of geophysical Earth. This is also a fruitful focus because most of them are 'geopolitical', in that they derive particular practical political agendas from the geographic realities they purport to embody. In making this geo-centered assessment, we employ three distinct sets of tools, first from 'critical geography', second from 'geopolitics' and third from what we refer to as 'geography criticism'.

First, we employ the tools of critical geography. The key insight of critical geography is that maps and spatial representations are slanted in ways that reflect the social and cultural assumptions and political and economic interests and ideologies of those who make and use them, to make parochial views and purposes seem natural, grounded in 'the way things are' (Cosgrove 2001; O'Tuathail 1996). During the Cold War, the stakes in global formulations were particularly high because they reflected fundamental conflicts of interest and ideology regarding the relationship between violence and the environment, national purpose, scientific and technological progress, and world order. Given that the fate of the Earth has been in play, the practical consequences of unmasking slanted geographies are great.

Second, we assess the extent to which these new Earth representations accurately capture the actual contours of the new global and planetary situation. Despite the prominence of the geographic aspects of these new Earths, their accuracy has not been extensively or systematically assessed.

Doing this entails what we refer to as geography criticism, by which we mean the assessment of the extent to which these geographic representations contained in new Earth formulations are accurate. Beyond assessing accuracy, geography criticism also seeks to identify what has been left out. Geography criticism evaluates the congruence between the representation and reality. Geography criticism is different from critical geography because it assesses the accuracy of claims about geography found in various socially constructed and politically motivated metaphors and arguments. In short, critical geography exposes the socially constructed and biased claims about geography, while geography criticism assesses what each formulation captures and misses about the material and geophysical new Earth.

Our third aim is to critically examine the implicit and explicit geopolitical dimensions of these new Earths. In combining claims about geography with political agendas, these Earth formulations are inherently geopolitical. Lacking any general theory of geopolitics, and making no effort to provide one here, we assess the nature and plausibility of the connections between mappings of planetary geographic materiality and claims about the appropriateness of particular political arrangements. The geographical is most commonly linked to the political in these Earth formulations because they descriptively characterize problematic, even catastrophic, aspects of the contemporary planetary situation. Problem-ridden images of the new Earth inexorably point toward particular solutions and their attendant political practices and authorities. In short, we attempt to examine how convincingly the problems that are emphasized or implied by various mappings connect to their accompanying political agendas.

Making and contesting 'one world'

Perhaps the simplest and most widespread characterization of the globality of the human situation is the simple expression 'one world'. The word 'world' is commonly associated with the place or space within which humans live, which at the broadest spatial scale was referred to as the 'oikoumene'. Geographers sought to map the dimensions of this habitation zone within the geophysical features of the Earth, which until the Middle Ages was understood as the lands and narrow waters in a broad crescent across Eurasia. The global reconnaissances of the 1500s and 1600s not only greatly expanded awareness of the vast reaches of inhospitable spaces on the planet but also revealed the presence of 'new worlds', most notably the Americas and Australia. By the later years of the nineteenth century, the combination of interstate rivalry, imperialism, and colonialism, fueled and amplified by the Industrial Revolution, made it increasingly clear to many observers that the previously fragmented and distant parts of the 'oikoumene' were merging together into 'one world'. The 'international relations theory' of this period, 'global geopolitics', extensively described this enlarged, interdependent, and interactive global human world and debated its main features and implications, particularly for military security (Deudney 2007). The advent of the airplane at the turn of the twentieth century, and its rapid diffusion and technological progression provided the most vivid and popularly resonant versions of the 'one world' insight (Jones 1955). In the works of science fiction writers and scientific-technological futurists, most notably H. G. Wells, the reality of 'one world' and the role of technology in creating it entered into wide popular awareness (Wong, Westfahl, and Chan 2005).

A major theme of the global geopoliticians had been the likelihood of 'world wars' whose spatial scope (and level of violence) would be unprecedented. Although earlier inter-state and imperial struggles, most notably the Seven Years' War, had been fought across multiple oceans and continents, the expression 'world war' came to be the universally employed designation for the two great twentieth-century conflicts during the years 1914–18 and 1936–45. The second of these conflicts, World War II, embroiled major combatants in all developed parts of the world and was fought across vast territorial, oceanic, and aerial 'theaters' of conflict. For a great many observers, this brought home the fact that military and economic interdependence had become so great that fundamentally new approaches to world order were necessary.

One world, anti-one world, and world government

During World War II and then the Cold War, the expression 'one world' became the central construct in a large body of theoretical, strategic, and popular writings and a leading rhetorical presence in American grand strategic public discourse. A key feature of these 'one world' formulations was the notion of a discrepancy between the 'one world' situation on the one hand, and popular consciousness and political arrangements on the other. The disjuncture between 'the way things really were' and the configuration of institutions was deployed to justify wide-ranging proposals for world order reform, limitations on national autonomy, and the establishment of effective forms of international cooperation, governance, and even government. The most significant institutional product of this way of thinking was the United Nations, which was advanced as a necessary step toward bringing world order into line with the material realities of the 'one world'. In addition to such structural programs and efforts, 'one world' thinkers also argued that human ideas and identities were dangerously obsolete. They advanced many proposals to replace provincial and parochial orientations with more cosmopolitan forms. UNESCO and a large and growing body of international NGOs and civil-society groups pursue this mission.

One world and its enemies

The development of nuclear weapons in the 1940s and their rapid technological maturation in the US–Soviet arms race further boosted the salience of 'one world' views of the global situation and greatly augmented the credibility of the claim that great disaster would occur unless political arrangements were radically altered. The United States and the Soviet Union, the two main victors of World War II, were locked in a struggle for global primacy, characterized by extreme ideological antagonism. Both believed that their ideology was universally applicable, and both feared the other as an extreme threat. This fueled rapid military, technological, and scientific innovation and competition to map and master the vast extra-territorial realms of the planet, and thus this era was particularly fertile in new formulations of the global whole.

Thinking about the implications of nuclear weapons for security and global political order has been fundamentally contested, and during the first half-decade of the nuclear era 'nuclear one world' views were especially salient. Theorists working from many different political orientations concluded that the development of nuclear weapons required some form of world government (Masters and Way 1946). Although they disagreed about its character, 'nuclear one world' thinking held that the elimination of system-level anarchy on a worldwide basis was necessary for the survival of civilization and that such an authoritative world political organization would be 'above' territorial states (Deudney 2007; Craig 2003, this volume). Thus, the expression 'one world' became transmuted from its core original notion of technological and material interdependence into shorthand for an agenda to address the resulting vulnerabilities by transferring authority 'upward' to a world government. In short, 'one world' came to refer to a program rather than a reality.

Once 'one worldism' became synonymous with a program for world government, the stage was set for the rise of a very strong 'anti-one worldism'. In the view of many observers, world government might itself become a peril of universal scope because such an entity would be potentially difficult to check and thus would tend to become a world totalitarian despotism. This fear of tyranny, combined with the growing realization that some form of nuclear balance of power or deterrence might greatly lower the prospects of nuclear war, diminished perceptions of the immediate peril. With the threat of world government elevated and the peril of nuclear war reduced, the stage was set for a Cold War American realist grand strategic orientation of navigating a middle path of deterrence and balancing between these two dangers. American strategy thus sought to steer between the twin perils of one world government and the 'no world' of nuclear annihilation. Nuclear war and 'one world' outcomes as world government were thus elevated to parallel status as ultimate *perils*. Across the long decades of the Cold War and after, 'anti-one world' government thinking and activism, often fueled to paranoiac heights by the suspicion that even modest forms of international cooperation and organization-building were on a slippery slope to world despotism, persisted as the central construct of ideological anti-internationalism.

The general failure to realize 'one world' ambitions of creating a unified human political and cultural community also reflects the limitations of the 'one world' narrative's account of the actualities of technological development.

'Nuclear one worldism' posited that a decisive material change had occurred. But its agenda of moving 'upwards' has been confounded and subverted by the rapidity, complexity, and unpredictability of ongoing technological, and therefore economic, political, strategic, and military change. It also neglects the ways in which material change has been uneven and stratified and the ways in which material interconnections and interdependence have served as conduits for new types power and competition.

Lifeboat Earth and cosmopolitanism ethics

Another 'one worldism' emerged during the 1960s and 1970s, with rising awareness of ecological and resource limitations and rates of population growth that seemed to be inexorably outstripping natural resources and local carrying capacities. Like its nuclear predecessor, ecological 'one worldism' linked a characterization of the global situation with an agenda for various forms of global cooperation and governance (Falk 1972). The 'lifeboat' seemed to many to capture the new human global predicament: 'we are all in the same boat' and will all sink if we do not collaboratively ration our finite resources and develop cooperative ways of getting along in our crowded and imperiled 'lifeboat world' (Brand 2009).

The 'anti-one world' argument and agenda also took new forms and deployed a competing 'lifeboat' geographic formulation. The pessimistic ecologist Garrett Hardin also likens the human situation to a 'lifeboat', but posits multiple lifeboats, each adrift in a pitiless and dangerous sea (Hardin 1974: 561). Hardin uses this analogy to argue against cosmopolitan 'one world' approaches. He observes that some lifeboats are better stocked and less crowded than others and argues that the better off should not attempt to rescue or assist those in impoverished lifeboats. In this analogy of rising but uneven ecological scarcity, global politics is segmented into territorial states ('lifeboats'), and has hardened into purely self-regarding political regimes. In Hardin's formulation an agenda of enhanced particularism and fragmentation, lack of concern for others, and indifference to the whole is transposed onto an anti-global geographic imaginary that combines disconnected built structures and an utterly undifferentiated, but perilous, nature.

Hardin assumes an imaginary geophysical that is essentially inaccurate, ignoring the basic reality of high levels of interdependence and interaction and grossly over-estimating the desire and capacity of different territorial groups to compartmentalize themselves from migrant flows, networks of production and exchange, and extended ecological footprints. A unit of carbon put into the atmosphere by anyone, anywhere on the Earth enters a global atmospherically circulated carbon reservoir. The consequences of such emissions manifest themselves globally. Similarly, a cache of plutonium anywhere, given modern transportation connectivity, is potentially a threat to anyone anywhere, but particularly to those in the wealthiest and economically strongest sectors of the world.

Furthermore, this extreme version of 'anti-one world' thinking tends to overlook the legacies of colonialism, imperialism, and militarism that at least partially explain why some lifeboats are less equipped than others. Far from recognizing these centuries of asymmetric interactions, Hardin simply blames the governments of less-advanced or less-resilient countries as less 'wise' than industrialized states. He also characterizes the needs of different lifeboats, and hence their claim to resources, as straightforwardly derivative of population size, thus obscuring the fact that consumption on the well-stocked boats is for luxuries, not necessities. Hardin's proposed 'lifeboat ethic' seals off the larger dilemmas about global resource distribution, providing no account of how and why the lifeboats became so different in their ability to support life. In short, Hardin's flawed formulation of globality is little more than an attempt to provide a foundation for policies of protectionism, nativism, and nationalism.

Spaceship Earth, laboratory Earth, and global techno-politics

By the later years of the twentieth century, modern scientific research, much of it funded for Cold War purposes, produced a revolutionary new view of the planet's geography. Spurred by Cold War rivalry, scientific study of the Earth grew rapidly. New weapons technologies such as submarines, airplanes, missiles, and satellites drew the military competition deeper into the extra-territorial realms of the ocean, atmosphere, and orbital space. As this happened, the performance of weapons systems and the conduct of war came increasingly to depend upon mapping and knowledge of the 'global commons' (Deudney 1983). This explosion in scientific investigation of the Earth was enabled by rapid improvements in the sensitivity of instrumentation, data processing, and platforms with synoptic coverage, most notably satellites. Furthermore, scientific investigation was stimulated in the 1960s and 1970s by growing awareness of environmental problems at global spatial scales and the connections between human health and large complex Earth systems. As science revealed new connections, worldwide environmental and anti-nuclear peace movements emerged and influenced scientific research agendas. Practical environmental problem-solving, like weapons deployments, increasingly came to hinge upon knowledge about the ocean, the atmosphere, and complex ecosystems.

Alongside this vast expansion in natural science, modern technological civilization has also pursued its core Baconian Enlightenment project of altering the material world to improve the human estate through the development, deployment, and operation of tools, machines, and systems of machines with successively increasing capabilities. Aspirations to re-fashion the natural world to serve human ends have been so effectively realized that human-built machines have become of global and planetary scope. In the destructiveness of weaponry, the range and speeds of communication and transportation, and in the scope of human exploitation of 'natural resources', the 'footprint' of humanity on the Earth has been transformed from almost undetectable to significantly determinative of the trajectory of life on Earth, ushering in what is now widely called the 'Anthropocene'. As this has happened, the Baconian Enlightenment project of mastering nature began to encounter limits rooted both in the features of the Earth and in the capacities of science to provide reliable information on which to base decisions of practical significance.

A primary feature of this 'new Earth' mapping is a greatly expanded understanding of human vulnerabilities to potential natural disasters and secular anthropogenic catastrophes of comprehensive planetary scope. Some of this new knowledge concerns a widened awareness of 'natural disasters' such as super-volcanoes, asteroidal collisions, sudden climate shifts, and new plagues. Some vulnerabilities stem from natural processes that humans did not cause, and in many cases can do little or nothing about, while some catastrophes, most notably nuclear war and climate change, have human causes and potential remedies.

Two formulations of globality, 'spaceship Earth' and 'laboratory Earth', encapsulate radically different understandings of the planetary situation produced by science and technology and their practical political implications.

Spaceship Earth and the politics of ships

Comparing the Earth to a 'spaceship' is one of the most evocative and salient new formulations of globality. Political theory provides a long lineage of analogizing 'ships' with political entities (Thompson 2001). The state as a ship, the 'ship of state', is a recurrent image in the realpolitik vision of separate polities maneuvering and struggling to survive and flourish in an essentially hostile and indifferent world of rivalrous states. Furthermore, 'ships' are complex machines that humans have built and operated to traverse the water realms of the Earth, and as their capabilities and ranges improved they became crucial links in the web of machines and activities of globalization (Paine 2013).

In the twentieth century, many spatially expanded applications of this basic analog were applied to the Earth as a whole in relation to the cosmos. In 1945 a nuclear one worlder, Ralph Barton Perry, said:

> As the heavens receded and merged with infinite and unknown regions beyond, the Earth began to fill their place. Man's growing sense of cosmic homelessness heightened attachment to his terrestrial home. The Earth became his ship voyaging in vast, uncharted seas. He became increasingly conscious of his dependence on its support and on its provisions, increasingly interested in its decks and cabins and in the fellow passengers with whom he was thus cast adrift.
>
> (Perry 1945: 19)

With the coming of the Space Age, the Earth-ship analogy becomes cast as the Earth itself being a 'space ship'. In an early use of this construct, the economist and peace researcher Kenneth Boulding contrasts two models for thinking about the relationship between humans and the environment. In the 'frontier' or 'cowboy' model, resources are taken from 'outside', consumed 'inside', and then dumped back 'outside'. In the 'spaceship' model everything is recycled and equilibrium is established between consumption and the yield of various natural stocks (Boulding 1966).

The most developed and widely circulated version of spaceship Earth is advanced by the American polymath inventor and designer R. Buckminster Fuller, most notably in his short book of 1969, *Operating Manual for Spaceship Earth*. Fuller's voluminous output of technological futurism and macrohistorical speculations bulges with wild and at times even unintelligible creative ideas. At the zenith of his career in the late 1960s and early 1970s, Fuller was the quintessential globe-trotting and 'jet setting' planetary futurist and his ideas reached wide audiences. In the scope of his intellectual ambition, in the outlandishness of many of his ideas, and in his public visibility, Fuller became the H. G. Wells of his time, and like those of Wells, Fuller's ideas are a further extrapolation of the core Baconian Enlightenment project of human advance through scientific-technological progress.

Fuller begins with a sweeping glance across human history, painting a highly simplistic story of human progress in which maritime activities and innovations play a decisive starring role. Ships empower what Fuller calls the 'top weapons sovereignties' by enabling piracy, plunder, and then trade on a global scale. But Fuller goes further and says the 'powers behind the throne' are maritime engineers. He argues that their mapping and navigational innovations, on successively larger scales, have created a generalized form of knowledge for planning large-scale projects. Fuller calls this generalized planning knowledge 'systems analysis', which he holds has advanced to the point where it can be used comprehensively as an 'operating manual' to allocate resources and direct human activity. Without this move to comprehensive planning, oblivion looms. But if embraced, it provides the path to a utopia of material prosperity beyond the grip of natural necessity (Fuller 1969).

In short, Fuller's program is to turn the Earth, as it travels through space, into increasing approximations of a 'ship'. Making the Earth into a spaceship entails the complete technological reconfiguration of the fabric of the planet, and the enclosure of its life-support systems (Deese 2009; Anker 2005; Anker 2007). Fuller's other works, and the literature of 'macro-engineering', set forth many schemes, such as diverting rivers, re-routing ocean currents, irrigating vast deserts, harvesting wind resources from remote windswept places, and building enclosed and floating cities. These schemes extend into 'outer space' around the Earth, and then beyond to lunar and asteroidal colonization. Visions of controlling the weather and 'geo-engineering' to alter planetary systems to prevent ice ages or arrest global warming essentially continue this spaceship Earth technological imaginary (Hamilton 2013; Fleming 2012; Masco, this volume).

The spaceship Earth formulation captures some essential features of the planetary situation but includes others that are quite illusory and even ominous. It starkly conveys key facts: the Earth's isolated position in a vast and inhospitable cosmic void and its essentially 'closed' character. It also registers the fact that interaction and interdependence are extensive, and extrapolates to a situation in which they are complete. Its call for an 'operating manual' also powerfully conveys the fact that the most important planetary questions are practical questions about the relationship between machines, humans, and material Earth. Its characterization of the situation as ship-like powerfully captures the fact that misguided steering choices can have catastrophic consequences and that all the activities of its human 'crew' must become significantly coordinated and based on the imperatives of the Earth as a whole.

But spaceship Earth also has misleading geophysical and political implications. It overstates the extent to which the human navigators of the Earth can 'sail' their 'ship' to varied and distant destinations. Fuller's globality vision oversimplifies in the way it subsumes the biological and political realms under the laws of mechanics (Noel 1986: 63). It also exaggerates the extent to which the contemporary Earth as a human habitat is built. The Earth, unlike a ship, has not been totally engineered and built to human specifications. The 'closed' spaceship model of the Earth is at least partially misleading because Earth systems depend on inputs from 'outside' in the form of solar energy and the Earth is periodically struck by exogenous asteroidal bodies.

Finally, the political implications of 'spaceship Earth' and government from an 'operating manual' are starkly anti-democratic and anti-liberal. Its suggestion of 'ship-like' and 'top-down' comprehensive hierarchical governance of the crew and passengers (and cargo) is frighteningly technocratic and totalitarian. In contrast to Fuller, Boulding uses the image to convey that the Earth is 'closed' but does not imply that it can or should be comprehensively or centrally directed and managed (Boulding 1966: 3).

Laboratory Earth and the ultimate experiment

Another globality formulation 'laboratory Earth', coined by the atmospheric scientist Stephen Schneider in 1997, encapsulates a fundamentally different message about the prospects for completing the 'conquest of nature' and converting the Earth into a completely *built*, ship-like system. In one sense, the Earth has long been the 'laboratory' of the natural sciences. But saying the whole Earth is a 'laboratory' suggests that humans are running a series of potentially dangerous experiments with the basic features of their habitat and that the potential for reliable scientific knowledge about the outcomes of these experiments is intrinsically limited.

The notion that humans are conducting a giant experiment, in effect making the whole planet a laboratory, appears prominently in discussions of both nuclear war and climate change. Jonathan Schell's 1982 book *The Fate of the Earth* powerfully synthetizes the evidence that nuclear war and nuclear testing constitutes a giant experiment. Reaching millions of people, his argument is credited by historians as helping to catalyze the global anti-nuclear movement that preceded the end of the Cold War and as a landmark statement on the singularity of the Earth (Wittner 2003). Similarly, humans are said to be 'unwittingly conducting a vast geophysical experiment' in one of the first official reports on climate change, presented to President Lyndon Johnson by his Scientific Advisory Committee in 1965 (President's Science Advisory Committee 1965: 126). And the report of the first international conference on climate change, the World Conference on the Changing Atmosphere held in Toronto in 1988 states that 'humanity is conducting an unintended, uncontrolled, globally pervasive experiment whose ultimate consequences could be second only to a global nuclear war' (Gardiner 2013: 78).

The 'laboratory' is the site for the production of reliable scientific knowledge, but the entire Earth as a laboratory signals the limits of scientists' ability to provide such knowledge. The modern scientific project deploys a method that in many areas of investigation yields reliable forms of knowledge, which have then been employed to alter and manipulate aspects of nature for human purposes. Most notably, this project has been spectacularly successful in material science and industrial processing. A large and growing complex of artifacts (hydro-electric dams, power plants, airplanes, ships, and submarines, enormous built spaces) and networks (communication, transportation, etc.) has been built on the reliable forms of knowledge that science has generated.

But in studying the Earth, science has reached an epistemological impasse rooted both in features of the Earth and the method of science. As more resources have been devoted to studying the Earth, and more knowledge accumulated about the Earth, science's ability to generate sound knowledge has proven to be limited because complexity and non-linear effects mark Earth systems. As a result, the ability to explain and make predictions about biological organisms, ecosystems of organisms, Earthquakes, severe storms, ocean circulations, and climate patterns has been frustrated. It is now widely recognized by theorists of the Earth sciences, and philosophers of science, that the Earth as an object of study presents insurmountable barriers due to the nature of the Earth itself (Botkin 1990).

Furthermore, scientific knowledge depends upon the study of multiple examples, which can be isolated and manipulated in controlled experiments. For the Earth, such procedures are impossible simply because there is only one Earth, and its major parts are all complexly interactive. In short, as Schell puts it, 'epistemologically the Earth is a special object' (Schell 1982: 76). Despite these epistemological impasses, the massive experiment on 'laboratory Earth' continues, with profound and unknowable consequences for human well-being and survival. In contrast to the analogy of 'spaceship Earth', the political implication of this epistemological impasse is that extreme caution, rather than technocratic optimism, should guide human actions.

In sum, these two globality formulations of 'spaceship Earth' and 'laboratory Earth' have radically different implications. Fuller's 'spaceship Earth' exaggerates technological possibilities, while 'laboratory Earth' points to the limits of science.

Gaia and Medea: Earth Mother, science and myth

Another cluster of post-1945 globality formulations draws on ancient bio-morphic and Earth-anthropomorphizing imagery of the Earth as biological and maternal. The surprising return of 'Earth Mother' conceptualizations as scientific and technological progress accelerated in the post-1945 era reflects the widespread feeling that something very basic and very important is being violated or put at dire risk by new technological empowerments. Recourse to such metaphors has emerged from the frontiers of modern sciences, a most unexpected move by scientists to harness the mytho-poetic resources of the past in order to find overarching images of the new global and planetary situation that capture the most important insights of scientific investigations and explorations. This late-modern appropriation draws on Earth Mother imagery that was extremely widespread in pre-modern societies all over the planet (Sjoo and Mor 1987; Neumann 2015).

Gaia: Earth as organism

A powerful and pervasive new globality derives from James Lovelock's 1979 Gaia hypothesis. This scientific hypothesis emerged from the late twentieth-century investigations of the atmosphere, ocean, lithosphere, and biosphere. These investigations have been revolutionized by the realization that Earth realms are not separate but rather complexly interacting and co-evolving. This means that realm-specific investigations must converge into one Earth system science, thus making a global scale perspective necessary to grasp and represent the interconnections between geophysical and biogeochemical Earth processes.

Lovelock's Gaia hypothesis is an argument about the character of the integrative Earth system. He holds that the Earth itself is 'alive' and functions as a 'single organism'. This Earth organism creates and maintains many of the conditions necessary for its own survival: the Earth is habitable for life because life has been making the Earth habitable for itself. Lovelock emphasizes that major Earth systems, such as the atmosphere, are extremely resilient because of their co-evolution with life. Thus, in his view humans can abuse the Earth and it can compensate in ways that humans will not necessarily recognize or benefit from. This is a design argument, in which processes immanent to the 'alive world' have teleological tendencies.

In labeling the living Earth system 'Gaia', Lovelock is stepping beyond science to draw on ancient understandings of a mythical 'Mother Earth' as a living being with a maternal relationship to the human species. The Gaian amalgamation of scientific, metaphysical, and spiritual orientations towards the Earth has facilitated different appropriations of the formulation that emphasize its different elements. Most notably, 'Gaia' has been adopted enthusiastically by parts of the environmental movement, eco-feminists, and 'New Age' groups, becoming a 'shorthand for holistic approaches' to health and human well-being (Heise 2008: 24). The anthropomorphic maternal Gaia facilitated the appropriation of the spiritual and mythical aspects of this 'new Earth' globality at the expense of its science and systems-based aspects. But this incorporation cannot be dismissed as misappropriation, because the ethical, religious, and teleological connotations of Gaia and its insights about Earth systems science are interconnected. Thus, Lovelock says that achieving homeostasis is an automatic process but requires intelligence, 'giving a sense of intentionality to objects that cannot have consciousness, desire, and purpose' (Botkin 2012: 136). Similarly, the relationship between humans and the 'Earth mother' is unclear because Lovelock holds that the human species is a part of Gaia, that Gaia is now 'awake and aware of herself' through humans, and that humans can serve to protect Gaia from mega-catastrophes like asteroid collisions (Lovelock 1979: 148). As a result of these controversies and ambiguities, the Gaia hypothesis has fractured into several different versions, each with different political implications (Schneider 2004).

Lovelock's globality formulation has diverse implications for human environmental policies and practices. The notion that Mother Earth has capacities to self-correct and re-establish homeostasis in the face of anthropogenic disruptions has quietist implications by encouraging a 'don't worry about it' orientation to contemporary environmental problems like climate change. Lovelock's claim that Gaia is a 'very democratic entity' in which the human species is a member but not a leader suggests that humans can pursue their own species interest because the other members of the organic Earth democracy will provide checks and balances in pursuing their own interests (Lovelock 1979: 145). But the idea that humans have an obligation to use technology to save Gaia from large-scale emergencies such as an asteroid collision or Ice Age contradicts the notion that the human species has no special status and seems to license macro-scale geo-engineering of the climate. Thus, these varied interpretations of the Gaia hypothesis imply that human interactions with the environment can be variously neutral, correctable, or good.

The Medea alternative

Responding to the Gaia 'new Earth' formulation, the scientist Peter Ward suggests that a more appropriate label for the role of life on Earth is Medea, a sorceress princess who killed her own children. Ward argues that recent discoveries about deep time, combined with extrapolations into the future, challenge Gaian notions of the role of life on Earth. Instead of life sustaining a planet's habitability, the Medea hypothesis posits that catastrophic losses of abundance and biodiversity experienced in the Earth's past were caused by life itself and will re-occur in the future, ultimately leading to the extinction of life and a return to planetary sterility (Ward 2009). Examples of biogenic disasters in the history of life on Earth include the 'methane crisis' of 3.7 billion years ago, the rapid oxygenation of the Earth due to the emergence of photosynthesis (resulting in massive die-offs of previously prolific oxygen-intolerant species), and the major temperature fluctuations, including extreme Ice Ages, or 'snowball Earths', caused by ecological evolution. Ward argues that most historical mass extinction episodes had internal microbial causes instead of external origins (such as an asteroid collision). Looking into the future, he suggests that the loss of carbon dioxide from the atmosphere is a high-probability scenario for total animal extinction in about 500 million years.

The Medea formulation, unlike Gaia, highlights the anthropogenic nature of major Earth systems disruptions like climate change. Paradoxically, it also has quietist political implications. If humans or another species are bound to generate a mass extinction through the natural course of ecological evolution, then a 'use it or lose it' orientation towards the Earth becomes more persuasive. An anthropomorphic Medea Earth 'mother' may serve to naturalize human disruptions, displacing responsibility for major anthropogenic alterations to the Earth. Medea, like Gaia, also fails to register the contestation between fragmented human communities, eliding the distinction between 'humans destroyed the biosphere with nuclear weapons' and 'the superpowers destroyed the biosphere in a world war'. In other words, assuming that life is self-destroying obscures the role of political choice, with inadvertent catastrophic consequences. This may also generate a practical political agenda of resignation to major risks.

Whole Earth, rare Earth, and cradle Earth: the politics of leaving

Another family of 'new Earth' globalities has emerged during the 'Space Age' from new technologies spurred by Cold War rivalry, most notably new transportation technologies enabling machines to go beyond the thin film of gasses hugging planet Earth and enter cosmic outer space. Many of the technological milestones, such as long-range missiles, Earth satellites, lunar landings, and inter-planetary probes, have been major public events, often involving high stakes international politics. Unexpectedly, new views of the Earth from space have gained wide currency for thinking about the planetary situation and the specialness of the Earth in the cosmos. The re-visioning of the Earth during the 'Space Age' has also been marked by an array of technological imaginaries and visionary schemes to leave the Earth behind. These re-visionings and futurist imaginaries have posed sharp questions about the tension between parochial nation-state objectives and the universality of global and cosmic perspectives.

Whole Earth and the pale blue dot

The 'Space Age' led to greatly expanded knowledge about the realms beyond the planet. But looking at the Earth from space has been a surprising and far-reaching consequence of the first human outer space activities. In 1950, the astronomer Fred Hoyle observed that 'Once a photograph of the Earth, taken from the outside, is available … a new idea as powerful as any in history will let loose' (Hoyle 1950: 9–10). The astronauts all reported that they were captivated, even mesmerized, by the panorama of the Earth, far more than vastly distant celestial bodies. The first 'whole Earth' photographs of the planet taken from space in the late 1960s were widely viewed as evocative and revolutionary in their implications, coming to symbolize a fundamentally novel human relationship with the planet and the cosmos and serving for many as a new master metaphor for the 'new Earth' (Poole 2008).

The whole Earth picture became a central icon for a variety of different schools of thought. For the emerging environmental movement the whole Earth images became powerful symbols of Earth system science, and they were prominently displayed at the first Earth Day in 1970. The whole Earth picture seemed to show the Earth 'as it actually was', showing the fluidity of the atmosphere and oceans and not showing sharp lines and compartmentalizations. Thus, it looked radically different from previous maps, particularly political mappings of state territorial borders. But the whole Earth imagery also obscured human activity as an immensely influential part of the planet, as well as political and cultural differences within and between human communities. Furthermore, the whole Earth photograph is ambiguous, sometimes connoting fragility, other times resilience (Cosgrove 1994).

The whole Earth image also was appropriated by 'New Age' spiritualists seeking to revive ancient claims about the Earth as possessing a mystic unity and sacred aura, and to re-establish artistic, religious, and mythological connections to the Earth in 'Space-Age consciousness' (Noel 1986: 199). This 'geo-mystic' understanding of the whole Earth can be seen as a reaction to the 'scientific literalism' associated with technological space sensing and measurement. There is, however, a contradiction between the geo-mythic anti-technological spiritualism and reliance on an image produced uniquely by advanced technology.

Another view of the Earth from space, taken decades later by probes in the outer solar system billions of miles away, showed the Earth to be a 'pale blue dot', in the words of the astronomer Carl Sagan. Sagan, whose ideas reached millions, described Earth as 'a lonely speck in the great enveloping cosmic dark' (Sagan 1995: 7). Since the time of Copernicus, the unfathomable size of cosmic outer space was known by astronomy, but the 'pale blue dot' was an actual photograph rather than an abstractly generated notion. The 'pale blue dot' suggests a twin message about the human situation – the planet is immensely significant from the human perspective, but from the cosmic perspective merely another planet of no particular import. Sagan drew a pointed political message from this image, arguing that its vulnerability 'underscores our responsibility to deal more kindly with one another and to preserve and cherish the pale blue dot, the only home we've ever known' (Sagan 1995: 7). Unfortunately, Sagan provides little guidance on translating the 'humility borne of our celestial demotion' into political arrangements that are more kind, cherishing, and preservationist (Ruprecht 1996: 463).

The limitations of the 'whole Earth' and 'pale blue dot' images are the flip side of the insights they contain: the images convey a natural geographic unity but obscure the stratifications and inequalities of the human world. Also, they give no guidance on how to realize planetary sustainability and human unity. The planet is indisputably one, but the lived worlds of humans are still fragmented and stratified.

Rare Earth

Another powerful and widely discussed understanding, the Earth as 'rare Earth', emerged out of the nascent field of astrobiology. The question of life in the universe beyond Earth has long fascinated. The Copernican Revolution led to the 'mediocrity principle' by displacing the Earth from the center of the universe and by establishing the vastness of cosmic space and the stupendously large number of 'other worlds' in it. Given the vast number of other worlds, it seemed logical to assume that life, and indeed intelligent life, existed on some other worlds, perhaps even in our own solar system (Dick 1992). Starting in the middle years of the twentieth century with the development of radio astronomy, a small network of scientists began an often underfunded but widely publicized systematic Search for Extraterrestrial Intelligence (SETI). Many serious astronomers, most notably Carl Sagan and Iosif Shklovskii, estimated that there were tens of thousands of technological civilizations in the Milky Way galaxy alone (Sagan and Shklovskii 1966).

The rare Earth image emerged to sum up a radical revision downward in the number of planets with intelligent life. In the classic formulation of the 'Rare Earth hypothesis', Peter Ward and Donald Brownlee argue that microbial life is likely to be present in many places, but that complex metazoic (i.e. functionally differentiated multi-cellular) life is likely to be extremely rare, and intelligent life even scarcer (Ward and Brownlee 2000). This argument is based on a greatly expanded knowledge of the history of the Earth and its life across deep time. According to Ward and Brownlee, the emergence and subsequent evolution of complex life on Earth has been made possible by a long list of very rare geophysical, solar, and galactic features. Furthermore, planetary disasters such as super-volcanism, climate change, and asteroidal collisions could have been more frequent and severe, suggesting that the persistence of complex life on Earth has been a matter of extraordinary luck. This argument thus reverses the previously dominant 'principle of mediocrity'.

One implication of the rare Earth view is that environmental decay, habitat loss, and species extinction are events of galactic importance. Instead of seeing the Earth as something common and potentially replaceable, this view provides a cosmic underpinning for the agenda of sustaining Earth habitability. It also supports human expansion into space and the development of technologies to protect Earth from asteroidal collision. Or, as the space expansionists put it, 'the dinosaurs became extinct because they didn't have a space program' (Chaikin 2001).

The 'rare Earth' formulation elevates low probability, high consequence events that might render the Earth uninhabitable at the expense of shorter-term, widely felt, often acute problems of on-going systemic oppression and environmental degradation. Furthermore, the rare Earth hypothesis will be subject to continuous potential challenge and modification as astrobiology advances. Despite presenting a view of the Earth as radically unique, the rare Earth hypothesis may err in confusing the rareness of a particular sequence with the rareness of a particular outcome.

Humanity's cradle and launchpad Earth

Another family of 'new Earth' globalities produced by the 'Space Age' focuses on leaving the Earth. The Russian inventor and space enthusiast Konstantin Tsiolkovsky, who sketched many of the basic stepping-stones for a trek to the stars, memorably referred to the Earth as 'humanity's cradle' (Tsiolkovsky 1960 [1906]). Similarly, the American counter-culture guru Timothy Leary spoke of the Earth as the 'womb planet' and 'nursery planet' (Leary 1977). These formulations encapsulate the elaborately developed vision of large-scale human expansion into space. 'Womb', 'cradle', and 'nursery' posit biological staging, collapsing all of human history into a preliminary stage for the actual maturation of the species through space expansion. The Earth home is transformed into an archaic stage in human evolution. Human advancement is measured by our ability to leave the Earth. This elides human development into technological development, turning the rocket and other space technologies into elaborate species prosthetics. This anthropocentric image leaves no role for other organisms or intrinsic value of the Earth. Cradle Earth becomes a launching pad for an inevitable human advance across a new frontier, which humanity must transgress to fulfill its species destiny.

These formulations seriously mischaracterize the human planetary situation. The 'nursery' metaphor is a mismatch with expansion into space. When infants leave the 'cradle' they move into a world that is still quite nurturing and hospitable, but the human species, on leaving the Earth, enters a harshly inhospitable realm. Furthermore, this cradle imagery fails to register the important fact that humans are despoiling their Earthly cradle. For some space expansion advocates, human ruination of the Earth justifies human expansion into space. Positing unlimited habitats across the 'final frontier' diminishes the significance of Earthly degradation. This framing of human possibilities values investments in space technology more than sustaining Earth's habitability. In this way, the 'cradle Earth' metaphor is essentially Earth-denying. It embraces a technological utopianism that obscures but cannot overcome the finitude, closure, and vulnerability of terrestrial Earth.

Global intelligence and global consciousness: meta-information politics

The rapid and accelerating growth of communications and computing technology, greatly stimulated by Cold War 'R&D', produced yet another entire family of 'new Earth' globality formulations centered on information, consciousness, and intelligence. In this large and diverse intellectual landscape, there are at least four roughly distinct variants of 'minded' Earth images.

Global biogenic brain

Starting at the broadest level is the theory that life itself is a type of 'super brain' in the sense that the genetic codes governing the forms and functions of all organisms constitute a vast library of information, which has been slowly accumulating across the billions of years of evolution. This natural informatic has been creative across time and has also been, through gene-swapping and reproductive descent, networked in such a way that individual organisms are mere manifestations of a collective, planet-spanning super-organism (Bloom 2000). The view that life is essentially a form of organized information implies that human artifacts and digital information are fundamentally similar in kind to life itself, captured in the adage that 'a chicken is a means by which eggs reproduce' (Dyson 1997). With this view of life, the new artificial information systems and the webbing together of increasingly powerful processing units can be seen as the next stage in the evolution of life and consciousness.

World Brain

The second cluster of 'global brain' formulations is much less comprehensive and cosmic. H. G. Wells articulates in his 1938 book *World Brain* the basic notion that dispersed human expertise and knowledges are accumulating and increasingly interconnected. Wells' conception of the locus of this knowledge and its role in human life is highly practical in character. He uses the language of a 'New Republic' to describe the worldwide network of scientific and technical experts, thus combining the Platonic notion of rule of the knowledgeable with a modern democratic commitment to universal dissemination and participation. Wells argues that only the accelerated emergence of the 'World Brain' enables humanity to avoid secular technological catastrophes. Wells speaks of a creating a 'networked encyclopedia' and eventually a 'World Brain Organization' to serve as the 'Competent Receiver' for the information required to direct world affairs by defining problems, forming solutions, building consensus, and coordinating implementation. Assembling, coordinating, and distributing the accumulated human knowledge will stimulate a 'gigantic and many-sided educational renascence' and civilizational advance (Wells 1937: xv).

Wells' argument is based on a rationalist assumption about the ability and willingness of groups to translate knowledge into appropriate action. The global brain as a path to problem-solving ignores the fact that knowledges, even scientific, can be deeply contested, that knowledge is used for conflicting agendas, and that a consensus about a global problem does not translate into uncontested solutions.

Telecommunications and the global electronic village

A third cluster of formulations centers on changes in communication technologies. The electric telegraph was widely discussed as marking an epochal alteration in the human relationship to space and time. Communication at distance previously depended upon the physical transportation of messages, but the telegraph, submarine cables, and satellites transmit at global distances nearly instantaneously. Successive innovations in communication technology, the 'wireless radio', cinematic 'motion pictures', the telephonic transmission of voice, and televised images also rapidly diffused and have been widely analysed for their implications for human life.

Perhaps the best known of these 'new Earth' metaphors focusing on the changes wrought by communications technologies, the term 'global village' was coined by the Canadian media theorist and public intellectual Marshall McLuhan (McLuhan and Fiore 1968). McLuhan wrote cryptic but widely read works on the new globalization spawned from new communications technologies, particularly the television. His key idea was that television, by transmitting full video images essentially everywhere nearly instantaneously, was rapidly creating a village-like communication environment analogous to historically face-to-face small communities. McLuhan argued that this was unifying human awareness and identity, making it a practical engine for the realization of a cosmopolitan human consciousness (McLuhan 1964, 1966).

While McLuhan emphasized this particular electronic unifying and space-compressing technology, the expression 'global village' has come to be widely deployed as shorthand for a more general world transformation. It does powerfully convey the central fact that the intensity of human interaction and interdependence on a global scale now matches that previously only experienced at the locale of a 'village'. This 'collapse of distance' insight implies the need for a 'good neighbor policy' to assure security and habitability. It also implies that a government for this 'village' would be essentially 'municipal' in character and thus attentive to the various 'mundane' and 'quasi-domestic' tasks of 'low politics' but on a vastly larger scale.

The 'global village' construct is deficient as an architectonic metaphor for the planetary condition because it fails to register the presence of 'combined and uneven' patterns of inequalities and differences, the dynamism and continuing acceleration of change, and the practical primacy of the machine and its governance. It is also deficient in its 'presentism', its inability to encompass any pattern of change or continuity across historical time, and thus occludes the enormous legacies from pre-'global village' times. 'Global village' also inaccurately connotes the slowness and stagnation typical of 'village life', whereas the electronic world is experienced as rapidly changing.

Global brain and the World Wide Web

The fourth major cluster of 'new Earth' information formulations centers on the 'World Wide Web' or 'internet'. The extraordinarily rapid advance of electronic digital computing technology since the 1950s has made possible the distribution and interconnection of increasingly powerful computers to support virtually every realm of human activity. Also, universal digitalization has transmuted all previous forms of information from the printed page, photographs, voice and musical recordings, and film into a common format that can be transmitted rapidly through the internet. The internet thus realizes a version of Well's World Brain, particularly its dispersed character and the role of users as both producers and consumers of information. It also further realizes McLuhan's global village vision by removing spatial barriers to substantive forms of interaction and community. Furthermore, sensing technologies now enable the networked communication among dispersed machines, making possible an 'internet of things'.

The internet has been accompanied by a pervasive set of political claims that making more information available would empower and liberate users. This has been amplified by the libertarian ideologies infusing the community of internet entrepreneurs and engineers. There are, however, problems with these expectations. The internet has been increasingly exploited as a tool for surveillance, espionage, and even sabotage. The internet globally interconnects, but the humans that it interconnects lack cosmopolitan consciousness and often pursue predatory and conflicting agendas. Furthermore, the internet has facilitated the monopolization of profits and centralization of power (Lanier 2010). And far from inherently producing liberation, these new information technologies may greatly enable autocratic and authoritarian regimes to tighten control to totalitarian levels (Deibert 2015). The internet as the realization of the global brain has produced connectivity and cumulation, but immense fragmentation rather than unification.

Conclusion

Each of the 'new Earth' formulations assessed here purports to capture the largest and most essential features of the actual new Earth. But these formulations are quite different in the features of the situation they select as most essential. And there does not appear to be any way in which they can be readily synthesized or hierarchically ordered. Despite their shared aspiration to overcome parochial and limited representations of space and place, these 'new Earth' formulations present us with a clash of alternative comprehensive perspectives. All of these 'new Earth' images have in common their attempt to make sense of the planetary condition of post-1945 globality. As such, these 'new

Earth' images are best viewed as embodying not an embryonic, unified understanding but rather a menu of influential but fundamentally contested alternatives. Given that so many aspects of the new Earth are in motion, incomplete and contested, it is premature to expect any one formulation to fully displace or subsume the others. Given this, we will have to make do with competing, radically different new universals while recognizing that these formulations remain valuable as mirrored shards of the essentially unsettled new Earth situation.

References

Anker, Peder (2005) 'The Ecological Colonization of Space', *Environmental History*, 10(2): 239–259.

Anker, Peder (2007) 'Buckminster Fuller as Captain of Spaceship Earth', *Minerva*, 45(4): 417–434.

Bloom, Howard K. (2000) *The Global Brain: The Evolution of Mass Mind from the Big Bang to the 21st Century*. New York: Wiley.

Botkin, Daniel B. (1990) *Discordant Harmonies: A New Ecology for the Twenty-first Century*. Oxford: Oxford University Press.

Botkin, Daniel B. (2012) *The Moon in the Nautilus Shell*. Oxford; New York: Oxford University Press.

Boulding, Kenneth E. (1966) 'The Economics of the Coming Spaceship Earth', in H. Jarrett (ed.), *Environmental Quality in a Growing Economy*. Baltimore, MD: Johns Hopkins University Press.

Brand, Stewart (2010) *Whole Earth Discipline: An Ecopragmatist Manifesto*. London: Atlantic Books.

Browne, Ray B. and Marshall W. Fishwick (eds) (1999) *The Global Village: Dead or Alive?*Bowling Green, OH: Bowling Green State University Popular Press.

Bunyard, Peter and Edward Goldsmith (eds) (1988) *GAIA, the Thesis, the Mechanisms and the Implications*. Wadebridge: Quintrell & Company.

Chaikin, Andrew (2001) 'Meeting of the Minds: Buzz Aldrin Visits Arthur C. Clarke', *Space Illustrated*, 27 February.

Christian, David, Cynthia Stokes Brown, and Craig Benjamin (2014) *Big History: Between Nothing and Everything*. New York: McGraw-Hill.

Cosgrove, Denis (1994) 'Contested Global Visions: One-World, Whole-Earth, and the Apollo Space Photographs', *Annals of the Association of American Geographers*, 84: 270–294.

Cosgrove, Denis E. (2001) *Apollo's Eye: A Cartographic Genealogy of the Earth in the Western Imagination*. Baltimore, MD: Johns Hopkins University Press.

Craig, Campbell (2003) *Glimmer of a New Leviathan: Total War in the Realism of Niebuhr, Morgenthau, and Waltz*. New York: Columbia University Press.

Deese, R. S. (2009) 'The Artifact of Nature: "Spaceship Earth" and the Dawn of Global Environmentalism', *Endeavor*, 33(2): 70–75.

Deudney, Daniel (1983) *Whole Earth Security: A Geopolitics of Peace*. Washington, DC: Worldwatch Institute.

Deibert, Ronald (2015) 'Authoritarianism Goes Global: Cyberspace Under Siege', *Journal of Democracy*, 26(3): 64–78.

Deudney, Daniel (2007) *Bounding Power: Republican Security Theory from the Polis to the Global Village*. Princeton, NJ: Princeton University Press.

Dick, Steven J. (1992) *Plurality of Words: The Extraterrestrial Life Debate from Democritus to Kant*. Cambridge: Cambridge University Press.

Dyson, George (1997) *Darwin among the Machines*. New York: Basic Books.

Edwards, Paul N. (1997) *The Closed World. Computers and the Politics of Discourse in Cold War America*. Cambridge, MA: MIT Press.

Falk, Richard A. (1972) *This Endangered Planet: Prospects and Proposals for Human Survival*. New York: Vintage Books.

Fleming, James Rodger (2012) *Fixing the Sky: The Checkered History of Weather and Climate Control*. New York: Columbia University Press.

Fuller, R.Buckminster (1969) *Operating Manual for Spaceship Earth*. Carbondale, IL: Southern Illinois University Press.

Gardiner, Stephen Mark (2013) *A Perfect Moral Storm: The Ethical Tragedy of Climate Change*. New York: Oxford University Press.

Hall, Stephen S. (1992) *Mapping the Next Millennium: The Discovery of New Geographies*. New York: Random House.

Hamilton, Clive (2013) *Earthmasters: The Dawn of the Age of Climate Engineering*. New Haven, CT: Yale University Press.

Hardin, Garrett (1974) 'Living on a Lifeboat', *BioScience*, 24(10): 561–568.

Heise, Ursula K. (2008) *Sense of Place and Sense of Planet: The Environmental Imagination of the Global*. Oxford and New York: Oxford University Press.

Hoyle, Fred (1950) *The Nature of the Universe*. Oxford: Blackwell.

Jones, Stephen B. (1955) 'Global Strategic Views', *The Geographical Review*, 45(4): 492–508.

Lakoff, George and Mark Johnson (1980) *Metaphors We Live By*. Chicago, IL: University of Chicago Press.

Lanier, Jaron (2010) *You Are Not a Gadget: A Manifesto*. New York: Alfred A. Knopf.

Laszlo, Ervin (2008) *Quantum Shift in the Global Brain: How the New Scientific Reality Can Change Us and Our World*. Rochester, VT: Inner Traditions.

Leary, Timothy (with R. A. Wilson and G. A. Koopman) (1977) *Neuropolitics: The Sociobiology of Human Metamorphosi*s. Los Angeles, CA: Starseed/Peace Press.

Lovelock, James E. (1979) *Gaia: A New Look at Life on Earth*. Oxford: Oxford University Press.

Masters, Dexter and Katherine Way (1946) *One World or None: A Report on the Public on the Full Meaning of the Atomic Bomb*. Oxford: Latimer House.

McLuhan, Marshall (1964) *Understanding Media: The Extensions of Man*. New York: Signet Books.

McLuhan, Marshall (1966) *The Gutenberg Galaxy: The Making of Typographic Man*. Toronto: University of Toronto Press.

McLuhan, Marshall and Quentin Fiore (1968) *War and Peace in the Global Village*. New York: Bantam Books.

Muir, Star A. (1994) 'The Web and the Spaceship: Metaphors of the Environment', *ETC: A Review of General Semantics*, 51(2): 145.

Neumann, Erich (2015) *The Great Mother: An Analysis of the Archetype*. Princeton, NJ: Princeton University Press.

Noel, Daniel (1986) *Approaching Earth: A Search for the Mythic Significances of the Space Age*. New York: Amity House.

O'Tuathail, Gerard (1996) *Critical Geopolitics: The Politics of Writing Global Space*. Minneapolis, MN: University of Minnesota Press.

Paine, Lincoln P. (2013) *The Sea and Civilization: A Maritime History of the World.* First edition. New York: Knopf.

Pelton, Joseph N. (1999) 'The Fast-Growing Global Brain', *The Futurist*, 3(7): 24–27.

Pemberton, Jo-Anne (2001) *Global Metaphors: Modernity and the Quest for One World.* London; Sterling, VA: Pluto Press.

Perry, Ralph Barton (1945) *One World in the Making.* First edition. New York: American Book-Stratford Press.

Poole, Robert (2008) *Earthrise: How Man First Saw the Earth.* New Haven, CT: Yale University Press.

President's Science Advisory Committee (1965) *Restoring the Quality of Our Environment.* Washington, DC: Government Printing Office.

Ruprecht, L. (1996) 'Pale Blue Dot: A Vision of the Human Future in Space', *Journal of the American Academy of Religion*, 64(2): 459–463.

Russell, Peter (1983) *The Global Brain: Speculations on the Evolutionary Leap to Planetary Consciousness.* Los Angeles:, CA J. P. Tarcher.

Sagan, Carl (1995) *Pale Blue Dot: A Vision of the Human Future in Space.* New York: Random House.

Schell, Jonathan (1982) *The Fate of the Earth.* New York: Knopf.

Schneider, Stephen Henry (1997) *Laboratory Earth: The Planetary Gamble We Can't Afford to Lose.* New York: Basic Books.

Schneider, Stephen Henry (ed.) (2004) *Scientists Debate Gaia: The Next Century.* Cambridge, MA: MIT Press.

Sagan, Karl and I. S. Shklovskii (1966) *Intelligent Life in the Universe.* New York: Dell Publishing.

Sjoo, Monica and Barbara Mor (1987) *The Great Cosmic Mother: Rediscovering the Religion of the Earth.* San Francisco, CA: HarperOne.

Thompson, Norma (2001) *The Ship of State: Statecraft and Politics from Ancient Greece to Democratic America.* New Haven, CT: Yale University Press.

Tsiolkovsky, Konstantin (1960 [1906]) *The Call of the Cosmos.* Moscow: Foreign Language Publishing House.

Turner, David P. (2005) 'Thinking at the Global Scale', *Global Ecology & Biogeography*, 14(6): 505–508.

Ward, Peter D. (2009) *The Medea Hypothesis: Is Life on Earth Ultimately Self-Destructive?* Princeton, NJ: Princeton University Press.

Ward, Peter D. and Donald Brownlee (2000) *Rare Earth: Why Complex Life Is Uncommon in the Universe.* New York: Copernicus.

Weart, Spencer R. (2008) *The Discovery of Global Warming.* Cambridge, MA: Harvard University Press.

Wells, H. G. (1937) *World Brain.* Garden City, NY: Country Life Press.

Willkie, Wendell L. (1943) *One World.* New York: Simon & Schuster.

Wittner, L. S. (2003) *Toward Nuclear Abolition: A History of the World Nuclear Disarmament Movement, 1971–Present.* Stanford, CA: Stanford University Press.

Wong, Kin-yuen, Gary Westfahl, and Amy Kit-sze Chan (2005) *World Weavers: Globalization, Science Fiction, and the Cybernetic Revolution.* Hong Kong: Hong Kong University Press.

2 Terraforming planet Earth

The age of fallout

Joseph Masco

Introduction

Being able to assume a planetary, as opposed to a global, imaginary is a surprisingly recent phenomenon.[1] Although depictions of an Earthly global sphere are longstanding and multiple (see Cosgrove 2001; Heise 2008), the specific attributes of being able to see the entire planet as a single unit or system is, I would argue, a Cold War creation. This mode of thinking is therefore deeply imbricated not only in nuclear age militarism but also in specific forms of twentieth-century knowledge production, as well as a related proliferation of visualization technologies (see Haffner 2013; Kurgan 2013). A planetary imaginary includes globalities of every kind (finance, technology, international relations) but also geology, atmosphere, glaciers, oceans, and biosphere as one totality. What is increasingly powerful about this point of view is that it not only relies on the national security state for the technologies, finances, and interests that create the possibility of seeing in this fashion but also, in a single image, exceeds the nation-state as the political form that matters. Thus, a planetary optic is not only a national security creation (in its scientific infrastructures, visualization technologies, and governing ambitions); it also transcends these structures to offer an alternative ground for politics and future making. Proliferating forms of globality – including the specific visualizations of science, finance, and environment – both achieve ultimate scale and are unified at the level of the planetary, which raises an important question about how collective problems and security can, and should, be imagined.

Today we live with unprecedented technical optics for assessing large-scale problems and are thus able to identify the as yet uncontrolled legacies of industrial-age capitalism on Earth, but we do not have political systems operating on the right scale to address truly planetary problems. This conundrum – of awareness exceeding political institutions and agency – can be profitably interrogated through an examination of the conceptual history, technoscience, and psychosocial effects of "fallout." Our radically changing environment is the unintended cumulative legacy of capitalism, militarism, and industrialism. A critical theory of fallout allows us to contemplate industrial effects as a cumulative form of planetary engineering, a remaking of Earthly domains that becomes visible only at certain scales. Attending to fallout thus not only enables new forms of globality but can draw our attention to emerging forms of violence across the global north/global south divide that operate on different time scales, thereby expanding our understanding of planetary process (see Parenti 2011). For even as Earth scientists generate increasingly precise and vivid depictions of ecological precarity on planet Earth, the immediate challenge is to collectively achieve a form of planetary governance that can fully recognize, let alone govern, escalating fallout. As we shall see, the "Age of Fallout" recasts historical categories and periodizations in favor of the future oriented ecological changes that have been put in motion by industrial activity. Rather than a bounded period, the Age of Fallout is thus an open-ended concept of futurity, a historical transformation unfolding on the scale of Earth systems, requiring new logics and optics to support a not yet achieved but necessary planetary process.

Figuring fallout

"Fallout" is a relatively recent term in the English language designating an unexpected supplement to an event, a precipitation that is in motion, causing a kind of long-term and unexpected damage: it is the aftermath, the reverberation, the negative side effect. We talk today about the fallout of the mortgage crisis or of official action or inaction, or of drone strikes and pre-emptions across the field of counterterrorism. Fallout comes after the event. It is the unacknowledged-until-lived crisis built into the infrastructure of a program, project, or process. Fallout is therefore understood primarily retrospectively but lived in the future anterior – a form of history made visible in negative outcomes. We live today, I think, in the Age of Fallout, inheriting from the twentieth century a vast range of problems linking ecologies with national security with science and technology and finance in an ongoing negative aftermath. For example, the nuclear disaster at the Fukushima-Daiichi plant in March 2011 produced literal fallout in the form of cesium-137 contamination but also was a combined technoscientific, financial, and regulatory failure.[2] Industrialism, militarism, and capitalism are each massive fallout-generating practices, producing reverberating crises, now consolidated in wide-ranging collective insecurities on issues ranging from energy to finance to war, each of which operates in a specific register of globality.

Fallout the noun comes to us from the verb to "fall out," which from the sixteenth century on has designated a social break or conflict. It is thus the fight that separates comrades, marking the end of intimacy, shared purpose, and social pleasure. Military personnel also fall out from being at attention, a marker of a return to individual activities after a collective review, a relaxing of the conditions of formal militarism. Falling out thus involves individual actions and lived consequences, a post-sociality, lived in isolation from the collective action of society or the war machine. To fall out is both to break with a friend and to relax from formal review; it is to burn a bridge and be off-duty all at the same time. Being off-duty matters today, as so many of our regulatory institutions are not doing their stated jobs, short-circuited by political agendas, lack of funding, or more generally misguided priorities. For example, in response to major reports from the Intergovernmental Panel on Climate Change and the U.S. Climate Assessment in 2014 detailing a disturbing future of ecological instability, the U.S. House of Representatives passed a bill prohibiting the Department of Defense from using any funds to respond to the vast range of security problems documented in these scientific studies, an effort to ban both science and the environment from defense policy in favor of short-term petrochemical profits (Koronowski 2014). We are living within an increasingly post-Foucauldian kind of governmentality, in which the project of improving and securing life is being overrun by a narrowly construed notion of profit, one that functions in the increasingly short lag between the engineered event and its fallout. Our notions of globality are thus also increasingly tied to tracking negative outcomes more than positive ones, as global flows of money, carbon, and information tend not to be recognized as infrastructural creations until they are in planetary crisis.

Fallout, the noun, is of course an invention of the nuclear age, appearing in the English language soon after the U.S. atomic bombings of Hiroshima and Nagasaki in 1945 (see Boyer 1998: xiii). Formally, fallout refers to the radioactive debris put into the atmosphere by a nuclear explosion, designating an atmospheric event with far-reaching consequences (see Glasstone and Dolan 1977). Marked as a precipitation, it involves a gradual settling of radioactive materials and effects over a wide area. Fallout thus formally links human actions, technological capabilities, atmospheres, and ecologies in a new configuration of contamination. Radioactive fallout is also made up of a wide range of possible nuclear elements – cesium, strontium, iodine, etc. – with radically different radioactive half-lives and environmental effects. It operates therefore on a wide range of temporal frames, and is both an immediate threat to health (radiation illness) as well as a long-term one (cancer or life shortening; see also Nixon 2011; Jain 2013). Fallout is, thus, always an act of coproduction, a simultaneously remaking of nature and society via collective injury.

With this in mind, consider how fallout was first presented to U.S. citizens, not long after the invention of the concept, in the largest propaganda campaign to date in American history, known as atomic "civil defense." In reaction to the first Soviet nuclear test, a new U.S. Federal Civil Defense Administration (FCDA) was created in 1950. The FCDA worked to transform U.S. citizens into Cold Warriors by saturating the public sphere with nuclear narratives, images, and themes (Masco 2014). An unprecedented effort to re-orient American society around the dangers of a new technology, the FCDA sought to create a productive fear of the nuclear age in order to achieve a permanent war posture (Oakes 1994). Figure 2.1, offers an emblematic illustration of the atomic civil defense campaign of the 1950s, presenting '"fallout" not simply as a new wartime threat to domestic life but also as a new structuring principle of American modernity.

Figure 2.1 "Facts about Fallout," Civil Defense handout
Source: Federal Civil Defense Administration, circa 1955.

In "Facts about Fallout" citizens learn that at home as well as on the street they are vulnerable to a new kind of invisible injury. Urban populations are no longer even the specific target of military attack; it is the environment itself which has been transformed into a potentially toxic space, remaking clouds and air as dangerous entities. The atomic bomb transforms the atmosphere on which living beings depend, converting it from a life support system into something now forever suspect, loaded at any moment with invisible and possibly deadly elements.

Part of a larger Cold War recalibration of American society through nuclear danger, the FCDA campaign attempted to shift responsibility for injury from the security infrastructures to the individual citizen, now positioned as properly informed about everyday risk via civil defense programs and expected to be both alert and resilient in a minute-to-minute confrontation with nuclear war. After 1945, Americans are increasingly recruited to normalize unprecedented forms of existential danger within an industrial atmosphere also undergoing radical change. "Facts about Fallout" illustrates this new kind of industrial awareness, offering a cloud that no longer brings the sustenance of rain but rather delivers deadly particulates that "you can seldom feel or see." Fallout is thus an environmental flow that matters to health and safety but also demands a new form of everyday perception and governance. Fallout, here, also implicitly positions the citizen less as national subject than as Earth dweller, increasingly at risk simply for being a "breather" (Choy 2011). This conversion of atmosphere from the most rudimentary domain of life into an uncertain circulation also directly challenges the territorial vision of the national security state system, as international borders and security states are rendered irrelevant by windborne industrial effects within Earth systems (see Sloterdijk 2009; also Beck 2007).

How many of our toxic industrial processes fall into this similar category of the unseen but cumulatively damaging or deadly? How many issues of toxicity now are also issues of scale and perspective – raising questions about not only visualization but also how to conceptualize danger? Fallout – in the form of radioactivity, synthetic chemicals, or the impacts of the carbon cycle – produces cumulative effects that only become visible in the destabilized organism or ecological system. The temporality of injury thus becomes central to the assessment of danger itself, as the industrial age generates "products" that install injury and crisis incrementally into the future, colonizing an ever-deeper time horizon (see Murphy 2008; Nixon 2011; Jain 2013).

In U.S. Cold War practice, fallout was initially constituted as the bomb's lesser form. This approach allowed a strange and perverse splitting of the nuclear event itself into the expected and planned detonation and its lingering atmospheric effects (see Eden 2004). Though it was understood in 1945 that the irradiated particulate matter that travels on wind patterns constituted a kind of weapon, enabling a new form of atmospheric terrorism, it was the explosive power of the bomb that was fetishized by the U.S. military and became the basis for nuclear war planning. A completely predictable aspect of any nuclear event, fallout was thus officially coded within U.S. practice as a side effect. Much as pharmaceutical companies today split the desired from the undesired effects of a molecule – the political economy of the side effect here has huge consequences, installing bizarre metrics and significant misrecognitions throughout nuclear national security logics – allowing certain forms of destruction to be recognized while others are marginalized. For example, while potentially deadly on a mass scale and constituting a new kind of chemical/biological weapon all in one, radioactive fallout was officially crafted as a secondary formation to the exploding bomb during the era of atmospheric nuclear testing.

The official project of producing a "safe" nuclear detonation involved evaluations of wind patterns and weather, as well as efforts to target radioactive fallout at unpopulated geographical regions. As history has repeatedly shown, the "unpopulated area" was rarely so, creating vast exposures that quickly undermined any notion of "national security" as a protection of populations (see Johnson and Barker 2008). Indeed, physicians and Earth scientists led a media crusade to publicize the health effects of atmospheric nuclear testing in the 1950s, directly challenging the logics of civil defense and national security. In the process, they help mobilize peace, justice, and environmental social movements (see Commoner 1958; Fowler 1960a). The first decades of the nuclear age were thus filled with both hemispheric exposures and new forms of social protest. These emergent social movements were met by an unsuccessful, if highly publicized, official effort to build a "clean bomb" at the U.S. weapons laboratories – a bomb, that is, which could explode without producing fallout.

A crucial development in the Cold War nuclear system was the move to underground nuclear testing. The 1963 Limited Test Ban Treaty (LTBT) – which stands as the first nuclear weapons treaty and the first global environmental treaty – both recognized the planetary consequences of nuclear testing and worked to preserve the nuclear arms race. By consolidating their energetic experimental test regimes underground, the U.S., British, and U.S.S.R. eliminated nuclear tests in the atmosphere, outer space, and the ocean while continuing to detonate nuclear devices feverishly through the 1980s. The LTBT also had the important effect of shifting the environmental register of nuclear test programs from atmospheric fallout to a different plane of ecological damage – one not borne on wind patterns but connected to underground seepage and flow.

The LTBT also significantly changed the visual politics of the nuclear age, allowing a shift from the iconic image of the mushroom cloud to diverse data sets produced by new technologies of global surveillance (devoted, for example, to detecting seismic signatures of nuclear tests). By the end of the 1960s, images from outer space, produced first by satellites and then by space missions, provided photographic images of planet Earth as a singular totality (Poole 2008; Kurgan 2013). These emerging visualization infrastructures were tied in direct and indirect ways to U.S. efforts to monitor foreign nuclear test regimes, as well as to develop more powerful infrastructures (from missiles, to early warning systems, to satellite based command and control technologies) for fighting nuclear wars.

The environmental legacies of Cold War nuclearism (from fallout, to environmental contamination, to nuclear waste) now stand as an iconic illustration of toxic industrialization and an emergent planetary politics. In what follows, I want to make a case for radioactive fallout as an emblem of industrial modernity but also invite you to think of it as an allegory for a larger set of processes now collectively gathered together under a rubric of climate change. The historical development of nuclear and climate dangers are complexly intertwined at the level of environmental effects, knowledge systems, and public perceptions (Masco 2010). The cumulative toxic fallout of the twentieth century continues to shift global and Earth systems, requiring a new politics of air, soil, water, energy, and finance, while also demanding new concepts of planetary security. Toxicity is now a planetary force, a realization that requires new critical theory as well as different concepts of the political (see Clark 2014). Thus, to be clear, for the remainder of this chapter, "fallout" is meant to be both material and conceptual, a way of talking about legacies and futures, toxics and natures.

A planetary stratum

It is easy to forget how radical the U.S. nuclear program was right from the beginning. Founded in secrecy, it quickly turned the entire planet into an experimental theater for nuclear science. The politics of radioactive fallout were key to the first efforts to regulate the bomb, as well as fomenting a wide-ranging social revolution, linking issues of war and peace to environment to public health in entirely new ways (see Egan 2007). Just consider the territorial scope of the nuclear complex for a moment, for as an ever-emerging global infrastructure its fallout exceeds any existing map.

Figure 2.2 is a U.S. Department of Energy map that details the geographical reach of its core facilities at the end of the Cold War. But even as it documents the formal U.S. nuclear weapons production complex at its height, this map fails to indicate the true scope of U.S. nuclearism, leaving out as it does nuclear power plants as well as sites of environmental contamination and nuclear waste storage across the continental United States. Nonetheless, the DOE map does suggest that, as infrastructure, the nuclear complex has always strained to achieve a kind of globality. It does so not only via the reach of nuclear weapons (via intercontinental missiles, nuclear submarines, bombers) but also via the extensive network of production and testing sites, linking a global uranium industry (Hecht 2012), vast experimental laboratories (Gusterson 1998), numerous test sites, with military support and delivery systems.

If we were to consider nuclear detonations – undoubtedly the single most destructive human enterprise to date – as a whole, we would start with a map like Figure 2.3, which also illustrates how the atomic bomb continually remakes relations between the global north and south. Constituting a new form of radioactive colonization, the build out of nuclear infrastructures and experimental regimes regularly impacted minority populations most directly

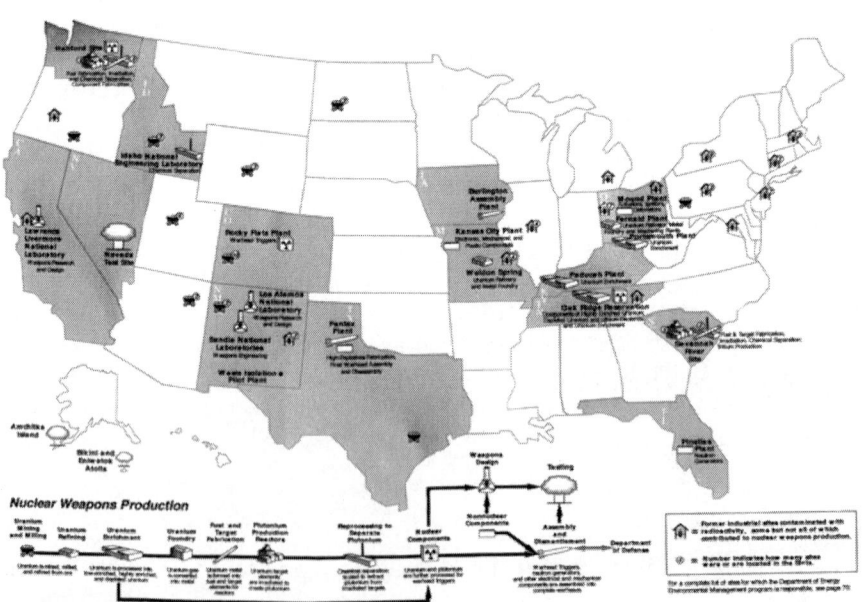

Figure 2.2 Map of the U.S. nuclear complex at the end of the Cold War
Source: Courtesy of the Department of Energy.

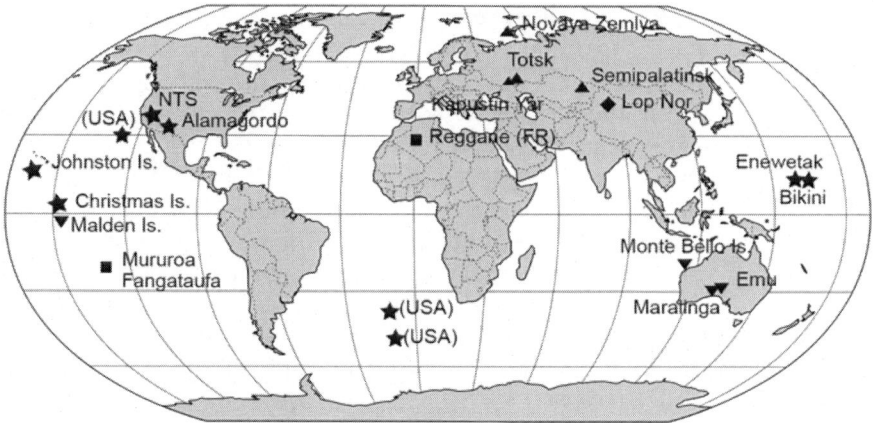

Figure 2.3 Locations of above-ground nuclear tests
Source: From Beck and Bennett 2002.

while also generating collective fallout effects. One of the most important aspects of fallout is that it can be both collectively and a symmetrically distributed, marking everyone to a degree while having a more immediate effect on specific communities, ecologies, and bodies. But even this map, with its global frame, is radically incomplete: one must add the wartime atomic bombings of Hiroshima and Nagasaki in 1945, as well as a half-century of underground nuclear explosions at test sites around the world, including those of newer nuclear powers – India, Pakistan, and North Korea. Think of each of these sites as a node in a global nuclear network of technologies, experiments, waste, and fallout – each radiating on a distinct frequency.

Fallout – in the form of accidents, contamination, and waste – has always been retrospectively diagnostic – forcing attention to how connected humans, non-humans, technologies, and environments have become in the industrial era. Indeed, Earth scientists used the radioactive signatures of strontium 90 and cesium 131 as means of mapping weather systems, food chains, and environmental complexity right from the start of the nuclear age (see Odum and Odum 1955 as well as Hagan 1992). What emerged in the first decades of the nuclear age was a powerful new vision of the biosphere as integrated ecological space, but this vision was only enabled by tracking radioactive contamination through it (Masco 2010). The planetary is emergent in these processes as fallout became the means of mapping ecological flows of every kind, moving from local exposures to regional contamination to global distributions of atmospheric endangerment.

Consider the first U.S. hydrogen bomb experiment conducted in the Marshall Islands as part of the IVY test series in 1952. Code-named "Mike," it produced a mushroom cloud that rose to over 120,000 feet and was 60 miles wide, and was quickly transformed by Earth scientists into a new kind of experimental lens. Here fallout quite literally became a primary means of empirically documenting stratospheric flows, ultimately revealing with a new specificity how Earth, ocean, and atmosphere interact.

The fallout produced by the Mike detonation was tracked by Machta, List, and Hubert (1956) in their foundational work on the stratospheric transport of nuclear materials (see Figure 2.4). It was among the first in a series of studies that followed the global transport of nuclear materials produced by atmospheric testing, offering increasingly high-resolution portraits of atmospheric contamination within an integrated biosphere. These wide-ranging studies directly challenged a national security concept that was no longer able to protect discrete territories but was instead generating, in Ulrich Beck's (2007) terms, new "risk societies" united not by territory, national identity, or language but by rather by air-borne environmental and health risks increasingly understood to be global flows.

Radioactive fallout studies helped to foment a new kind of planetary vision in several ways. Most importantly, the effort to understand fallout involved the creation of new surveillance systems and comprehensive data sets in the Earth sciences, generated in the name of understanding nuclear environmental effects and for tracking the Soviet nuclear program. The Cold War produced a massive investment in air, ocean, geology, the ice caps, and, increasingly, outer space research. This was an effort to track and investigate every possible kind of nuclear event and also to research how to militarize nature itself for national advantage (see Fleming 2010 and Hamblin 2013). In every case, nuclear injury was both the motivating logic and the experimental lens for producing a new set of national security Earth sciences. These data sets become, as Paul Edwards (2010) has argued, a kind of global infrastructure, allowing new portraits of planetary process – particularly climate change – to be possible. The effort to understand nuclear injury (for both war fighting and civil defense) thus generated a conceptual frame for engaging a

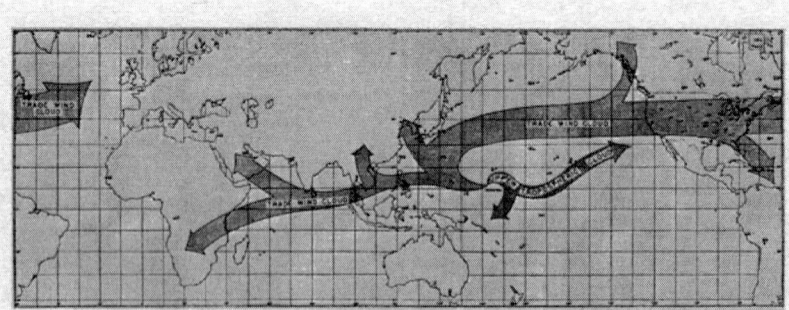

Fig. 2. Early history of the Mike cloud. The figures indicate the number of days between detonation and the first ground observation of fission products.

Figure 2.4 Fallout study of Mike fallout cloud
Source: From Machta, List, and Hubert 1956.

planetary space that was simultaneously being transformed by nuclear industry. As Sloterdijk (2009) has argued, a militarization of environment in the twentieth century also enabled new forms of environmental thinking, enabling a scalar multidisciplinary commitment to connecting locality with global infrastructures with planetary processes.

By 1960, for example, Machta and List are exploring a more expansive vision of fallout, pulling our field of view increasingly off planet in their effort to illustrate the scale and scope of nuclear effects. Figure 2.5 is an illustration from Fowler's (1960a) important edited collection, *Fallout: A Study of Superbombs, Strontium 90, and Survival,* published at the height of the public health debate over atmospheric nuclear testing. In it, Machta and List (1960) document the stratospheric height of fallout and its ability to travel on wind patterns for great distances, essentially merging the global north and global south as irradiated space. The development of U.S. national security in the form of the hydrogen bomb was thus linked to the production of (1) an entirely new global ecological danger and (2) a new technoscientific and environmental investment in understanding integrated environmental spaces and ecological transport. The Earth sciences become a national priority in this early Cold War moment, as efforts to study the bombs' material effects connected researchers to the defense department in a major new way, leading to revolutions in biomedicine, computing, geology, oceanography, and atmospheric sciences (see Doel 2003; Edwards 2010; Farish 2010; Hamblin 2013).

The fallout danger created many research programs that continue to this day, including biomedical studies of exposed populations (from Hiroshima and Nagasaki to the Marshall Islands, to the vast population of workers with the nuclear complex itself, see Lindee 1997; Johnson and Barker 2008; Makhijani and Schwartz 2008). These forms of internal and external sacrifice became embedded within Cold War national security practices (see also Kuletz 1998; Petryna 2002; Brown 2013), raising basic questions about what kind of a human population was emerging via the encounter with nuclear technologies and accumulating forms of fallout. Consider James Crow's (1960) contribution, "Radiation and Future Generations" to Fowler's *Fallout* anthology, contemplating the genetic consequences of atmospheric nuclear explosions for men and women. He underscored the uncertainty in measuring the relationship between radioactive fallout and mutation rates across generations and species (humans, flies, mice), and projected alternative futures of genetic damage across species based on different degrees of nuclear testing. Thus, as Machta and List considered the atmospheric reach of nuclear effects, Crow investigated the accumulating force of exposure itself within the human genetic pool. Space and time are thus radically reconfigured in these fallout studies to constitute a vision of a collective future incrementally changing in unknown ways through cumulative industrial effects. The logics of a national security state (with its linkage of a discrete territory to a specific population) becomes paradoxical in the face of mounting evidence of genetic damage on a collective scale, not from nuclear war but rather from atomic research and

THE GLOBAL PATTERN OF FALLOUT   29

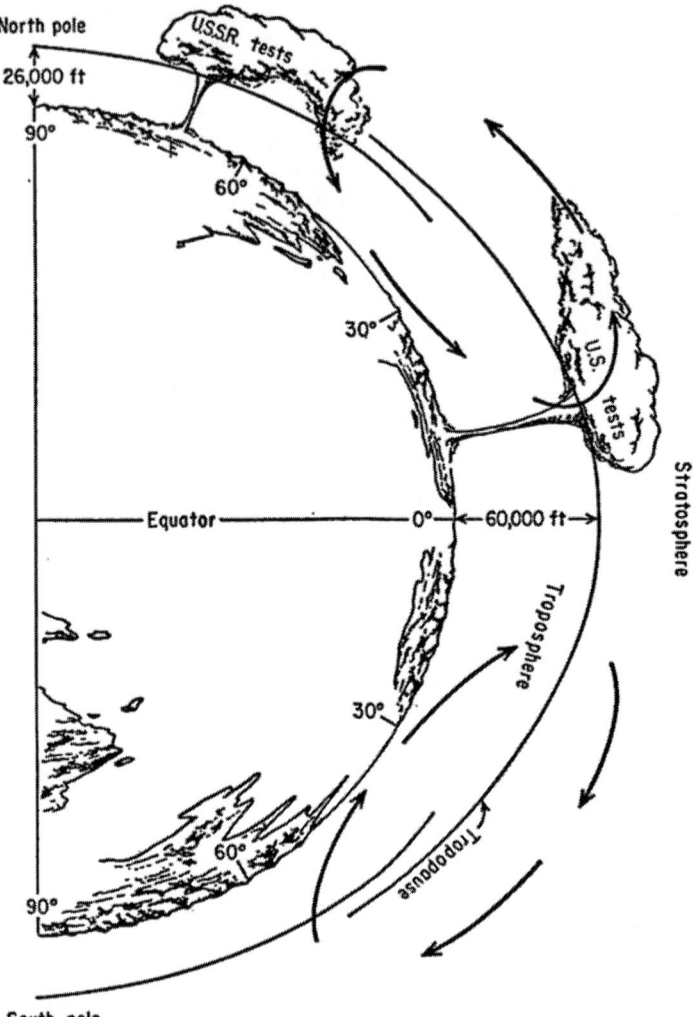

FIG. 3. Model of the air circulation between the troposphere and the stratosphere, showing the probable routes of global travel of fallout. Most of the large United States bomb tests took place at tropical latitudes; the Soviet tests, at northerly latitudes.

Figure 2.5 Illustration of the global travel of fallout
Source: From Machta and List 1960.

development programs. It is important to recognize that while cast as "experiments," U.S. atmospheric detonations were in reality planetary environmental events with wide-ranging consequences.

Fowler (1960b), for example, was able to calculate the amount of Strontium 90 from nuclear testing in the New York food supply, across milk, cereal, meat, fruits, and vegetables. This is a remarkable moment in an emergent planetary consciousness, given that the nuclear age was only 15 years old in 1960 and already understood to be a transformational industry in terms of ecology and public health. Fowler, and the many Earth scientists tracking similar flows, documented how military science, atmospheric conditions, plants, animals, and people were connected both systemically and increasingly via toxicity. Put differently, radioactive fallout was recognized as a planetary industrial signature by 1960, one being inscribed at different levels into every living being.

Figure 2.6 is a National Cancer Institute chart of the Iodine-131 contamination from Cold War-era nuclear tests conducted at the Nevada Test Site. This county-by-country chart remakes the continental United States – the territorial space thought to be secured by nuclear defense – as a new kind of sacrifice zone, with citizens remade by varying degrees of exposure (see also Beck and Bennett 2002). To this day, exposure from the atmospheric nuclear weapons tests is measureable, an environmental fact so ever present as to become a literal biological stratum in the human population (Bennett 2002). This "stratum" is not a recognized health risk today, even though the National Academy of Sciences concluded in its most recent study that there is no "safe" level of radiation exposure (National Research Council 2006; Simon et al. 2006). Consider Figure 2.7, a chart of the "background radiation" rate, judged by medical science and the nuclear industry to be the baseline exposure rate for contemporary human populations. This nominal exposure rate (involving a small but measurable contribution from atmospheric nuclear testing and nuclear accidents) constitutes in its ubiquity a new form of industrial "nature."

In other words, since 1945 human beings have become post-nuclear creatures, marked with the signature of nuclear weapons science (Masco 2006: 294). What is in question is not the material fact of radioactive fallout or exposure but rather our perception of its effects and implication. This lag between the environmental event and the recognition of its long-lasting effects is a major psychosocial achievement of the industrial age, where – in the name of commerce or security – consequences are loaded into an uncertain future and thus expelled from the realm of formal political discourse. Fallout nonetheless constitutes a new planetary process after 1945. This makes the nuclear age the era in which the planet first becomes an object of comprehensive scientific study in its Earth systems totality and the moment when human beings first become an existential threat to themselves. Due to the scale and scope of human industrial activities and their cumulative impact on the geological record, atmospheric chemist Paul Crutzen (2002)

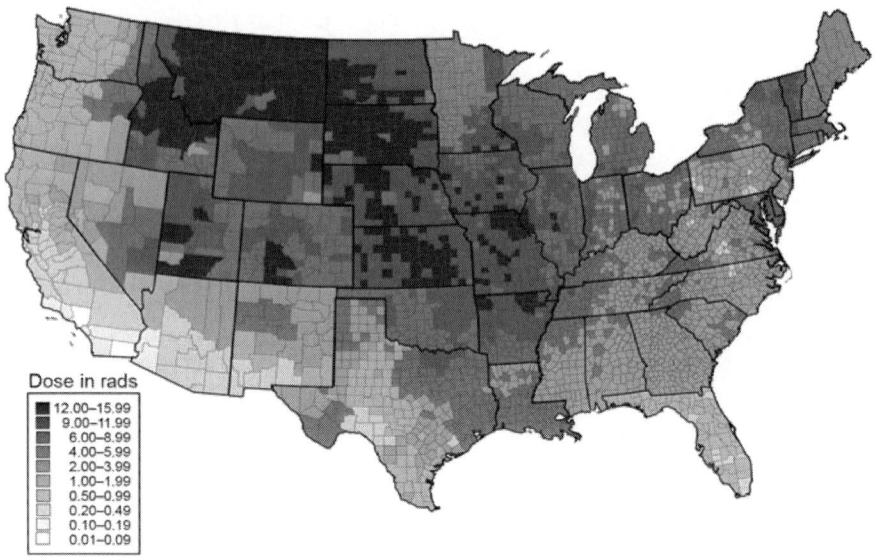

Figure 2.6 Cumulative iodine contamination from nuclear detonations at the Nevada
          Test Site
Source: Courtesy of the National Cancer Institute.

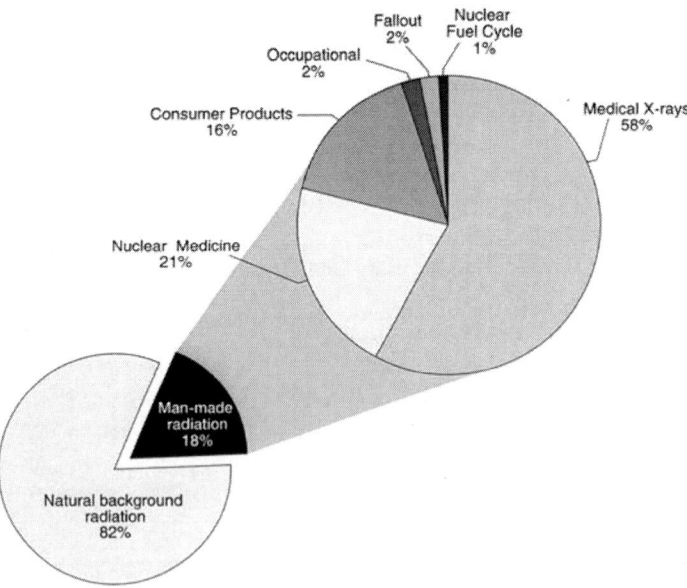

Figure 2.7 Background radiation rates for U.S. populations
Source: From National Research Council 2006.

has suggested that the Holocene has ended and Earth is now in the era of "the Anthropocene." With this in mind, we might productively use 16 July 1945, the date of the first nuclear detonation, as the start of a new planetary ecological regime, one in which everyday life is increasingly structured by the "fallout" effects of human industry (see Steffen et al. 2011) amplified across nuclear, petrochemical, and synthetic chemical regimes. What is important to underscore about these effects is their claim on an ever-deeper future, making industrial fallout an ever unfolding temporal as well as physical force.

Geoengineering/nuclear testing/terraforming

In the early twenty-first century, rising ocean levels, shifting weather patterns, and intensifying storms are generating wide-ranging problems across food production, public health, and urban spaces (see e.g. Costello et al. 2009). In the face of these emerging dangers, various schemes for geoengineering our way out of climate crisis have been proposed (see Caldeira et al. 2013; Keith 2013). Geoengineering is an effort to consciously shift the dynamics of Earth systems, and as a conceptual enterprise often draws on imaginative schemes to "terraform" another planet – that is, create an atmosphere on it capable of supporting human life. Geoengineering envisions a profound understanding of planetary systems even as its proponents negotiate the cumulative *unintended* environmental consequences of human industry (across nuclear, petrochemical, and capitalist-consumption regimes) on Earth. Programs for massive carbon capture (underground and in the oceans) compete with imaginative chemical proposals to shift the atmosphere by injecting sulfur particles into the upper stratosphere or changing the composition of clouds to reflect back heat from the sun. Other proposals look to space, with a view to creating mechanical means of diffusing sunlight and cooling the planet. In all, these proposals consider reengineering the oceans, air, forests, ice caps, and outer space to handle carbon dioxide and heat differently, in hopes of cooling the planet, imagined as a complex thermostat that needs to be adjusted (Schneider 2008; Robock et al. 2009; Hamilton 2012). What is attractive to many about these schemes is the idea of "correcting" an atmospheric imbalance caused by human activity, of now consciously treating the biosphere as a mechanism that can be tuned to optimal human outcomes.

For those versed in the history of the U.S. nuclear program, these projects sound eerily familiar, mirrored in the scientific efforts to understand nuclear effects on land, sea, air, and the upper atmosphere during the long Cold War (see Hamblin 2013). Each of these "experiments" was a form of geoengineering in its own right, producing specific planetary optics tied to desires for new forms of power while also producing environmental problems of a new kind and scope. There was, for example, the Atomic Energy Commission's project Plowshare, which ran from 1957 to 1975 and sought to expand the utility of the bomb in novel ways. Plowshare was a research and development program to utilize nuclear explosives as an engineering tool – to convert the military bomb from a city killer into a civilian Earth-moving technology. Plowshare scientists sought gigantic Earth works projects, promising literally to "move mountains" and build "new harbors" in the name of economic progress, albeit with little attention to the fallout that would inevitably occur. A filmic introduction to the project by the Atomic Energy Commission entitled "Excavating With Nuclear Explosives" offered this vision of the near future (see Atomic Energy Commission 1968):

> Excavations of new harbors, big dams, canals, passes through rugged mountainous terrain – these and other massive, imaginative Earth-moving projects may soon be ours, created in seconds with the tremendous energy of the peaceful atom. Nuclear explosives for large projects that are simply not feasible with conventional methods, and at considerably less expense. Scientists and engineers today are carefully working toward these goals with a series of nuclear excavation experiments, designed to increase their knowledge and skills in this exciting new concept. They call their program Plowshare. And the emplacement and detonation of a nuclear explosive is only the midway point in each succeeding project. Before any nuclear detonation, the project is first thoroughly explored and proven, in exhaustive theoretical analyses, researched and tested in laboratory mockup, and often tested again with conventional chemical explosives in the field. The detonation itself serves to refine the predictive capability and provide support data for the next related experiment. It is a deliberate, careful, scientific program.[3]

This "exciting new concept" involved turning the planet into an imaginative space for nuclear engineering, as proponents sought a project big enough to sell to the mass public as well as to industry and government the idea of converting the bomb from weapon of mass destruction to engineering tool. The repeated invocation of care in planning, of rigorous scientific judgment, and good governance was at odds with the radical nature of the project, which sought to detonate atomic bombs no longer in "test sites" officially designated as unpopulated but rather anywhere that geology could be made to correspond to commercial needs.

As Plowshare proponents looked across the globe, they found an ideal project in Panama, one that would utilize military technology to enhance global commerce by casting environmental destruction as civil engineering (see Figure 2.8, and Lindsay-Poland 2007). The "peaceful atom" would thus redeem the bomb as a force for public good and commercial profit. Plowshare scientists and engineers imagined that the atomic bomb would no longer represent a legacy of war, irradiated bodies, or damaged environments but rather be the key to civil engineering and new continental scale Earth works. The commercial promise of nuclear powered civil engineering is depicted in a 28-minute AEC promotional film called *Plowshares* (Atomic Energy Commission 1973), which offered this portrait of the need for a new canal:

> But there is no doubt that most applications of nuclear excavation would be, not in the United States, but in other countries. The most dramatic example so far is in Central America: the blasting of a sea level, Atlantic-Pacific interoceanic canal. Studies are being planned for both conventional and nuclear excavations on four possible routes for such a cut across Central America to supplement, and eventually replace, the Panama Canal, where ships now wait long hours to strain through the narrow complex lock system and others can't make it through at all. Before long it will be inadequate. Even before it was built half a century ago, the complexities and limitations, of this lock type were realized. Men dreamed of a sea level canal but it remained a dream. Plowshare may be able to make that dream a reality. And it is being considered. It is estimated that for certain routes, nuclear explosives could excavate the sea level canal at one-third the cost of conventional excavation and in considerably less time. The end result would be a much wider and much

Figure 2.8 Depiction of nuclear blast sequence for a new Panama Canal, from *Plowshares*
Source: Atomic Energy Commission 1973.

deeper channel. A nuclear excavated route across Central America could produce a navigable channel 1000 feet wide and up to 200 feet deep at mid-channel, offering a virtually unlimited capacity. No wonder this enormous project has so stimulated the imagination of the world. For a canal of this immensity, representing years of planning and development, complex engineering, and precise execution would be one of the greatest civil engineering feats of all time.

This plan to build a new Panama Canal, along with other Plowshare proposals, were ultimately defeated by the work of global environmental activists, specifically by an alliance of indigenous activists from the Pacific to the Americas now well versed in fallout effects (O'Neill 2007). The risk communities of the nuclear age, armed with examples of both fast and slow-moving forms of violence, as well as populations abandoned to injury in the industrial age, mobilized against civilian nuclear power in all its forms (see Berlant 2007; Nixon 2011). In other words, the fight against future fallout linked populations across race, class, and national lines in opposition to the AEC's Plowshare program, which was ultimately shut down in 1975 (see Kirsch 2005; Kaufman 2012).

However, the legacy of Plowshare continues in unexpected ways. One of the least remembered aspects of Plowshare was a series of nuclear experiments conducted using underground explosions to unlock natural gas reserves – a kind of pre-hydraulic fracturing (or "fracking"), natural gas–nuclear energy economy (Woodruff 1967). Some of the scientists and engineers originally involved in Plowshare shifted their focus from contemplating nuclear Earth moving to novel energy economies, pushing technical developments in extractive industries that become key elements in anthropogenic environmental change. This history is a profound illustration of the imbrication of militarism, industrialism, and capitalism in the United States. Today, the emerging hydraulic fracturing shale economy – which proponents say will make the United States the largest energy producer on the planet by 2017 – is also constituting radical future fallout risks, as the gigantic scale of the extraction infrastructure, with its well-known leakage rates, will place much of the American water supply in doubt over the coming decades (see Dumit 2013).

The (nuclear-petrochemical) industrial state has thus been geoengineering since 1945, remaking both atmospheres and ecologies, creating problems impossible to remediate or clean up. The Nevada Test Site today (see Figure 2.9) contains valley after valley of radiating nuclear test craters – a monumentally changed environment only visible in its entirety from a stratospheric point of view. Here, industrial injury demands a new planetary vision, one that sees cumulative environmental effects over and against national boundaries and short-term profit making.

Fallout – across nuclear and extractive energy regimes – has proliferating forms as well as temporalities (see Masco 2006; Brown 2013). The 1986 Chernobyl accident offered an iconic image of industrial disaster, a failed technology that created an airborne global environmental danger but also created a permanent regional crisis (Petryna 2002). Today, a gigantic engineering effort is underway to build a new containment vessel for the damaged reactor, one that hopes to prevent further radioactive releases for the next 100 years (the expected life of the facility). Chernobyl illustrates the profound consequences of technological failure in the nuclear age; but it is only one permanent danger-zone among many nuclear disaster sites around the world. Hanford, for example, is devoted today not to producing nuclear materials for U.S. weapons (as it did from World War II through the Cold War) but rather to observing the accumulated radioactive sludge of the twentieth century both ages and chemically transform into unknown substances. As one of the most contaminated spaces in North America, Hanford engineers devote each day to managing gigantic holding tanks of Cold War-era radioactive waste that to this day resists both chemical assessment and full containment. As these holding tanks continue to leak, there is a slow-moving transformation of the Columbia River region underway derived from Cold War-era American commitments to the bomb. Fukushima-Daichi presents a similarly long-lived problem, as the combined effects of Earthquake, tsunami, and fire transformed the nuclear power plant into a nuclear crisis in 2011 and revealed how few technical options there are for undoing the fallout of failed nuclear technologies. One might say that industrial failure on this scale is a form of geoengineering in its own right, just one operating without a planetary plan.

In applying the lessons of the twentieth-century nuclear complex to contemporary geoengineering schemes to manage climate change, we might question 1) the claim to both newness and absolute crisis, that installs a state of emergency and suspends normal forms of law and regulation; 2) a process that rhetorically reproduces the split between the event and its fallout so completely; and 3) the suggestion that geoengineering is a novel activity, that it is not an ancient practice with many examples to think of in assessing our current moment. We might also interrogate how the past half century of multidisciplinary work to create detailed visualizations of the planet now installs a dangerous confidence in globality itself, as increasingly high-resolution visualizations come to stand in for objectivity and sovereignty (see Daston and Galison 2010), thus enabling psychosocial feelings of control over what are still vastly complex Earth systems that remain, at best, only partially understood.

Geoengineering schemes today also refuse to recognize the long-term co-evolution of human and natural systems by suggesting that ecologies are simply machines that can be tuned by people to better outcomes. This high modernist position (assuming an external relation to nature) is the same one that created the nuclear infrastructure in the twentieth century that continues to generate new forms of fallout. It refuses to acknowledge the logic or history of fallout or to accept that in the era of big data we do not have a single planetary vision but rather a proliferation of planetary optics tied to specific sciences and projects, which may not align. Concepts like "the

Figure 2.9 Craters produced by nuclear detonations at the Nevada Test Site
Source: Courtesy of the Department of Energy.

Anthropocene" – which have been highly useful in alerting us to the scale of environmental change on planet Earth – nonetheless suggest that human agency is all that is involved in producing our increasingly complex world of organisms, ecological flows, technologies, and toxics (see e.g. Kosek 2010; Orff and Misrach 2012). The term flattens the complexity of human/non-human interactions, as well as natural systems, even as it recognizes the planetary scale of cumulative industrial effects. One unintended but pernicious effect of "the Anthropocene" is the suggestion that we are living in an entirely human-made ecology, or alternatively that a pristine state of nature could be recovered through planetary reverse engineering. These claims discount the history and inevitability of the coevolution of human and nonhuman systems.

Anthropologist Hugh Raffles (2002), for example, has documented that what appears to us today as giant tributaries of the Amazon River are in fact the collaborative work of people and river ecologies, as small canals cut by people for easier canoe navigation have grown to become massive waterways, now only visible in their entirety from outer space. The first satellite images of North America revealed ancient road systems connecting what is today the U.S. Southwest to Mexico, etched into the landscape. Similarly, cities are geoengineering projects of the most direct kind, foundationally effecting landscapes, ecologies, weather patterns, and resources. The problem is thus less the fact of human agency as a geological force (an ancient phenomenon) than the cumulative scale and scope of industrial toxicity. The human population has grown to more than seven billion, mostly living in megacities, enmeshed in nuclear, petrochemical, and synthetic chemical regimes. Toxicity, the cumulative fallout of the industrial age, has now achieved planetary agency. As these collective environmental concerns scale up past the nation-state form to the global, a new threshold is being reached for visualizing problems as planetary (see DeLoughrey 2014). Consider, for example, the "Science on a Sphere" project run by the National Oceanic and Atmospheric Administration (Figure 2.10), an educational program involving projecting complex big data visualizations onto a six-foot sphere. This project makes the unit of analysis the planet itself but with an added temporal dimension coded into each visualization.[4] Thus, planetary optics are proliferating in the twenty-first century and taking on new forms, as big data sets, emerging visualization technologies, and the cumulative force of toxicity generate both the need and the capacity for new visions of ecological process.

Transforming the atmo-bio-geo-sphere

Contemporary geoengineering discourse emerges from a consideration of how to build an atmosphere capable of supporting human life on other planets, terraforming for human survival and comfort. Mars is often the center of these imaginative efforts, but they are also often motivated by the idea that environmental damage on Earth – the end of fossil fuels, a destabilized climate, nuclear war, overpopulation, disease, or food scarcity – will drive

Figure 2.10 National Oceanic and Atmospheric Administration "Science on a Sphere"
visualization of sea surface temperatures and currents
Source: Courtesy of NOAA.

interplanetary research (see, for example, Pixar's *WALL-E* from 2008 or the
2014 Christopher Nolan film, *Interstellar*). The escape pod to Mars has a
long history in science fiction and as an imaginative project is intellectually
stimulating and often quite entertaining. But this idea rehearses the American
modernist story of self-invention, of the ability to start over somewhere else,
to break with the past and begin anew, to escape fallout by simply relocating
to a new frontier. Nature once again becomes an experimental laboratory,
endlessly changeable, a denial of co-constitution to enable new visions of exo-
planetary industry and potentially endless colonial space projects. Before
such an endeavor is launched (conceptually or in practice), we might well

interrogate the ecological and health impacts of the introduction of synthetic chemicals and other long-lived toxins into the biosphere over the past half-century (see Murphy 2008; Orff and Misrach 2012). In short, through the combined efforts of industry and the nuclear state, people have been feverishly terraforming planet Earth for generations, creating an atmosphere increasingly precarious for human life, rather than tuned to its creature comforts. This means that we are living in the unintended aftermath of cumulative industrial, military, and financial projects, remaking bodies and atmospheres on a planetary scale, and in ways that we have yet to fully account for, let alone govern.

On this difficult point, which asks us to think on scales and in temporalities that are radically different from our everyday embodied experience (see Chakrabarty 2012), consider Isao Hashimoto remarkable visualization of the nuclear age, "Nuclear Explosions 1945–1998" (see Figure 2.11; and also Hashimoto 2015).[5] His video animation shows in chronological order the 2053 nuclear detonations on Earth between 1945 and 1998. The video is straightforward, offering a global map and a chronological sequence of nuclear detonations, each marked by a white flash and beeping noise, with the

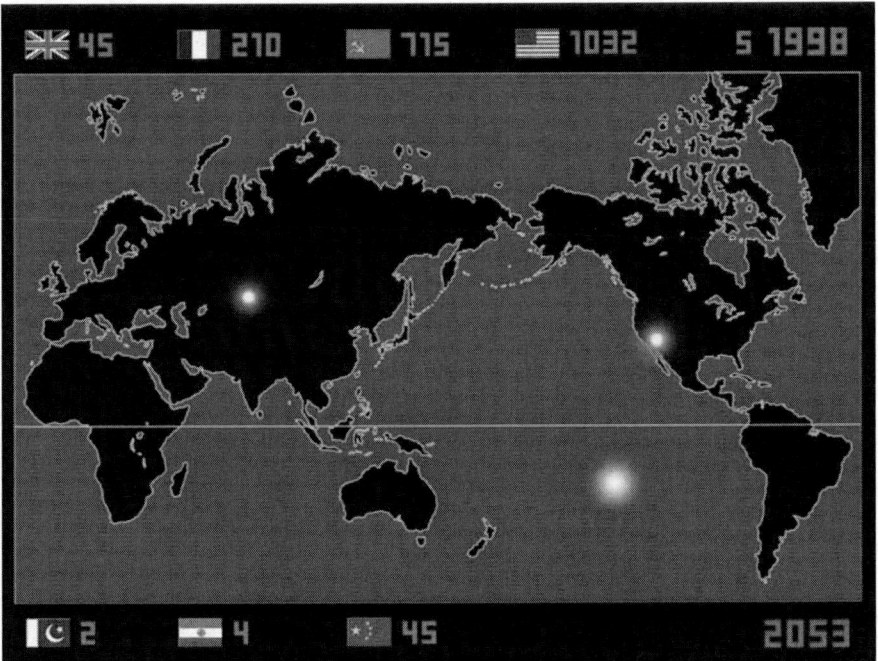

Figure 2.11 Still image from Isao Hashimoto's art installation, "Nuclear Explosions 1945–1998"
Source: With the permission of Isao Hashimoto.

date recorded in the upper right corner. In the margins, counters tally the detonations for each nuclear state, as well as the total count. It takes 13 minutes to move month by month from 1945 to 1998, offering an extremely precise illustration of nuclear politics in the twentieth century, documenting the expansion of both nuclear industry and national power. In certain years – 1957, 1962, or 1984, for example – it appears that nuclear explosions are the only things happening on planet Earth, with multiple continents flashing white and beeping at a feverish pace. The disturbing power of the video is that it both recognizes the nation-state form and renders it irrelevant to the cumulative planetary force of the bomb.

Hashimoto shows us the planetary logics of the nuclear complex and allows us to reconsider the temporality of nuclear war itself. In the Cold War competition between the U.S. and Soviet Union, nuclear war – the ultimate and final disaster – was conceived of as brutal and short. It was a matter of hours and minutes, as always on-alert weapons systems (still active today) made war possible every second of the day. Thus, we've inherited an idea of nuclear war as extremely short, fast, and totalizing – literally the end of everything. But Hashimoto reorients our point of view, showing that a nuclear war was fought in the twentieth century: it started in the summer of 1945 with three explosions – in New Mexico, Hiroshima, and Nagasaki – and was then fought vigorously in "test sites" around the world. Hashimoto's video is elegantly devastating in displaying the planetary politics of the bomb. He gives us access to the long-term violence that accumulates effects over decades, offering us a new perspective on a global industry that – in the name of energy, security, and profit – has performed as a radioactive geoengineer.

Given the ever-present material reality of environmental toxics, there is no need to project geoengineering with its specific planetary optic into a distant future or require travel to other worlds. We can look closer to home for an example of a planetary atmospheric politics. There has been a long-term terraforming project conducted on planet Earth – one that is drawn from the cumulative effects of industrialism, militarism, and capitalism. That climate change – despite such imaginative industrial activity and scientific insight across generations – was not planned or intended is precisely the point. Constituted as a side effect of the industrial age, it articulates the ongoing challenge to conceptualizing an ecological security *not* based on the split between the engineered event and its aftermath, between the boom and the bust of capital, between the pre-emptions and blowbacks of counterterror. Such a project requires instead many new planetary optics as well as a politics of complexity capable of assuming a post-national form of security and a new understandings of the collective future. This recognition of the accelerating environmental changes brought on by decades of human industrial activity destabilizes our existing notions of bounded technological ages of historical periods. Indeed, to consciously engage radically changing Earth systems in the early twenty-first century formally inaugurates the Age of Fallout.

Notes

1 This chapter first appeared in *History of the Present* (Copyright 2015 by the Board of Trustees of the University of Illinois. Used with permission of the University of Illinois Press) and has been revised for this volume. I am grateful to Casper Sylvest and Rens van Munster for their editorial care, as well as to all the participants in the Assembling the Planet project for their critical engagement.
2 See Winiarek, Bocquet, Roustan, Birman and Tran (2014) for a 30-day simulation of the global cesium fallout from the Fukushima-Daichii nuclear accident as it traversed the Pacific Ocean. Available at: http://cerea.enpc.fr/en/fukushima.html.
3 The two AEC Plowshare films I discuss in this chapter are available for viewing on youtube.com as one contained file. See: www.youtube.com/watch?v=ZGXS_Qgfqno.
4 For detailed information about Science on a Sphere visualizations and NOAA's larger public education project, see: http://sos.noaa.gov/What_is_SOS/index.html.
5 Hashimoto's video instillation is available for on-line viewing at: www.ctbto.org/specials/1945-1998-by-isao-hashimoto/.

References

Atomic Energy Commission (1973) *Plowshare*. 28-minute film. Washington, DC: Atomic Energy Commission.

Atomic Energy Commission (1968) *Excavating with Nuclear Explosives: Technology Status Report Plowshare Program*. 9-minute film. Washington, DC: Atomic Energy Commission.

Beck, Harold L. and Burton G. Bennett (2002) 'Historical Overview of Atmospheric Nuclear Weapons Testing and Estimate of Fallout in the Continental United States.' *Health Physics*, 82(5): 591–608.

Beck, Ulrich (2007) *World at Risk*. Cambridge: Polity Press.

Bennett, Burton G. (2002) 'Worldwide Dispersion and Deposition of Radionuclides Produces in Atmospheric Tests.' *Health Physics*, 82(5): 644–655.

Berlant, Lauren (2007) 'Slow Death (Sovereignty, Obesity, Lateral Agency).' *Critical Inquiry*, 33 (Summer), 754–780.

Boyer, Paul (1998) *Fallout: A Historian Reflects on America's Half-Century Encounter With Nuclear Weapons*. Columbus, OH: Ohio State University Press.

Brown, Kate (2013) *Plutopia: Nuclear Families, Atomic Cities, and the Great Soviet and American Plutonium Disasters*. Oxford: Oxford University Press.

Caldeira, Ken, Govindasamy Bala, and Long Cao (2013) 'The Science of Geoengineering.'' *Annual Review of Earth and Planetary Sciences*, 41 (May), 231–256.

Chakrabarty, Dipesh (2012) 'Postcolonial Studies and the Challenge of Climate Change.' *New Literary History*, 43(1): 1–18.

Choy, Tim (2011) *Ecologies of Comparison: An Ethnography of Endangerment in Hong Kong*. Durham, NC: Duke University Press.

Clark, Nigel (2014) 'Geo-politics and the Disaster of the Anthropocene.' *Sociological Review*, 62(S1): 19–37.

Commoner, Barry (1958) 'The Fallout Problem.' *Science*, 127(3305): 1023–1026.

Cosgrove, Denis (2001) *Apollo's Eye: A Cartographic Genealogy of the Earth in the Western Imagination*. Baltimore, MD: Johns Hopkins University Press.

Costello, Anthony et al. (2009) 'Managing the Health Effects of Climate Change.' *The Lancet*, 373(9676): 1693–1733.

Crow, James (1960) 'Radiation and Future Generations.' in Jon M. Fowler (ed.) *Fallout: A Study of Superbombs, Strontium 90, and Survival*. New York: Basic Books, pp. 92–105.

Crutzen, P. J. (2002) 'The "Anthropocene".' *Journal de Physique IV*, 12(10): 1–6.

Daston, Lorraine J. and Peter Galison (2010) *Objectivity*. Cambridge, MA: MIT Press.

DeLoughrey, Elizabeth (2014) 'Satellite Planetarity and the Ends of the Earth.' *Public Culture*, 26(2): 257–211.

Doel, Ronald (2003) 'Constituting the Postwar Earth Sciences: The Military's Influence on the Environmental Sciences in the USA after 1945.' *Social Studies of Science*, 33(5): 635–666.

Dumit, Joseph (2013) 'Earth Possessed.' Paper delivered at the Society for Social Studies of Science Annual Meeting, San Diego, 10 October.

Eden, Lynn (2004) *Whole World On Fire: Organizations, Knowledge, and Nuclear Weapons Devastation*. Ithaca, NY: Cornell University Press.

Edwards, Paul (2010) *A Vast Machine: Computer Models, Climate Data, and the Politics of Global Warming*. Cambridge, MA: MIT Press.

Egan, Michael (2007) *Barry Commoner and the Science of Survival: The Remaking of American Environmentalism*. Cambridge, MA: MIT Press.

Farish, Matthew (2010) *The Contours of America's Cold War*. Minneapolis, MN: University of Minnesota Press.

Fleming, Roger (2010) *Fixing the Sky: The Checkered History of Weather and Climate Control*. New York: Columbia University Press.

Fowler, John M. (ed.) (1960a) *Fallout: A Study of Superbombs, Strontium 90, and Survival*. New York: Basic Books.

Fowler, John M. (1960b) 'The Rising Level of Fallout.' in Jon M. Fowler (ed.) *Fallout: A Study of Superbombs, Strontium 90, and Survival*. New York: Basic Books, pp. 51–67.

Glasstone, Samuel and Philip J. Dolan (eds) (1977) *The Effects of Nuclear Weapons*. Third edition. Washington, DC: Government Printing Office.

Gusterson, Hugh (1998) *Nuclear Rites: A Weapons Laboratory at the End of the Cold War*. Berkeley, CA: University of California Press.

Haffner, Jeanne (2013) *The View From Above: The Science of Social Space*. Cambridge, MA: MIT Press.

Hagen, Joel (1992) *An Entangled Bank: The Origins of Ecosystem Ecology*. New Brunswick, NJ: Rutgers University Press.

Hamblin, Jacob Darwin (2013) *Arming Mother Nature: The Birth of Catastrophic Environmentalism*. New York: Oxford University Press.

Hamilton, Clive (2012) *Earthmasters: The Dawn of Climate Engineering*. New Haven, CT: Yale University Press.

Harley, Naom (2002) 'Laboratory Analyses: Environmental and Biological Measurements.' *Health Physics*, 82(5): 626–634.

Hashimoto, Isao (2015) 'Artwork as the Interface Between People and Problems.' *Harvard College Review of Environment & Society*, 2 (Spring): 14–16.

Hashimoto, Isao (2003) *"Nuclear Explosions 1945–1998"* 13-minute video. CTBTO Preparatory Commission. Available at www.ctbto.org/specials/1945-1998-by-isao-hashimoto/ (accessed 1 April 2014).

Hecht, Gabrielle (2012) *Being Nuclear*. Cambridge, MA: MIT Press.

Heise, Ursula (2008) *Sense of Place and Sense of Planet*. Oxford: Oxford University Press.

Jain, S. Lochlann (2013) *Malignant: How Cancer Becomes Us*. Berkeley, CA: University of California Press.

Johnson, Barbara Rose and Holly M. Barker (2008) *The Consequential Damages of Nuclear War: The Rongelap Report*. Walnut Creek, CA: Left Coast Press.

Kaufman, Scott (2012) *Project Plowshare*. Ithaca, NY: Cornell University Press.

Keith, David (2013) *A Case for Climate Engineering*. Cambridge, MA: MIT Press.

Kirsch, Scott (2005) *Proving Grounds: Project Plowshare and the Unrealized Dream of Nuclear Earth Moving*. New Brunswick, NJ: Rutgers University Press.

Koronowski, Ryan (2014) 'House Votes to Deny Climate Science and Ties Pentagon's Hands on Climate Change.' *Thinkprogress.org*, 22 May. Available at http://thinkprogress.org/climate/2014/05/22/3440827/mckinleyclimate-pentagon-climate-change/.

Kosek, Jake (2010) 'Ecologies of Empire: On the New Uses of the Honeybee.' *Cultural Anthropology*, 25(4): 650–678.

Kuletz, Valerie (1998) *The Tainted Desert: Environmental Ruin in the American West*. New York: Routledge.

Kurgan, Laura (2013) *Close up at a Distance: Mapping Technology, and Politics*. Cambridge, MA: MIT Press.

Lindee, M.Susan (1997) *Suffering Made Real: American Science and the Survivors at Hiroshima*. Chicago, IL: University of Chicago Press.

Lindsay-Poland, John (2007) *Emperors in the Jungle: The Hidden History of the U.S. in Panama*. Durham, NC: Duke University Press.

Machta, Lester and Robert J. List (1960) 'The Global Pattern of Fallout.' in John M. Fowler (ed.) *Fallout: A Study of Superbombs, Strontium 90, and Survival*. New York: Basic Books, pp. 26–36.

Machta, L., R. J. List and L. F. Hubert (1956) 'Worldwide Travel of Atomic Debris.' *Science*, 124(3220): 474–477.

Makhijani, Arjun and Stephen I. Schwartz (2008) 'Victims of the Bomb.' in Stephen I. Schwartz (ed.) *Atomic Audit*. Washington, DC: Brooking Institution Press , pp. 375–431.

Masco, Joseph (2014) *The Theater of Operations: National Security Affect from the Cold War to the War on Terror*. Durham, DC: Duke University Press.

Masco, Joseph (2010) 'Bad Weather: On Planetary Crisis.' *Social Studies of Science*, 40(1): 7–40.

Masco, Joseph (2006) *The Nuclear Borderlands: The Manhattan Project in Post-Cold War New Mexico*. Princeton, NJ: Princeton University Press.

Murphy, Michelle (2008) 'Chemical Regimes of Living.' *Environmental History*, 13: 695–703.

Murphy, Michelle (2006) *Sick Building Syndrome and the Problem of Uncertainty: Environmental Politics, Technoscience, and Women Workers*. Durham, NC: Duke University Press.

National Research Council (2006) *Health Risks From Exposure to Low Levels of Ionizing Radiation: BEIR VII Phase 2*. Washington, DC: National Academies Press.

Nixon, Rob (2011) *Slow Violence and the Environmentalism of the Poor*. Cambridge, MA: Harvard University Press.

Oakes, Guy (1994) *The Imaginary War: Civil Defense and American Cold War Culture*. Oxford: Oxford University Press.

Odum, Howard T. and Eugene P. Odum (1955) 'Trophic Structure and Productivity of a Windward Coral Reef Community on Eniwetok Atoll.' *Ecological Monographs*, 25(3): 291–320.

O'Neil, Dan (2007) *The Firecracker Boys: H-Bombs, Inupiat Eskimos, and the Roots of the Environmental Movement*. New York: Basic Books.

Orff, Kate and Robert Misrach (2012) *Petrochemical America*. New York: Aperture.

Petryna, Adrianna (2002) *Life Exposed: Biological Citizens after Chernobyl*. Princeton, NJ: Princeton University Press.

Poole, Robert (2008) *Earthrise: How Man First Saw the Earth*. New Haven, CT: Yale University Press.

Parenti, Christian (2011) *Tropic of Chaos: Climate Change and the New Geography of Violence*. New York: Nation Books.

Raffles, Hugh (2002) *In Amazonia: A Natural History*. Princeton, NJ: Princeton University Press.

Robock, Alan, Allison Marquardt, Ben Kravitz and Georgiy Stenchikov (2009) 'Benefits, Risk and Cost of Stratospheric Geoengineering.' *Geophysical Research Letters*, 36(19).

Sloterdijk, Peter (2009) *Terror From the Air*. Los Angeles, CA: Semiotext(e).

Schneider, Stephen (2008) 'Geoengineering: Could We or Should We Make It Work?" *Philosophical Transactions of the Royal Society A*, 366: 3843–3862.

Simon, Steven L., Andrea Bouville, and Charles E. Land (2006) 'Fallout from Nuclear Weapons Tests and Cancer Risks.' *American Scientist*, 94(1): 48–57.

Steffen, Will et al. (2011) 'The Anthropocene: From Global Change to Planetary Stewardship.' *Ambio*, 40(7): 739–761.

Winiarek, Victor, Marc Bocquet, Yelva Roustan, Camille Birman and Pierre Tran (2014) 'Atmospheric Dispersion of Radionuclides from the Fukushima Daichii Nuclear Power Plant.' Centre d'Enseignement et de Recherche en Environnement Atmospherique. Available at http://cerea.enpc.fr/en/fukushima.html (accessed 1 April 2014).

Woodruff, Wayne (1967) *Nuclear Operation: Project Gasbuggy*. Livermore, CA: Lawrence Livermore National Laboratory.

3 Classical realism for the twenty-first century[1]

Responding to the challenge of globality

Campbell Craig

Introduction

The advent of transnational and supranational threats to human security raises a fundamental challenge to conventional theories of International Relations (IR) that focus upon interstate relations. The most prominent of these theories (though not the only one) is structural realism, which possesses no means of analysing such threats, nor a praxeology for contending with them. Structural realism, sometimes also called 'neorealism,' regards international relations as, fundamentally, an interminable conflict among nation-states characterized by the ever-present possibility of great power war (the most important recent studies are Mearsheimer 2001 and Glaser 2010). Structural realists cannot incorporate threats posed by something other than nation-state predation into their theorizing; nor can they, therefore, suggest political strategies suitable for dealing with such threats. For some scholars, these shortcomings, together with other structural realist failings (which are discussed later) foretells the end of realism itself.

This chapter argues that realism, considered as a political philosophy that regards security from external threats as the first objective of collective policy, remains the most effective means of understanding international politics. Here I suggest that this is true even for a conception of the politics of globality in which the sociopolitical realm has now reached a planetary level: the advent of transnational and supranational problems, ranging from climate change, to nuclear proliferation, to sub-national terrorism, to a volatile globalized capitalism that no single state can regulate, has made the traditional framework of interstate politics far less important (though certainly not irrelevant). But the form of realism that most directly speaks to this realm is not structural realism, but its twentieth-century predecessor, classical realism, as it was advanced by Hans Morgenthau, the American scholar widely regarded as the founder of the modern discipline of International Relations.

The classical realism outlined below restates Morgenthau's development of realist principles during early Cold War America, and it is here that I contend with extant interpretations of classical realism (and of Morgenthau himself) that attribute to it an idealistic progressivism which I argue is anachronistic. I then add to these principles some key implications of recent international history and an engagement with contemporary threats to human security. The result is to stipulate a realism that regards external dangers as being global and existential in nature, and collective policy as now to be conceived on behalf of humanity itself rather than distinct national societies.

Morgenthau's Cold War realism and the nuclear revolution

To develop a school of classical realism that is relevant to our present era, it is necessary to distinguish it not only from structural realism, but also from the classical realist tradition that was so vigorously established by several leading intellectuals in the middle of the twentieth century. A modern classical realism that simply reiterates the arguments of Morgenthau *et al.* would have nothing new to offer.

Recognizing this, many political theorists interested in classical realism have argued over the past decade or so that the founders of the school were influenced far more fundamentally than previously acknowledged by continental political theories and progressive political programs.[2] This new work clearly shows, for instance, that key realist intellectuals were far more comfortable with ideas about radical political change, and especially those related to the transformation of the interstate system, than their successors; that they concerned themselves with emotive and psychological factors, such as lust, pride, love, and other things one does not usually read about in *International Security*[3]; and that they were highly skeptical of, if not hostile to, attempts to understand international politics in any kind of formal scientific fashion.[4]

This recent move gives us the means to found a new classical realism for the current era, because it provides further material to draw clear boundaries between its founders and the structural realists who followed them, and an avenue to reconceptualize the tradition by explicitly incorporating into it the theories and argumentation of the continental intellectuals who so clearly influenced it.

But the move accomplishes a third purpose as well. It allows its exponents to suggest that classical realism was actually much less 'realist' than commonly believed, and that its founders can be seen as anticipating, or sympathetic to, or even paving the way for, conceptions of international politics that are clearly antagonistic to modern IR realism (Tjalve 2008: 7–9). Moreover, it allows these contemporary scholars to de-emphasize the great international crisis of the West in the 1940s – World War II, and the decision to wage the Cold War – as the central problematique of classical realism. By aligning the original classical realists with both pre-war continental and contemporary theorizing, we can consider them in a train of thought that transcends that kind of historical context. Classical realism may therefore be used as a means of developing what Quentin Skinner (1969: 9–12; 1974) called a 'Mythology of Doctrine': an instance of regarding past political writing as a part of a natural trajectory to one's own position rather than as an attempt to comprehend problems of the time.

I do not at all wish to claim here that the large body of recent scholarship addressing classical realism as a political philosophy on its own terms is wrong or misguided, but rather that by downplaying historical setting this work can misread its reformist nature. This runs the risk of Skinner's ahistoricism, to be sure, but my main point here is to argue that a de-emphasis of the Cold War context deprives us of the most promising means of redefining classical realism for the contemporary period.

The classical realists established their school of thought in the 1930s and 1940s, in response to the crises in Europe and then the post-Second World War order, and to an idealistic conception of international relations developed in the interwar period which they thought dangerous. They accepted the inter-state system as it existed and believed that the West had to be willing to play power politics, and so run the risk of major war, if it were to survive. The foundational texts of classical realism all make this same argument.[5]

Since then, two events occurred which threatened to undermine these central tenets of classical realism: the nuclear revolution, and the peaceful end of the Cold War. The nuclear revolution happened on their watch, so to speak: it took place just as soon as they had laid out a new case for power politics in the 1930s and 1940s. The end of the Cold War, on the other hand, did not occur until after (almost) all of the original classical realists were gone. This chapter will proceed by first showing how Hans Morgenthau responded to the nuclear revolution while it unfolded and how his reaction permits us to reconceive classical realism as an historical episode.

To understand how the nuclear revolution forced an evolution of Morgenthau's realism, it is necessary first to summarize his general approach to the Cold War – his overarching vision of international politics during the first decade after World War II and its implications for US foreign policy. Amidst all of the recent theoretically oriented literature on Morgenthau it is easy to lose sight of the fact that he dedicated himself in the late 1940s and early 1950s to demanding that the United States confront the Soviet Union, particularly in Europe, and that he aimed his argumentation primarily towards the left. It was this campaign that elevated classical realism to the heights of intellectual power, at least in the US: we would have long forgotten it otherwise.

Morgenthau, as well as other classical realists like Reinhold Niebuhr, George Kennan, and Walter Lippmann, regarded their primary task after World War II as one of persuading the American public, and particular the liberal elite that had dominated US politics since the early 1930s, that it would be necessary for the United States to engage in the kind of peacetime power politics it had consistently eschewed since the early nineteenth century (Rosenthal 1991). It is hard to imagine today, but in 1945, even after the victory over Japan and Germany, most Americans, including many elites, desired nothing more than to return to isolationism. The Republican Party, and especially its broad constituency in the rural midwest and west, was mostly dominated by fiscal conservatives who wished to roll back the size of the federal government, slash military spending, and return to a cheap hemispheric foreign policy. More important, the Democratic Party and the middle-class urban liberals who largely ran it remained wedded, with some exceptions, to Roosevelt's ideal of the grand alliance with the Soviet Union and Great Britain, and hoped to cooperate with these allies (especially the USSR) to forge a collective international order that could eliminate power politics once and for all.[6]

A key objective of Morgenthau's writings during the second half of the 1940s and early 1950s was to demolish these liberal hopes. A good part of his case, of course, focused upon the naïveté of those who fancied global cooperation with Stalin. More important for our purposes, however, was his larger argument that the abolition of power politics would be impossible in any case. The only way to reliably do so is to create a world government, and Morgenthau made it clear (before the advent of the nuclear revolution) that this was an impossibility.

The way he advanced this argument was classic Morgenthau. In the first two editions of *Politics Among Nations* he acknowledges the logic of a world state, seeing it as a hypothetical necessity in a world of total nationalism and the erosion of international society and diplomacy in the twentieth century, a phenomenon that reached its apogee in World War II, the atomic bombing of Hiroshima and Nagasaki, and the rise of totalitarian states such as Nazi Germany and the Soviet Union (Morgenthau 1948, 1st edn: 392–400) Like many other students of international politics during the early years of the Cold War, Morgenthau took from the atomic bomb and the legacy of total war the general idea that things ought not to continue as they were indefinitely (van Munster and Sylvest 2016).

But Morgenthau then pointed out that a world state could not come into being until a truly supranational society developed that could provide it with political legitimacy. Morgenthau applied John Stuart Mill's test of workable government to the supranational level and found that none of Mill's three essential requirements was even remotely at play (see Scheuerman 2009: 127). No one felt loyalty to a supranational entity, could expect justice from it, or could imagine supporting its military power over that of the nation-state. As he wrote in the first edition of *Politics Among Nations* in 1948:

> Under the present moral conditions of mankind, few men would act on behalf of a world government if the interests of their nation would require a different course of action. On the contrary, the overwhelming majority would put the welfare of their own nation above everything else, the interests of a world state included … . The odds are to such an extent in favor of the nation that men who might be willing and able to sacrifice and die that the world state be kept standing do not even have the opportunity to do so in the world as it is constituted today.
>
> (Morgenthau 1948: 400–401)

What was Morgenthau trying to do by postulating the logical need for a world government, and then shooting it down with such force? He was attempting to show, as he did with many issues, the difference between abstract reason and political reality. It was not difficult to demonstrate abstractly why a world government made sense in an era of total war and global technologies. The job of a political realist was to point out that such ideas could not work before they gained traction among liberals.

Because Morgenthau demanded that the West confront the Soviet Union and rejected the possibility of world government, his scope for political dissent from US Cold War foreign policy was limited. Indeed, it was difficult for him, despite frequent disavowals, to criticize *any* policy that purported to strengthen the western commitment to the Cold War and the defence of Europe; this was reinforced by the political culture of McCarthyism in the first half of the 1950s, something from which Morgenthau was not immune (Craig 2003: chs 2–3; viz. Scheuerman 2011).

His conservative bent in the 1950s reached its apex in the second aspect of his Cold War realism relevant to this chapter: the embrace of the idea of winnable nuclear war. In 1949, the USSR tested an atomic bomb; by 1953 both nations had tested thermonuclear devices. This meant that anyone who believed that the West must continue to confront the USSR had now to accept the possibility of a nuclear war. For Morgenthau, this represented a decisive moment. It was one thing to demand that the West contend with the Soviet bloc when America possessed an atomic monopoly, the Soviet Union was still recovering from the war, and direct conflict was unlikely. Now it portended dozens of Hiroshimas and Nagasakis. Throughout the Western world many began to rethink their support of the Cold War (van Munster and Sylvest 2016).

Not Morgenthau. Maintaining his belief that the West had to be willing to fight rather than back down, he plainly embraced the idea of winnable nuclear war – and its necessary corollary, nuclear strategy – during the middle part of the decade. If anything, he was even more determined to maintain the *ultima ratio* of war in the face of the new nuclear condition. Between 1954 and 1958 he wrote on many occasions that the United States must develop new weapons to wage and win a war with the USSR; that it must adopt more flexible strategies of limited conflict, including tactical nuclear war; that Eisenhower administration accommodation of the USSR (during the Suez crisis, for example) amounted to appeasement; and that, following the *Sputnik* test of October 1957, the US must embark upon a massive campaign of rearmament and mobilization. It was necessary, in short, to meet the Soviet threat with the conventional tools of military power and a determination to fight. The 'United States,' he wrote in January 1956, 'must prepare for, and fight if necessary, a clearly limited atomic war' (Morgenthau 1956: 9; see also Craig 2003: 94–101).

On the eve of the nuclear revolution, therefore, Morgenthau's classical realism cannot be described as anything but orthodox. Yes, he wrote in a style that was more humanistic and attentive to a wide range of political philosophies than did his neorealist successors; yes, he was willing to entertain ideas about a world beyond nationalism and power politics. But when it came to the contemporary Cold War enterprise, he adhered to a mainstream, hawkish line. His acceptance of nuclear strategy epitomizes this position. Had he been committed to serious global reform, he would have rejected such an enterprise from the outset. He would have been repulsed by the highly retrograde, if not perverse, nature of nuclear strategizing (as he would be a decade hence); more important, he would have recognized immediately that the whole point of nuclear strategy was to sustain the interstate order as it was in the face of a technology that threatened to make it obsolete. It represented the exact opposite of progressive international reform.

The nuclear revolution took place in the late 1950s and early 1960s. It was during this period that the two Cold War superpowers produced large numbers of thermonuclear bombs and began to deploy them on intercontinental missiles. An all-out war waged with such weaponry could now effectively kill off both nations and much of the planet as well. That outcome was not possible earlier in the Cold War, when both sides wielded atomic weaponry and delivered them on manned bombers. Equally important, especially with respect to public perceptions, it was at this time that the US and the USSR faced off against one another in several nuclear crises, characterized above all by a common fear that they might explode into a general war no one wanted. From the second Quemoy-Matsu crisis in 1958 to the Cuban Missile Crisis in 1962, the world experienced four major showdowns, each of which could easily have resulted in a major nuclear conflict – an ordeal that brought home the unique spectre of nuclear war to everyone.[7]

Between 1958 and 1962, Morgenthau changed his tune. By that I mean not only that he revised his views about the immutability of the Cold War interstate order and the notion of justifiable nuclear war but also that his tone of argumentation on these issues became far more anguished, radical, and unhesitant. On the one hand, Morgenthau renounced his flirtation with nuclear strategy in violent language, accusing Strangelovian strategists like Herman Kahn of regarding human society 'like a primitive ant society' (Morgenthau 1962a, vol. 1: 70) and dissecting his and Henry Kissinger's plans for winnable nuclear war clinically in a 1962 essay in *Commentary* and a 1964 article in the *American Political Science Review*. There is 'no way of overcoming the immensity of nuclear destruction,' Morgenthau stated (Morgenthau 1962b: 155).

On the other, Morgenthau began to argue in the early 1960s that the nuclear revolution had made the interstate system obsolete. It is 'obvious,' he maintained, that 'the nuclear age has radically changed man's relation to nature and his fellow men.' The nuclear revolution, he wrote, had changed everything: 'no such radical transformation of the structure of international relations has ever occurred in history,' he wrote. The threat of nuclear war, he declared, 'suggests the abolition of international relations itself through the merger of all national sovereignties into one world state which would have a monopoly of the most destructive instruments of violence' (Morgenthau 1961: 231; Morgenthau 1962a, vol. 3: 174–175). In the space of a couple of years, while the Berlin Wall and Cuban crises raged, Morgenthau argued very specifically that nuclear weapons – not anything else – had undermined the conventional realist understanding of international politics and great power war (Craig 2003: ch. 5; see also Scheuerman 2009: 77–79).

The importance of this shift, with respect both to structural realism and contemporary revisions of classical realism that play down the Cold War context, is paramount. It is crucial in distinguishing the classical realists from their neorealist successors, and in particular the founder of structural realism, Kenneth Waltz, for the simple reason that Morgenthau recognized that a realism which reified interstate anarchy amounted to a justification of omnicidal nuclear war: rather than accepting this as a regrettable fact, he declared, for the first time in his life, that the interstate system was inviable and must be transformed. It would be hard to devise an issue that more fundamentally separates the classical realists from the neorealists than that.

The move is also key in our consideration of the current literature on classical realism because it was driven by a response to material, technological, and geopolitical conditions. Morgenthau did not advance global reform and the idea of a world state because he had always been well-versed in and sympathetic to the writings of continental thinkers opposed to modern nationalism and total power politics and was finally coming around to their views; he did so because he reluctantly concluded that the spectre of omnicidal war had made his conventional Cold War realism obsolete. The timing and logic of his intellectual shift is too precise to have any doubts about this. Before the nuclear revolution, he adhered to the interstate model, going so far as accepting the notion of winnable nuclear war so as to preserve it; his abandonment of this model happened afterwards, and in his writings after 1960 he states quite clearly that his only reason for doing so was because the possibility of nuclear holocaust forced his hand.[8] The radical element of Morgenthau's classical realism derives from his encounter with the nuclear revolution: the historical record on this is simply indisputable.

This latter point is strengthened further by the final part of the story. Despite his conclusion that the nuclear revolution necessitated a transformation of the international order, Morgenthau never put forward any kind of sustained argument showing how this might happen. Why? Surely, his growing and eventual public opposition to the Vietnam War in the 1960s and the fading of nuclear danger after the Cuban Missile Crisis redirected his attentions. There was also the problem that advocates of ending the interstate system run the risk of being caricatured as eccentric, and, in high Cold War America, dangerous.

Morgenthau, however, did try to address the issue, and the impasse he reached illustrates well how his classical realism, at least, had not turned in a wholly ideational direction. He had long understood quite well that the solution to the nuclear dilemma could not be achieved by piecemeal reform. If the world were to be rid permanently of the spectre of nuclear war, nothing short of a world government capable of verifying and enforcing total global disarmament would do. Without it, nations would be able to cheat, to with-hold nuclear weapons secretly, and the fact that everyone knew this was possible would stop a more modest initiative in its tracks. 'Effective over-all disarmament,' he told a subcommittee of the Senate Foreign Relations Committee in early 1957, 'is tantamount to the establishment of a world government' (Morgenthau 1962a, vol. 3: 142). Why then did he not advocate just that?

The problem, he perceived, lay in the structure of Cold War politics. Nuclear peace could not be had without a serious world government, but such a government could not come into being unless the two Cold War superpowers were willing to establish a new entity that had more power than either of them did. The situation by the early 1960s was particularly tragic: on one hand, the danger of war had now become omnicidal, making the creation of a world government an urgent task; on the other, the USSR was now an established power, with its own massive nuclear arsenal, and so could be even less expected to agree to a world government that would be acceptable to the United States. There was no other way: a political resolution to the Cold War had to occur before the nuclear dilemma could be solved. In the third edition of *Politics Among Nations*, published in 1960, Morgenthau put it like this:

> Competition for armaments reflects, and is an instrument of, competition for power. So long as nations advance contradictory claims in the contest for power, they are forced by the very logic of the power contest to advance contradictory claims for armaments. Therefore, a mutually satisfactory settlement of the power contest is a precondition for disarmament.
>
> (Morgenthau 1960: 411)

The two superpowers could, and should, Morgenthau incessantly argued, reach negotiated settlements on outstanding issues, pursue arms control, and resume diplomatic contacts. They should act more like the European states of the nineteenth century. But actual disarmament was a different issue entirely. That would require a mutually satisfactory settlement of the power contest, and this, he presciently stated in 1959:

> cannot be settled by the give-and-take of negotiations. It will be settled, after negotiations have done their work on the political plane, by the nobler and weightier act of performance. Which system will prove capable of meeting basic human aspirations for itself and for mankind?
>
> (Morgenthau 1962a, vol. 3: 322)

William Scheuerman suggests that in the last years of his life Morgenthau moved toward a more radical view: he 'jettisoned any remaining doubts about the necessity of multilateral nuclear disarmament' and insisted that the two superpowers 'possessed a rational common interest in reducing existing arsenals as well as the creation of new weapons of mass destruction.' Those who 'assumed the Soviets would necessarily pursue the most diabolical course,' Scheuerman adds, 'not only failed to provide sufficient evidence that the Russians either could get away with cheating or even possessed an incentive to do so, but disregarded the even more horrendous risks of an unlimited arms race increasing the probability of war' (Scheuerman 2009: 160–161).

This discussion, however, conflates arms control, arms reduction, and non-proliferation with the very different end of complete nuclear disarmament. Morgenthau was of course in favor of the first three objectives, and had been since the 1950s. But this did not mean, at all, that he had abandoned any doubts about the necessity of nuclear disarmament. That much harder task could not happen until a world government was established, and that in turn required an end to the Cold War.

The only solution remaining was to buy time until the Cold War came an end. As Reinhold Niebuhr put it in 1967, in a joint interview of him and Morgenthau, 'I don't know whether we'll ever have perfect peace. What we've got to do now is avoid Hell and nuclear disaster.' Morgenthau noted that the two superpowers could establish a 'condominium over all the world' to avoid such a disaster, but said nothing about how this might come about. In the meantime, he added, the US and the USSR would have to rely upon effective diplomacy (Niebuhr and Morgenthau 1967: 4–7; see also Craig 2003: 115).

Morgenthau had nothing more to offer not because the Soviets were 'diabolical' or were bent upon getting away with cheating but because the anarchical condition of Cold War international politics, which he believed still prevailed, would prevent either superpower from disarming completely without being sure that the other side was doing the same. In the nuclear age, the only way to be sure that the other side is not cheating is to construct a world government, and that could not happen as long as the two sides 'advanced contradictory claims in the contest for power' (Morgenthau 1960: 411). The only other logical alternative to waiting for the Cold War to end was for the United States to disarm unilaterally and hope for the best. This Morgenthau could not, and never did, advocate.

Morgenthau's engagement with the nuclear dilemma during the height of the Cold War compels us to modify our historical conception of classical realism. It indicates that he recognized that interstate anarchy was inviable in the nuclear age, thus placing him squarely not only against structural realists who regard anarchy as an immutable condition but also against common perceptions of realism more generally.[9] It shows that his move toward a transformational global agenda is explained not by his location within a progressive chain of ideas inexorably leading to the present but by his historically contingent encounter with the possibility of omnicidal war in the late 1950s and early 1960s. Finally, it demonstrates that he recognized that the transformation of interstate politics that he sought could not take place until the Cold War came to an end – but, as he perceived, it *could come to an end* without the usual catalyst of systemic war. These recognitions take on new and vivid salience in the aftermath of the events of 1989–91.

Classical realism and the end of the Cold War

Scholars across the IR spectrum have long regarded the demise of the Cold War rivalry between the United States and the Soviet Union and the peaceful collapse of the USSR during the period 1989–91 as an authentically revolutionary event in the history of international politics. There is an enormous and growing literature on its relevance to every major subfield in IR, together with ongoing historical inquiry into the decision-making of leaders and peoples in the two Cold War superpowers, every nation in Eastern Europe, and elsewhere.[10]

In the second section of this chapter I intend to identify two implications of the end of the Cold War that are particularly relevant to a reconceptualization of classical realism today. The aim here, as in the first section, is to suggest that such a reconceptualization rests on firmer ground when it is informed by a rigorous engagement with historical events.[11] The difference, of course, is that the events in question here did not affect the development of classical realism as it was initially put forward; what they ought to affect is how we think about it now.

As is well known classical realism as a scholarly project faded away in the 1960s, supplanted by a structural realism, pretty much invented by Kenneth Waltz, which sought to explain the nature of international politics by adopting the methodology and epistemology of modern social science, particularly microeconomics. I have suggested elsewhere that a key factor behind this shift was precisely the nuclear revolution and the impasse it created for the major classical realists (Craig 2003: ch. 6). A theoretical approach to international politics which sought merely to explain, not try to solve, problems such as global nuclear war could avoid such an impasse. Other factors, including larger trends in US social science toward behavioralism and structural analysis, certainly played a role (Bell 2002; Wohlforth 2011; Kirshner 2012, 2013).

Structural realism reached its apex in the late 1970s and early 1980s with the publication of two books, Waltz's *Theory of International Politics* (1979) and Robert Gilpin's *War and Change in World Politics* (1981). Though the two books present substantially different theses, and indeed the latter is not universally regarded as a work of structural realism, they share three key assumptions relevant to our understanding of the end of the Cold War. First, both books assume that great powers seek above all else to maintain this position, and will wage war, if they must, to keep it. Second, they argue that international systems are defined by the rivalry of great powers, and that these systems come to an end only as a consequence of systemic war. After such wars, some powers decline, others rise, and the process begins anew. Both Waltz (in his 1959 tour de force *Man, the State and War*) and Gilpin explicitly insist that this phenomenon had not been made obsolete by nuclear weapons (see Craig 2012).

Third, both authors believe that a useful theory of international politics ought to be predictive: it ought to foresee major shifts in the general direction of great power politics. Prediction, after all, is one of the few ways one can test the validity and explanatory power of a formal social science theory. Waltz predicted that the bipolarity of the Cold War made it exceedingly stable and likely to last for a long time. Gilpin suggested that the US faced a future of hegemonic decline and worried that this could trigger a war between itself and its rising challengers (see Wohlforth 2011).

As many critics have pointed out – the best analysis remains Richard Ned Lebow's (1994) article in *International Organization* – the end of the Cold War constituted a major blow to all of these central assumptions.[12] The Soviet Union, a vast empire that still wielded massive military power, chose in the late 1980s to allow its client states in Eastern Europe to collapse and in 1991 put an end to its own existence, effectively committing superpower suicide. A great power wielding formidable military might simply surrendered in its Cold War rivalry with the US, a rivalry it had spent fifty years, trillions of Roubles, and fought many minor wars to maintain.[13] Accordingly, because the USSR surrendered peacefully, the Cold War came to an end without the catalytic war that is supposed to terminate all great power systems and give birth to new ones. This had never happened in modern international history.

What is more, neither Waltz, nor Gilpin, nor any other structural realist predicted the end of the Cold War, or anything like it. It would not be fair to have expected them to foresee the events exactly, of course, but if prediction is to have any meaning as a feature of social science, to fail to anticipate the collapse of the Soviet Union and the peaceful demise of an international system, and indeed to predict precisely the opposite, must be judged as a critical failure (Lebow 2007).

Structural realism's comprehensive inability to account for the end of the Cold War created an opening for the rise of competing international relations theories, and in particular constructivism (see Reus-Smit 2008). Constructivists point to the agency of key actors in Eastern Europe and Russia during the 1989–91 period and to the influence of ideas and ideals upon their behavior as a clear validation of their thesis that ideational factors trump material ones in the course of international events (English 2000). 'Anarchy' may have meant one thing to American and Soviet leaders in, say, 1946, but it meant something quite different to Gorbachev and Yeltsin in 1990 and 1991.

It is here, between the structural realist and constructivist debate, that a new classical realism must position itself. In responding to the nuclear dilemma, Morgenthau advanced ideas that proved far more prescient with respect to the end of the Cold War than anything produced by his neorealist successors. He argued that the nuclear revolution had made the interstate system inviable, the prospect of World War III unacceptable, and, crucially, that therefore international politics would have to adapt, something that could only be done by human action at the 'unit level.' Indeed, in his amazing 1959 comment he recognized that the Cold War would have to be fought with 'soft power' and that such a struggle could constitute a third way of international politics that temporarily finessed the existential problem of nuclear holocaust. In these respects, he was a kind of 'proto-constructivist.'

But not in others. Morgenthau's conclusion that the nuclear dilemma could not be permanently solved while the Cold War raged shows clearly that he rejected the claim that international politics is entirely socially constructed and hence can be transcended by human ideas: in his view, there was no way, short of unilateral disarmament, to eliminate nuclear danger while the US and the USSR continued their contest for power (Levine 2013: 101–102).

And as he explicitly stated, the underlying reason why the nuclear problem could not be solved once and for all during the Cold War was because the only way to do so was to construct a serious world government that possessed all nuclear weaponry and the power to prevent other parties from getting their hands on it, an impossible task while the US and the USSR still sought global preponderance. In contrast, disarmament movements during and after the Cold War (a contemporary example is the 'Global Zero' campaign) advance the 'constructivist' claim that nations can divest themselves of their nuclear weaponry and trust others to do the same if leaders come around to the idea that it is possible. Total nuclear disarmament can happen without supranational verification and enforcement, because people around the world can choose to make it so. Because there is nothing physically preventing that from occurring, all that is necessary is a shift in beliefs, and the nuclear spectre can therefore be eliminated without the grim work of building a world state.[14]

To this, Morgenthau would have bared his realist teeth. His objection would have focused not upon the irrelevance or impotence of ideas and human agency as such but upon the dangers of misplaced idealism. For Morgenthau, and for all realists, including contemporary classical ones, the political world remains bedeviled by mistrust, cynicism, and exploitation. And when it comes to nuclear disarmament, the stakes of forgetting this reality are at their highest. A campaign of unenforced and unverified nuclear disarmament, one based upon nothing but trust that all nuclear nations will disarm completely and remain disarmed, no matter what, opens the door for exploitation by cynical powers, whom Niebuhr called the 'Children of Darkness' (Niebuhr 1944). A state that secretly withheld its nuclear weapons while others disarmed would find itself in a position of supreme power; acutely aware of this fact, and of the fact that such weapons are both easy to hide and strategically decisive, at least some other nations would never disarm completely. A process of unenforced disarmament would disintegrate therefore into a condition of recrimination and conflict – it would be worse than doing nothing. This is why Morgenthau stated in 1957 that disarmament equals world government, and why he never proposed that the West unilaterally disarm (see Scheuerman 2009: 123). Politics, as Max Weber argued a century ago, cannot work without a government in possession of all war-making weaponry: today, those weapons are nuclear, and so the government must be global. This is a realist argument.

Classical realism for the twenty-first century

Our first use of the end of the Cold War has been as a kind of heuristic tool: as a means of distinguishing further classical realism from structural realism, as well as from a constructivism which it might otherwise resemble.[15] The second way to use the end of the Cold War to sharpen classical realism as a praxeology: as a means of giving it a political blueprint, of defining exactly what it stands for. This second objective wholly follows the lead of the original classical realists, who rarely tried to pretend that they were not interested in influencing the course of world politics (Jervis 1994).[16]

To do so, it is necessary to summarize the key conclusions made so far in this chapter. We have, I hope, established three key points about Morgenthau's classical realism. First, he remained wedded to the interstate model of international politics, despite some passing interest in more radical political concepts, until the nuclear revolution compelled him to embrace a supranational ideal. Second, he recognized that only a world government could permanently eliminate the specter of an omnicidal nuclear war, but believed that such a government was impossible until the Cold War came to an end. Crucially, and in vivid contrast to the structural realists, he did believe that it could come to an end short of a systemic war, in which case a world government would have been too late.

Third, the end of the Cold War permits us to draw vivid lines between classical realism and its structural realist and constructivist rivals. We do so by insisting that structural realism was essentially undermined by its failure not only to predict but also to explain the peaceful surrender of the Soviet Union, but that realism as a political philosophy about international relations was not. The ability of Morgenthau to grasp the revolutionary implications of the nuclear revolution and to therefore foresee a peaceful end to the Cold War came about not because of his abandonment of realist principles, but rather because he recognized that these principles had to be modified in the face of a technology that invalidated previous realist prescriptions. Morgenthau continued to believe that politics at the collective level was characterized by insecurity, cynicism, and fear; he continued to believe that this unfortunate reality created a kind of international structure which made reform qualitatively more difficult to achieve than at the domestic level. This was precisely why he was unable to provide a solution to the nuclear dilemma in the 1960s – and an important reason why classical realism faded away.

These three conclusions together establish an obvious agenda for contemporary classical realism. If the threat of omnicidal nuclear war still remains and only world government can permanently end this threat and if the structural impossibility of attaining such a government during the Cold War has now passed, then it becomes clear that contemporary classical realism must adopt as its core concern the development of a supranational politics which applies realist principles to a post-interstate order. This is not to make the facile and unprovable assertion that if Morgenthau were alive today this is what he would be calling for. Rather it is to argue that it is an inescapable implication of his writing.

If contemporary classical realism is to reject the structural determinism of neorealism and argue that history and learning can be used by today's leaders to improve the practice of international politics,[17] it will have no means of ruling out world government on its own terms. To reject this agenda, it must either claim that the dangers of establishing a world government are greater than persisting in nuclear anarchy, or assert that it is a practical impossibility. In the former objection lies an important debate which could form a basis of contemporary classical realist discourse. In the latter objection lies a reification of interstate anarchy by the back door.

This intra-realist debate lies at the heart of a politics of globality interested in supranational threats to human security and the kind of state necessary to contend with such threats. If Morgenthau had anything to say about such a state, it was that intermediate or half-hearted attempts to conceive of it – what van Munster and Sylvest (Introduction, this volume) nicely call 'more shady forms of global governance' – will not only be insufficient to contend with the transnational and existential problems we are facing, but that proposing an ameliorative solution to a fundamental condition may well be worse than doing nothing. Such ameliorative solutions can be found not only amidst the cosmopolitan/poststructuralist centre, in which power politics somehow disappears even as the stakes of success become absolute. They are also implied by the recent move on the left towards an anti-cosmopolitan nationalism, in which the solution to global threats is to stick one's head in the sand of national/ethnic solidarity; and, on the right, towards a reliance upon an eternally competent regime of US hegemonic management.

A classical realism informed by Morgenthau's insights will have little patience with these kinds of responses. It recognizes that the impossibility of uninventing military technology and the continuing possibility of cynical behavior by egoistic global actors make anything short of a Weberian global state an insufficient aim of the politics of globality. At the same time, it also recognizes that the attainment of such a state becomes possible only when we develop an ideal of supranational political solidarity, one unified not against other states or peoples but rather the threat of extinction.

Early in his presidential term, John F. Kennedy, struck by the absurdity that the two superpowers seemed ready initiate a global thermonuclear war even though it was obvious that both sides were desperate to avoid it, muttered: 'And we call ourselves the human race' (cited in Reeves 2011: 230). A supranational politics of globality may take from Kennedy's comment two related imperatives. First, that catastrophe can and will happen if we do not act, even if everyone understands that it ought be avoided. Second, that the way to prevent this is to begin thinking about what Kennedy meant by the word 'we.'

Notes

1　The title heeds the call of Schweller (2011).
2　See Williams (2004; 2007; 2013), Tjalve (2008), Scheuerman (2009; 2011), Rösch (2014). For critiques, see Levine (2013) and McQueen (2013).
3　An excellent overview of emotive factors in classical realism is Ross (2013).
4　See Jervis (1994) and Brown (2012).
5　By foundational texts I refer to Niebuhr (1932; 1944), Carr (1939) and Morgenthau (1946).
6　Rosenthal (1991); Craig (2003: Chs 1–3).
7　For overviews, see Jervis (1989) and Craig (2013).
8　*Pace* Scheuerman (2009: 101; 2011: 91–92).
9　On this perception, see Scheuerman (2011: ch. 1).
10　See e.g. Lawson et al. (2010) as well as the special issue of *International Politics* (2011).
11　Humphreys (2011), Suganami (2008) and Guilhot (2012).
12　Two other interesting pieces written soon after the Soviet demise are Gaddis (1992) and Baldwin (1995).
13　William Wohlforth, in the special edition of International Politics (2011), argues that realism can explain the end of the Cold War because Gorbachev undertook his economic reforms and relaxed control over Eastern Europe in order to rebuild Soviet power. This may well be so, but Wohlforth's important analysis still does not explain why the USSR, when these reforms spiraled out of control, chose to surrender and end its contest with the US while it still maintained massive military power. For further discussion, see Craig (2012).
14　See the global zero website: www.globalzero.org/get-the-facts/gzap (accessed 5 November 2014). For a constructivist argument that rejects this idealism, see Wendt (2003).
15　See Humphreys (2011) on the use of history to inform international relations theory; and vice-versa.
16　On the unacknowledged normative dimension of structural realism, see Oren (2009) and Craig (2003: Ch. 7).
17　See Linklater (2004) and Kirshner (2012; 2013).

References

Baldwin, David A. (1995) 'Security Studies and the End of the Cold War,' *World Politics*, 48(1): 117–141.
Bell, Duncan S.A. (2002) 'Anarchy, Power and Death: Contemporary Political Realism as Ideology,' *Journal of Political Ideologies*, 7(2): 221–239.
Brown, Chris (2012) 'Practice, Prudence and International Relations Theory: Bourdieu, Aristotle and the Classical Realists,' *Spectrum: Journal of Global Studies*, 4(1): 27–46.
Carr, Edward Hallett (1939) *The Twenty Years' Crisis*. New York: Harper.
Craig, Campbell (2003) *Glimmer of a New Leviathan: Total War in the Realism of Niebuhr, Morgenthau and Waltz*. New York: Columbia University Press.
Craig, Campbell (2008) 'The Resurgent Idea of World Government,' *Ethics and International Affairs*, 22(2): 133–142.
Craig, Campbell (2012) 'The End of the Cold War and Soviet Collapse: The Limits of Realism and Liberalism,' *International Politics*, 49(3): 383–387.
Craig, Campbell (2013) 'The Nuclear Revolution,' in Richard Immerman and Petra Goedde (eds) *Oxford Handbook of the Cold War*. New York: Oxford University Press, pp. 360–376.

Deudney, Daniel (2007) *Bounding Power*. Princeton, NJ: Princeton University Press.

Deudney, Daniel (2013) 'Burying World Government: Planetary Geopolitics, the World State and Republican Green Peace,' paper prepared for International Studies Association workshop on World Government, San Francisco, 30 March.

English, Robert D. (2000) *Russia and the Idea of the West: Gorbachev, Intellectuals and the End of the Cold War*. New York: Columbia University Press.

Frei, Christoph (2001) *Hans J. Morgenthau: an Intellectual Biography*. Baton Rouge: Louisiana University Press.

Gaddis, John Lewis (1992/3) 'International Relations Theory and the End of the Cold War,' *International Security*, 17(3): 5–58.

Gilpin, Robert (1981) *War and Change in World Politics*. New York: Cambridge University Press.

Gismondi, Mark (2004) 'Tragedy, Realism, and Postmodernity: Kulturpessimismus in the Theories of Max Weber, E. H. Carr, Hans Morgenthau, and Henry Kissinger,' *Diplomacy and Statecraft*, 15(3): 435–464.

Glaser, Charles L. (2010) *Rational Theory of International Politics: The Logic of Competition and Cooperation*. Princeton, NJ: Princeton University Press.

Guilhot, Nicholas (2012) 'American Katechon: When Political Theology Became International Relations Theory,' *Constellations*, 17(2): 224–253.

Humphreys, Adam R. C. (2011), 'The Heuristic Application of Explanatory Theories in Internation Relations,' *European Journal of International Relations*, 17(2): 257–277.

International Politics (2011) Special issue on the end of the Cold War, 48(4/5).

Jervis, Robert (1989) *The Meaning of the Thermonuclear Revolution*. Ithaca, NY: Cornell University Press.

Jervis, Robert (1994) 'Hans Morgenthau, Realism, and the Scientific Study of International Relations,' *Social Research*, 61(4): 853–876.

Kirshner, Jonathan (2012) 'The Tragedy of Offensive Realism: Classical Realism and the Rise of China,' *European Journal of International Relations*, 18(1): 53–75.

Kirshner, Jonathan (2013) 'The Economic Sins of Modern IR Theory and the Classical Realist Alternative,' paper prepared for Reppy Institute workshop on Classical Realism, Cornell University, 4–5 May.

Lawson, George, Chris Armbruster and Michael Cox (2010) *The Global 1989: Continuity and Change in World Politics*. Cambridge: Cambridge University Press.

Lebow, Richard Ned (1994) 'The Long Peace, the End of the Cold War, and the Failure of Realism,' *International Organization*, 48(2): 249–277.

Lebow, Richard Ned (2007) 'Classical Realism,' in Tim Dunne, Milja Kurki and Steve Smith (eds) *International Relations Theories*. New York: Oxford University Press, pp. 52–70.

Levine, Daniel (2013) 'Why Hans Morgenthau Was Not a Critical Theorist (and Why Contemporary IR Realists Should Care),' *International Relations*, 27(1): 95–118.

Linklater, Andrew (2004) 'Norbert Elias, the Civilizing Process, and the Sociology of International Relations,' *International Politics*, 41(1): 3–35

McQueen, Alison (2013) 'Realism as Rationalization?,' paper prepared for Reppy Institute workshop on Classical Realism, Cornell University, 3–4 May.

McQueen, Alison (2013) 'Hans Morgenthau and the Postwar Apocalyptic Imaginary,' unpublished book chapter.

Mearsheimer, John (2001) *The Tragedy of Great Power Politics*. New York: Norton.

Morgenthau, Hans (1946) *Scientific Man versus Power Politics*. Chicago, IL: University of Chicago Press.

Morgenthau, Hans (1948/1960) *Politics Among Nations*, First and Third Edition. New York: Knopf.

Morgenthau, Hans (1961) 'Death in the Nuclear Age,' *Commentary*, 32(3): 231–234.

Morgenthau, Hans (1962a) *Politics in the Twentieth Century*, vols 1–3. Chicago, IL: University of Chicago Press.

Morgenthau, Hans (1962b) 'Love and Power,' *Commentary*, 32 (March): 247–251.

van Munster, Rens and Casper Sylvest (2016) *Nuclear Realism: Global Political Thought during the Thermonuclear Revolution*. Abingdon: Routledge.

Niebuhr, Reinhold (1932) *Moral Man and Immoral Society*. New York: Scribners.

Niebuhr, Reinhold (1944) *The Children of Light and the Children of Darkness*. New York: Scribners.

Niebuhr, Reinhold (1949) 'The Illusion of World Government,' *Foreign Affairs*, 27(3): 379–388.

Niebuhr, Reinhold, and Hans Morgenthau (1967) 'The Ethics of War and Peace in the Nuclear Age,' interview in *War/Peace Report*, 7 (February): 3–8.

Oren, Ido (2009) 'The Unrealism of Contemporary Realism: The Tension between Realist Theory and Realists' Practice,' *Perspectives on Politics*, 7(2): 283–301.

Reeves, Richard (2011) *President Kennedy: Profile of Power*. New York: Simon & Schuster.

Rösch, Felix (2014) 'Pouvoir, Puissance, and Politics: Hans Morgenthau's Dualistic Concept of Power?,' *Review of International Studies*, 40(2): 349–365.

Rosenthal, Joel (1991) *Righteous Realists*. Baton Rouge: Louisiana University Press.

Reus-Smit, Christian (2008) 'Reading History through Constructivist Eyes,' *Millenium— Journal of International Studies*, 37(2): 395–414.

Ross, Andrew A. G. (2013) 'Realism, Emotion, and Dynamic Allegiance in Global Politics,' *International Theory*, 5(2): 273–299.

Scheuerman, William (2009) *Hans Morgenthau: Realism and Beyond*. Cambridge: Polity.

Scheuerman, William (2011) *The Realist Case for Global Reform*. Cambridge: Polity.

Schweller, Randall L. (2011) 'Rational Theory for a Bygone Era,' *Security Studies*, 20(3): 460–468.

Skinner, Quentin (1969) 'Meaning and Understanding in the History of Ideas,' *History and Theory*, 8(1): 3–53.

Skinner, Quentin (1974) 'Some Problems in the Analysis of Political Thought and Action,' *Political Theory*, 2(3): 277–303.

Speer, James (1968) 'Hans Morgenthau and the World State,' *World Politics*, 20(2): 207–227.

Suganami, Hidemi (2008) 'Narrative Explanation and International Relations: Back to Basics,' *Millenium – Journal of International Studies*, 37(2): 327–356.

Tjalve, Vibeke (2008) *Realist Strategies of Republican Peace: Niebuhr, Morgenthau and the Politics of Patriotic Dissent*. New York: Palgrave Macmillan.

Waltz, Kenneth (1959) *Man, the State and War*. New York: Columbia University Press.

Waltz, Kenneth (1979) *Theory of International Politics*. Reading: Addison-Wesley.

Wendt, Alexander (2003) 'Why a World State is Inevitable', *European Journal of International Relations*, 9(4): 491–542.

Williams, Michael C. (2004) 'Why Ideas Matter in International Relations: Hans Morgenthau, Classical Realism, and the Moral Construction of Power Politics,' *International Organization*, 58(4): 633–665.

Williams, Michael C. (2005) 'What is the National Interest? The Neoconservative Challenge in IR Theory,' *European Journal of International Relations*, 11(3): 307–337.

Williams, Michael C. (2007) 'Introduction,' in Michael C. Williams (ed.) *Realism Reconsidered: The Legacy of Hans J. Morgenthau in International Relations*. New York: Oxford University Press.

Williams, Michael C. (2013) 'The Irony of Realism,' paper prepared for Reppy Institute workshop on Classical Realism, Cornell University, 3–4 May.

Wohlforth, William C. (2011) 'Gilpinian Realism and International Relations,' *International Relations*, 25(4): 499–511.

4 Mastering the globe

Law, sovereignty and the commons of mankind

Tanja Aalberts and Wouter Werner

Introduction

One of the perennial questions of international law concerns the delimitation of territory under sovereign jurisdiction from areas beyond the (exclusive) control of states, the so-called non-sovereign spaces. Where should the line be drawn between sovereign state territory and spaces belonging to 'human society' (Vattel 1758: para. 283)? International law, in other words, is not just about the 'regulation of relations between sovereign states'[1] – as the commonplace shortcut description would have it – but also about the identification and regulation of the so-called commons of mankind.[2] The delineation between sovereign territories and the commons of mankind takes place on the basis of specific legal imaginaries of the globe as a whole. It is this triad globe–sovereignty–mankind that is central to this chapter.

In contemporary debates on human rights, environmentalism and humanitarian intervention, sovereignty is often treated as the antipole of mankind and/or the global. However, as we will illustrate below, the meaning of sovereignty in fact is intrinsically bound up with both imaginaries of globality and projections of the nature of the commons of mankind. Rather than juxtaposing sovereignty, the global and mankind, this chapter looks into their mutually constitutive relationship. More specifically, it elaborates how sovereignty and mankind are central but shifting reference points in the politics of globality. This transpires clearly from the post-1945 introduction of the 'common heritage of mankind' principle, as will be discussed in the second part of this chapter. But in order to show the different kinds of politics that emerge through the conceptual pairing of sovereignty and mankind, we first need to go further back into history to what Sloterdijk (2004) has identified as the second epoch of globalization.[3] He locates this at the shift from the classical mediative sphere speculations to practices of 'globe management' or 'mastering the globe' that emerged in the age of discovery, as a constitutive moment of the transformation to modernity. This concept of 'mastering' encompasses the emerging intelligibility of the globe as a single space, on the one hand, and practices of its control and management – and, by extension, its domination – on the other. In other words, it is the idea or conception of the Earth as a globe that ignites a legal politics of globality.

The pairing of sovereignty and mankind is a central component of very different practices of 'globe management' in both the sixteenth and the twentieth century. The gradual opening up of the globe and (by now) outer space has evolved into different understandings of mankind as a governing concept in international law. These variant notions of mankind, in their turn, have affected understandings of sovereign membership of the global legal community. Relating the modern debate on the commons of mankind back to its emergence as a politico-legal discourse in the Age of Discovery hence enables us to elaborate various legal politics of globality.

It is in this regard that sovereignty and mankind function as mutually constitutive elements within legal rationalities that combine notions of space, mankind and sovereignty in particular constellations of global ordering. We identify three such rationalities. The first is driven by the logic of appropriation, the second by a logic of laissez faire, and the third by a solidaristic logic. The *first* rationality imagines non-sovereign spaces as opportunities for (imperial) expansion; as 'empty lands' available for appropriation and sovereignty claims. In the *second* rationality the commons of mankind are constructed as open, free spaces, available for beneficial use to all sovereigns. The paradigmatic example of this understanding can be found in the notion of *Mare Liberum*. This emerged in the sixteenth century as a space of non-sovereignty, governed by a residual principle of freedom – to navigate, explore and exploit these non-sovereign spaces – as a natural right of mankind for individual sovereigns. In the *third* rationality the commons of mankind are conceived, to the contrary, as spaces that are to be nourished, protected and exploited for the benefit of all states as a collectivity, including future generations of their respective populations. This understanding turns sovereigns into mankind's guardians via the principle of common heritage. This rationality can be found most prominently in post-1945 law governing the deep seabed, Antarctica and outer space, as will be elaborated below.

While these different rationalities emerged in different eras, we want to emphasize at the outset that these should not be understood as successive stages in the evolution of international law. Indeed, the idea of *Mare Liberum* has survived up to the present day and has been codified in e.g. the UN Convention on the Law of the Sea (1982). These readings of mankind and sovereignty thus should be understood as partly overlapping, partly conflicting rationalities. As we will show in this chapter, these rationalities inform contemporary understandings in international law of how sovereigns are to behave in relation to the commons of mankind. They constitute, in other words, the legal dimension of the politics of globality.

Before we move on to substantiate this idea, we would like to make one preliminary remark on the use of the concept of 'mankind' in this chapter. Our focus is on the use of 'mankind' as a *spatial* notion, or more specifically on its use in relation to the legal presentation of *space* or *territory*. This means that we do not discuss how notions of 'mankind' or 'humanity' are invoked in debates pertaining to the position of individuals per se (e.g. in human rights law, humanitarian law, bio-law or international criminal law). Nor do we examine how the notion of 'mankind' is invoked to protect cultural objects and sites. What we are interested in are basically three questions: (i) How is 'mankind' used to define the status of certain spaces or territories? (ii) How do these definitions relate to understandings of sovereignty? (iii) How is the relation between sovereignty and the commons of mankind embedded in legal imaginaries of globality? Through these questions this chapter analyses the legal idiom and rationalities in which the politics of globality is and has been conducted.

The commons of mankind as free space

From its early development from the sixteenth century on, questions pertaining to the differences between territories under state jurisdiction and the commons of mankind have been centre-stage in international law. Initially, these debates primarily revolved around access to the high seas. In the Age of Discovery, the 'mastering of the globe' originally was paired with competing claims of exclusive jurisdiction for imperial powers versus claims to freedom by rising merchant powers. Against this background, the first understanding of the commons of mankind portrays them as free, open spaces; a freedom that comes with specific powers and limited restraints for sovereigns. More specifically, non-sovereign space in this context entailed a natural right of mankind – executed by sovereigns and private companies – to free travel, exploration and exploitation and, as a corollary, the negative duty to respect the freedom of other sovereigns to do the same. If they fail to do so, they violate not only the rights of their fellow sovereigns but also those of 'mankind'. In addition, states enjoy powers to act against pirates, who spoil the freedom of the high seas and undermine the peaceful co-existence of states.[4] Finally, there has been a gradual recognition that considerations of humanity limit the freedom of states on the high seas, by allowing for a right to visit and search suspected foreign ships.

The rationale of disciplined freedom can be found already in the writings of the 'founding fathers' of international law, Francesco de Vitoria (1486–1546) and Hugo Grotius (1583–1645). Both argued against imperial claims to exclusive jurisdiction over the high seas and undiscovered territories. Such claims were laid down, for example, in the Papal Bull of Donation (1493) and the Treaty of Tordesillas (1494). These documents were the first to take the globe as a whole as their reference point, dividing the Earth as an empty space for Spanish and Portuguese expansion, trade and conquest. Interestingly, the Treaty is based on an abstract knowledge of space, and its geographical division includes yet undiscovered and unknown places that are nevertheless brought under one regulatory regime.[5] In this respect exploration, cartography, politics and law went hand in hand in the production of globality. As observed by Carl Schmitt (2003: 86), '[n]o sooner had the contours of the Earth emerged as a real globe – not just sensed as myth, but apprehensible as fact and measurable as space – than there arose a wholly new and hitherto unimaginable problem: the spatial ordering of the Earth in terms of international law'.[6]

Similar to the Treaty of Tordesillas, the works of Vitoria and Grotius are based on an abstract knowledge of the globe as a whole as basis for international legal ordering. Confronted with the same issue of imperial expansion, they present an alternative imagery and legal rationality for such ordering. Rather than seeing the globe as a sphere of influence to be divided between great powers, they present it in terms of a dual spatial order, based on a natural division between *terra firma* – including both sovereign territories and *terra nullius,* i.e. territory free for appropriation by imperial powers[7] – and open, free spaces belonging to mankind as a whole.[8] The idea of the high sea as an open space free from the exclusive jurisdiction of states was by no means uncontroversial at the time. Even authors such as Selden (1635), who was critical of Spanish and Portuguese claims, still held that the seas could sometimes be appropriated and brought under sovereign control.[9] The works of Vitoria and Grotius seek to free the high seas from such claims to exclusive jurisdiction.[10] At the same time, the sovereign and non-sovereign spatial orders are inherently related at a conceptual level. Within legal discourse they are brought together in legal rationalities that constitute sovereign subjectivity through imageries of mankind and its relation to non-sovereign spaces – and thus also to imageries of the globe as such.

Obviously, it is notably Grotius who is known for his construction of the high seas as the *Mare Liberum,*[11] which – contrary to common interpretations – refers not to its condition as an unregulated space but rather to its condition of being 'insusceptible of physical appropriation'. That is to say, as a matter of law and of their natural materiality the high seas 'cannot become a possession of any one' and are 'adapted for the use of all' (Grotius 1916: 39, 28).[12] Based on these two infinite characteristics, the seas, like the air, are public goods: they are non-exclusive, non-appropriable, non-exhaustible, lying 'open unto all' and therefore belonging to the 'whole of society of mankind' (Grotius 1916: 26, 55).[13] Grounded in its natural limitless condition, this identification as a common of mankind informs a legal rationality based on the combination of freedom and discipline. This rationality serves to guarantee a fundamental principle of natural law: the right to global travel and trade, based on mankind's pre-given liberty of 'going hither and thither and [of] trading' (Grotius 1916: 6).

Here Grotius builds on Vitoria's discussion of the so-called *ius communicationis,* the natural, universal right to communicate.[14] The right to communicate implies three important constraints for political communities: they cannot set aside the right to travel, the right to trade and the right to preach the Christian faith. Those that hinder the harmless exercise of the *ius communicationis* violate natural law, the interests of mankind and the rights of other political communities. They could become the targets of a just war, provided no other means are available and waging a war helps to effectively vindicate the rights of the injured party (Vitoria 1917 [1539]: Part III). In similar fashion (albeit for a different political project altogether),[15] Grotius claims that when states hinder others' natural right to trade and communicate, they frustrate the constitution of a global human community (*humani generis societas*) and could even be put on a par with pirates, as *hostes humani generis*. All states (and even private persons) could then enforce the laws of mankind against its enemies.

While originating in a natural law doctrine (in which law is grounded in transcendental and universal values), the tying together of mankind and sovereignty through a logic of freedom and discipline has survived international law's transition to legal positivism (in which law is derived from state consent). As a natural law doctrine the freedom of the high seas even popped up in the writings of predominantly consent-based theories of international law,[16] while it was gradually adopted as the default position in state practice as well. Thus, when the British started to visit, search and confiscate ships engaged in the transatlantic slave trade in the nineteenth century, their actions were criticized as incompatible with the freedom of the high seas as codified in contemporary law. The critique not only came from the flag states of the targeted ships but also from British prize courts. Even courts that applauded the good cause of fighting slave trade held that under positive international law states could not search and visit foreign ships in peacetime. This followed, as Sir William Scott (Lord Stowell) put it in the case of the French slave ship *Le Louis*, from two foundational principles: the equality of states and the principle of access to non-sovereign space, namely that:

> all (states) have an equal right to the uninterrupted use of un-appropriated parts of the ocean for their navigation. In places where no local authority exists, where the subjects of all states meet upon a footing of equality and independence, no state, or any of its subjects has a right to assume or exercise authority over the subjects of another.[17]

With the freedom of the high seas firmly rooted in the equality of states, the only way to modify international law under legal positivism was through state consent and new state practice. This is indeed what Great Britain sought to do through an ever-growing web of bi- and multilateral agreements (sometimes backed up by gunboat diplomacy), eventually culminating in the acceptance of a limitation of the freedom of the high seas when it comes to slave trade (Allain 2007; Martinez 2012). As the 'crowning accomplishment' of this system, the Quintuple Treaty (1841) concerns an agreement between Great Britain, France, Russia, Prussia and Austria for the reciprocal, peacetime right of visitation of their merchant ships when justifiably suspected of slave trade (Grewe 2000 [1984]: 561–562). This was restricted to carefully delineated zones, thus confirming the default freedom of the high seas, but at the same time it was now recognized that cosmopolitan considerations of humanity (as opposed to Grotius' communitarian reading of the interests of mankind) could limit the sovereign freedoms within the commons of mankind.[18]

The current UN Convention on the Law of the Sea to a large extent reflects the same position. While its starting point remains the freedom of the high seas, it recognizes that considerations of common interest and humanity sometimes require a redefinition of what this freedom entails. This means not only a limitation of the room for manoeuvre via the traditional principle of reciprocity but also a reformulation of what it means to be a sovereign member of the international community. As formulated by the International Court of Justice in the *Fisheries Jurisdiction* cases (1974):

> It is one of the advances in maritime international law, resulting from the intensification of fishing, that the former *laissez faire* treatment of the living resources of the sea in the high seas has been replaced by a recognition of a duty to have due regard to the rights of other States and the needs of conservation for the benefit of all.[19]

This was further regulated by the 1982 Convention on the Law of the Sea (UNCLOS), which reconfirms the traditional freedoms of the high seas but qualifies it along the same lines of reciprocity (article 87) and community values. For example, when it comes to slave trade all states are put under an obligation to prevent and punish ships flying their flag, whereas it allows warships to visit suspected foreign ships in peacetime (article 99, 110 UNCLOS). At the same time, there is a paradox in UNCLOS as one of the 'most momentous recent developments' in the global codification of natural resources law, as Sand (2004: 47) points out. For it concomitantly resulted in a net expansion of territorial jurisdiction by the introduction of 'exclusive economic zones' (EEZ), which enclosed another 35 per cent of the oceans' surface under sovereign control (Brundtland Commission 1987: para 17). This paradox can be understood from the dual rationalities that permeate the contemporary debate on the 'global commons': a freedom-based logic of access and a proactive logic of protection, as will be discussed in the next section.

The commons of mankind as vocation

During the second half of the twentieth century, rapid technological developments of global reach and the concomitant growing potentiality of catastrophes produced an alternative understandings of the commons of mankind that supplemented older, essentially freedom-based readings. This second understanding of the commons of mankind views them as spaces that need to be nourished and protected by shared efforts of the community of sovereign states. We use the term 'supplemented' deliberately here, since the idea of mankind's commons as free spaces has by no means disappeared. In addition, however, new, more protective, proactive and solidarist understandings were developed. This shift in legal rationality is part of larger socio-political developments in the post-1945 period, which – as in Sloterdijk's second epoch of globalization – are driven by further scientific discoveries and shifts in technological capabilities, now combined with growing perceptions of scarcity and vulnerability, and the pursuant unfolding political debate on the global commons in the 1980s (Brundtland Commission 1987; Vogler 2012).[20]

This debate is taking place on the basis of two different parameters.[21] On the one hand, there is the framing of the global commons in terms of access. As formulated by geostrategist Alfred Thayer Mahan at the end of the nineteenth century: 'The first and most obvious light in which the sea presents itself from the political and social point of view is that of a great highway; or better perhaps, a wide common, over which men may pass in all directions' (Mahan 1918 [1890]: 25; quoted by Kraska 2011: 157). Like a modern, geopolitical variant of Vitoria's *ius communicationis* the focus is on guaranteeing the rights of innocent passage through the commons as non-sovereign spaces.[22] Similar to Grotius' *Mare Liberum*, the commons are presented as a crucial infrastructure or 'key enabler' for global hegemony (Posen 2003).[23] As the publisher's blurb of a recent volume on *Securing Freedom in the Global Commons* tells us:

> Now, more than ever ... national security and prosperity depend on the safekeeping of a global system of mutually supporting networks of commerce, communication, and governance. The global commons ... serve as essential conduits for these networks, facilitating the free flow of trade, finance, information, people, and technology.[24]

On the other hand, there is a predominantly environmentalist discourse on the global commons as vulnerable and unique spaces that – precisely because of their open access – are in danger of overuse, congestion and degradation. This was the central message of Hardin's (1968) diagnosis of the 'tragedy of the commons', which more specifically is a 'tragedy of freedom in the commons' that is self-defeating for mankind. It also forms the parameters of the Brundtland Report (1987), which reflects a new, protective and proactive understanding of the commons of mankind.

One way to counter the 'tragedy of the commons' would be to restrict access to the *res communes*, e.g. by further (sovereign) enclosure – subdividing the commons and distribute private property rights over its parts (Wijk 1982; Ostrom 1990; Shackelford 2009).[25] While this at face value seems to be the case with regard to the introduction of the Exclusive Economic Zones in the 1982 UNCLOS, these do not contain so much an extension of sovereignty rights to the benefit of national interest, as they establish a specific sovereign responsibility over such zones, which states manage on behalf of all mankind.[26] Hence they are more akin to a public trusteeship with fiduciary rights rather than property rights (Sand 2004).[27]

Such fiduciary logic or trusteeship also underlies another solution that expresses a protective, proactive and solidarist understanding of the commons: the development of the concept of the 'common heritage of mankind' to govern different spaces outside the national jurisdiction of states. The principle has been applied in particular to the deep seabed and to outer space, and to a lesser extent the Antarctic. It first emerged in the preamble to the 1954 Hague Convention for the Protection of Cultural Property in the event of Armed Conflict, but was pronounced as positive duty under international law in the 1967 Outer Space Treaty and the 1979 Moon Treaty. It was also adopted by the UN GA Resolution 2749 (XXV) (12 December 1970) *Declaration of Principle Governing the Seabed and Ocean Floor* and then incorporated into the 1982 UNCLOS (art 136 and 137).

   Like the environmentalist discourse on the global commons, the common heritage of mankind as a governing principle combines a growing awareness of the vulnerability and fragility of the Earth and its natural resources with a realization that this is a transnational issue par excellence, rendering the reciprocity principle and laissez faire logic insufficient for globe management. As one of the leading proponents of the identification of the seabed as common heritage stated:

> Many modern technologies require international cooperation at unprecedented levels if they are to be used with benefit to the user and without harm to others. … In the situation as it existed in the 1960s, neither sovereignty nor traditional freedom were suitable to constitute the bases for a viable and reasonably equitable legal regime in ocean space. However, the only recognized alternative to a regime of freedom (*res communis*) was either territorial sovereignty or a regime of *res nullius* which permitted the acquisition of sovereignty or property rights over appropriable areas or things.
>
> (Pardo 1984: 566)[28]

Drawing upon a longer discussion on common properties of the human race that goes back to the 1948 Draft World Constitution and the contributions of Elisabeth Mann Borgese (Taylor 2011),[29] Pardo proposed the common heritage principle to the UN General Assembly as a third rationality to manage the global commons, focusing in his case on the seabed and the ocean floor.[30] While the common heritage doctrine is by no means well developed or clearly defined, it is generally conceived to encompass three elements: starting from their condition as non-sovereign space, it (i) regulates the exploration, exploitation and conservation of the global commons of mankind (including the prohibition of military activity); (ii) seeks to distribute the benefits of such activity based on the principle of equity;[31] and (iii) establishes management mechanisms (Shaw 2003: 454). As an international governing regime, it however relies on rather weak mechanisms of enforcement. It would be beyond the scope of this chapter to enter into a detailed discussion of the many problems and controversies related to the common heritage principle. Let us just give one example of a problem that affects the functioning of the common heritage principle: how to determine where the jurisdiction of states ends and the commons of mankind begin? In the case of the deep seabed, this is still largely left to the coastal state, whereas the demarcation between air space and outer space is a largely unsettled question (Oduntan 2003). In other words: while the legal differences between sovereign rights and the heritage of mankind are fundamental, in practice it is often difficult to determine where the one ends and the other begins.

Having said that, the introduction of the common heritage principle remains an important shift in the legal imagination of space (see also Mickelson 2014). Take for example the way in which outer space is conceptualized in international law. In the years following the launch of the first Sputnik in 1957, the Soviet Union and the United States engaged in a series of missions to outer space. Legally speaking, the move to outer space posed specific problems related to sovereign jurisdiction over territory. Under international law as it stood in the 1950s, the territory of the state included the air column, to the effect that each state enjoyed the sovereign right to permit or refuse entry into its territorial space. Now what would this imply for the new missions carried out by the Soviet Union and the US? Would it be necessary to obtain permission for over-flight from all states concerned? How would astronauts landing on foreign territory be legally qualified in case such permission had not been obtained? Notwithstanding these legal issues pertaining to what may be considered one of the core aspects of state sovereignty (legal entitlements to control over territory), neither the Soviet Union nor the United States bothered to request permission for their operations. Looming largely in the back of these legal issues were anxieties about the promises of the newly discovered space and fears that the exploration of outer space would open up new battlefields between the two superpowers. As Agar (2002) has argued, one of the ways to deal with these anxieties was to mobilize the seemingly neutral role of science as somehow standing above parochial interests. Outer space (just like for example Antartica) would be a space for scientific activities that would benefit 'mankind' and thus go beyond narrowly defined national interests.[32]

Another solution would have been to follow the example of the high seas regime and declare outer space as *res communis* that is free and open for all states. State practice and international treaties, however, started to introduce alternative imageries of what spaces beyond sovereign control could look like. This became clear in the UN General Assembly adoption of the 1962 *Declaration of Legal Principles Governing the Activities of States in the Exploration and Use of Outer Space.*[33] The basic principles and rules of the Declaration were subsequently codified in a series of treaties on the use of outer space, including the Outer Space Treaty (1967),[34] the Agreement pertaining to Astronauts and Objects launched in Space (1968),[35] and the Moon Treaty (1979).[36] The UN General Assembly Declaration, state practice and the subsequent treaties established nothing short of a new legal conception of the globe. Up until then, not even the sky had been the limit to sovereign jurisdiction over the air column; theoretically speaking, while it was horizontally demarcated, states could extend their jurisdiction endlessly in a vertical direction. With verticality no longer a mere fantasy or abstraction but coming within technological and visual reach – apprehensible as fact and measurable as space, to paraphrase Schmitt – the problem of spatial ordering of 'space' in terms of international law re-emerged. This resulted in a legal separation of the air column (air space) from outer space; relegating the first to sovereign jurisdiction and the latter to mankind.

The Outer Space Treaty, for example, declares outer space as the 'providence of mankind' (article 1) and prohibits national appropriation through sovereignty claims by means of use or occupation, or by any other means (article 2). Yet it also reconfirms the default freedom principle: 'Outer space … shall be free for exploration and use by all States without discrimination of any kind, on a basis of equality and in accordance with international law, and there shall be free access to all areas of celestial bodies', including freedom of scientific investigation. At first sight, this invocation of 'mankind' seems to echo the way in which Grotius and Vitoria used the concept to defend the freedom of the seas. And indeed, there is considerable overlap in the ways in which early thinkers and the Outer Space treaty attempt to bar sovereignty claims by defining certain areas as belonging to mankind.

However, the Outer Space Treaty does more than just prohibiting claims to sovereignty or exclusive jurisdiction. It also inserts a solidarist notion in the conception of mankind demanding that 'The exploration and use of outer space, including the moon and other celestial bodies, shall be carried out for the benefit and in the interests of all countries, irrespective of their degree of economic or scientific development …' (article 1). Here, mankind's territory is not just a *res communis* that should be respected as such; it turns into a space that can be explored and exploited in the interest of mankind.[37] In other words: in addition to the traditional laissez faire approach that came with the *res communes* or commons of mankind, there is now a regulatory approach that seeks to guide exploration and exploitation in the interests of environmental and social justice. This is even more pronounced in the 1979 Moon Treaty, which, unlike the Outer Space Treaty, makes explicit reference to the notion by identifying the Moon as the common heritage of mankind. This means the Moon cannot and shall not be appropriated and its exploration and possible future exploitation shall be in the 'province of all mankind', which – crucially – also takes this to encompass future generations (article 4). Where for example Grotius invoked 'mankind' to argue for an obligation not to interfere with the freedom of others, treaties such as the Outer Space Treaty also use the concept of mankind to bring states actively together in a common effort to tackle global problems. The commons of mankind nowadays hold promises of scientific and economic progress when exploited properly.[38] At the same time, they are seen as vulnerable and exhaustible. The commons of mankind, in other words, are as much a burden as a potential benefit. Both the promises and the vulnerability of the commons call for cooperation and supervision, as to make sure that mankind's territories will sustainably benefit humanity at large.

This shift from a freedom logic, based on territorial sovereignty, to a rationality of responsibility towards spaces of mankind also transpires in the qualification of astronauts in the Outer Space Treaty. Instead of treating them as nationals of a fellow sovereign state, states should conceive of astronauts as 'envoys of mankind in outer space' (article 5). This implies that astronauts may not be treated as intruders in sovereign territory but should be regarded as envoys of the same global community to which the state and its nationals also belong. In more practical terms this implies that astronauts should be given 'all possible assistance in the event of accident, distress, or emergency landing on the territory of another State Party or on the high seas' and a safe and prompt return to state of registry of their space vehicle (article 5).

While thus portrayed as heralds and diplomats of mankind, it is note-worthy that none of the treaties pertaining to outer space or astronauts identifies potential violators as 'enemies of mankind'. As was set out above, this category of 'enemies of mankind' played a pivotal role in the writings of Grotius and Vitoria; for them the flip side of defining the high seas as the providence of mankind was that he who violates the freedom of the seas can be treated as *hostis humani generis*. While this term has survived up until the present day in relation to piracy, the concept is noticeably absent in all treaties dealing with outer space (as well in those pertaining to the deep seabed, the ocean floor or Antartica). One of the core points of regimes regulating contemporary global commons is that areas belonging to 'mankind' cannot be used for military purposes. Apparently, military usages are seen as beneficial to individual states, or coalitions of states at best, but not to mankind as such.[39] The main focus of the treaties in question is on cooperation, exchange of information, reporting, etcetera, not on measures that should be taken against those that disrespect the commons of mankind. Of course, this does not mean that the issue of norm violation has become totally irrelevant. Sometimes the treaties explicitly identify those that are responsible (liable) for injuries[40] and the general rules on state responsibility still apply to breaches of treaty obligations. All this, however, does not turn the violators of the rules pertaining to the commons of mankind into *hostes humanis generis* against whom military force may be used. In other words, while the cosmopolitan ambitions of contemporary international law are much greater, the means to discipline those that violate mankind's law are much more limited.

Concluding remarks

As the introduction to this volume has set out, globality can be understood in different ways. It traditionally is used to refer to the condition of the world as a universality, totality and single place. While this understanding usually (if problematically) identifies globality as the endpoint of globalization (van Munster and Sylvest, this volume), from a legal perspective it would mean that modern international law has always already operated in some state of globality. From its early days, legal imageries of the globe as a whole have informed regimes that set sovereign territories apart from the commons of mankind. However, as pointed out by the editors, globality can also be used in a more specific sense, as the result of developments that make 'the world (appear) small, manageable, tame, and, hence, ripe for new types of polities' (van Munster and Sylvest, this volume, footnote 5). This form of globality is a relative newcomer in international law. The idea that the world as such is a space to be managed and nourished has given rise to new legal rationalities that deviate significantly from older, albeit still surviving, legal imageries and orderings of the world.

Different imageries of the globe as a whole or global space(s) have given rise to different understandings of both sovereignty and the nature of the commons of mankind. We have traced three legal rationalities to order, master and nourish the globe through particular constellations of sovereignty and the commons of mankind. The first presents the globe as a sphere divided between sovereign territories on the one hand and 'formless and empty' spaces on the other, as *terra nullius,* freely available to be appropriated by imperial powers.

In the second rationality the commons of mankind are presented as *res communes,* spaces where states meet each other as free and equal and attempts at appropriation are seen as violating the rights of mankind. The accompanying understanding of sovereignty is basically twofold: a principle of reciprocity, i.e. mutual respect for sovereignty as a freedom to manoeuvre, combined with a conditional understanding of this freedom insofar as it cannot be (ab)used to undermine universal community values. A good example of the latter is the gradual acceptance of the illegality of slave trade on the high seas and the accompanying right of other states to search and visit suspected ships. In this context, the freedom of the high seas is accompanied by arguments that freedom cannot be used in ways that violate principles of 'humanity'.

The third rationality comes closest to the condition of globality in the narrow sense, alluded to above. As this volume makes clear, it is no coincidence that this rationality is a post-1945 phenomenon. It redefines *res communes* from spaces of freedom and laissez faire to spaces that are to be nourished, managed and exploited in the interests of inter-state solidarity and mankind as a whole, including its future generations.[41] Sovereignty, under this understanding, means responsible participation in the exploration and exploitation of vulnerable territories. In other words, mankind is now also mobilized to activate states in a common effort to secure and nourish areas that are of interest to the world as a whole. This shift in the understanding and constellation of space, sovereignty and mankind informs a legal rationality where non-sovereign space and the commons of mankind seek to discipline sovereigns in a positive and proactive duty to protect the global commons as the common *heritage* of mankind and hence incorporates a temporal dimension to mankind as a spatial notion.

The latter two rationalities dominate current international law with regard to the commons of mankind. They help explain the tension that is present in contemporary understandings of what it is to be a sovereign state under international law – both a free and independent authority *and* a responsible agent of a world community.

Notes

1 The phrase is taken from the classical case of *Lotus; S.S. Lotus* (Fr. v. Turk.), 1927 P.C.I.J. (series A) No. 10 (Sept. 7).
2 Closely related to this issue is the way in which international law has classified and regulated colonial territories. In this chapter, however, the main focus will be on territories that are defined as part of the commons of mankind. For a discussion of international law and colonial territories, see Anghie (2005).
3 In his philosophical theory of globalization contemporary phenomena like network governance, rapacity of capitalism and the collapse of space/time at the expense of modern territoriality and sovereignty is only a late and figurative moment of a longer process of engaging with global imaginaries, proceeded by classical productions of metaphysical and theological spheres and the mastering the globe as the first and second epoch of globalization.
4 Yet at the same time, pirates were sometimes co-opted by sovereign powers in their imperial conquests. For a fascinating account of these legal practices and legal geography of the oceans, see Benton (2010, notably Chapter 3).
5 As Strandsbjerg (2010: 94) argues, '[I]t was already decided that Brazil would belong to the crown of Portugal even prior to its "discovery" in 1500 and it was thus the Treaty based on a cartographic reality of the world that came to decide "the reality on the ground" and not the other way around.' See also Schmitt (2003: 88–89), who also distinguishes between different ways of global linear thinking in the Age of Discovery.
6 While pinpointing the link between politics and geography, Schmitt upholds the idea of geography and cartography as an objective knowledge of reality.
7 As such *terra nullius* has both a descriptive and normative aspect: the description of an actual lack of ownership is coupled with the legal possibility of a future claim to such ownership (Mickelson 2014). While there were further distinctions between European territory and non-European space as the basis for the European legal order (including the notorious standard of civilisation), these are less relevant for the argument we pursue here, which focuses on the notion of freedom.
8 As Schmitt (2003: 54) notes: 'The antithesis of land and sea as an anthithesis of diverse spatial orders is a modern phenomenon. It governed the structure of European international law only after the 17th and 18th centuries, i.e., only after the oceans had opened up and the first global image of the Earth had emerged.'
9 It was a response to Grotius' *Mare Liberum* to address the right of Dutch fishermen to fish at the English coast. In contemporary international law the *mare clausum* principle is translated in the concept of territorial waters (12 nautical miles from a coastal state's baseline, see article 3 of the 1958 Geneva Convention on the Territorial Sea and the Contiguous Zone, and article 5 of the 1982 United Nations Convention on the Law of the Sea, UNCLOS) and 'exclusive economic zones' (EEZ) of 200 nautical miles from the coastline (article 55 and 56 UNCLOS), which gives states special rights over the exploration, exploitation and conservation of its marine sources.
10 Note that also under Roman law, the sea (like the air, the rivers, and the seashore) was conceived as open space, incapable of private ownership and dedicated to the

use of the public. See also Public Trust doctrine under English and American common law. See further Sand (2004), who discusses the sovereign rights of states over environmental resources within and beyond their territory as fiduciary rights.

11 The book originally was published in 1609 under the title *Mare Liberum, sive de jure quod Batavis competit ad Indicana commercia dissertation*. Here we use the translation by Ralf van Deman that was published in 1916.

12 Grotius (1916: 27): 'all that has been so constituted by nature that although serving some one person it still suffices for the common use of all persons, *is today and ought in perpetuity to remain the same condition as when it was first created by nature.'*

13 The logic is terrestrial insofar as Grotius links claims to property to the factual or possible ('susceptible of') occupation of space (Grotius 1916: 27).

14 Parts of what follows in this paragraph are taken from Werner (2013).

15 Whereas Vitoria's project ultimately was the propagation of Catholic faith and the freedom of overseas Christian missions, Grotius' focus was on countering the British (and earlier Spanish and Portuguese) claims to maritime monopoly, ownership of the seas and/or right to navigate it, to further profit and power politics of the Dutch East India Company.

16 For an analysis of the natural freedom of the high seas in the work of Emerich de Vattel, see Werner (2013) and Mickelson (2014).

17 Le Louis (1817) 2 Dodson's Admirality Reports 210, 344–345, quoted in Allain (2007).

18 Noteworthy in this regard is Britain's persistent effort to have slave trade recognized as an act of piracy, in order to move beyond the contractual basis of its maritime policing authority against slave trade. This would also entail a radical transformation of the underlying logic of piracy, insofar as Grotius linked it to the violation of a negative right of freedom of access to the high seas as a non-sovereign space, whereas the British tried to link it to an emerging proactive duty to combat slave trade on the high seas as an alleged cosmopolitan space. The efforts by one of the advocates of abolition, Lord Castlereagh, to categorize slave trade as an exercise of piracy at the Congress of Vienna failed (Reich 1965), but the British did succeed in incorporating it in bilateral treaties. This was for instance the case in the 1826 Treaty with Brazil, as well as in article 1 of the 1841 Quintuple Treaty, which declares 'un tel traffic crime de piraterie' (Grewe 2000 [1984]: 562).

19 Already in the seventeenth century Grotius – somewhat ambivalently – recognized the possibility that fishing resources of the oceans might indeed not be limitless (Grotius 1916: 43; as quoted by Schrijver and Prislan 2009: 173).

20 See also other chapters in this volume, in particular the Introduction and Chapter 1 by Deudney and Mendenhall.

21 See also Vogler (2012).

22 See UNCLOS articles 37–44, the US national space policy (White House, United States 2010), and NATO's new strategic concept with regard to the global commons (NATO 2011), cited by Vogler (2012).

23 See also the conception of *res communes* as 'common pool resources' (Ostrom 1990).

24 www.sup.org/book.cgi?id=18677 about Jasper (2010).

25 Another option within the sovereignty paradigm would be to turn it into *terra nullius* and thus make it available for sovereign appropriation (Pardo 1984).

26 For the conceptualization of sovereignty as a way to organize responsibility, see Werner (2004); Aalberts and Werner (2008).

27 However, it is noteworthy that both the exploration, exploitation, conservation and management of the EEZ are defined as 'rights' in article 56(1) of the UNCLOS; also article 55 on the specific legal regime of the EEZ speaks only of rights and jurisdiction of the coastal states, and rights and freedoms of other states. The

reference to duties is only mentioned in residual or general terms: 'other rights and duties provided for in this Convention' (article 56(1)c); 'in exercising its rights and performing its duties' (article 56(2)). In practice, states indeed appear to emphasize the rights logic and use it as part of a traditional sovereignty game, as transpires clearly from the mobilization of the Continental shelf provisions of the UNCLOS (articles 76–85) to lay claim to a bigger EEZ in the Arctic Oceans. Vogler (2012) identifies this as a practice of 'creeping appropriation'. Shackelford (2009) in this context refers to the tragedy of the common heritage of mankind principle itself, as it is being unravelled through reinterpretation of treaty systems by sovereign states in order to expand property rights for private entities under their jurisdiction.

28 Mr Pardo was the Maltese Ambassador at the United Nations, who used the term 'common heritage of mankind' in his speech to the UN General Assembly, First Committee 1515th meeting, Wednesday 1 November, 1967 (Official Records, A 22nd session, UN Doc A/C.1/PV1515 1967, available at www.un.org/depts/los/convention_agreements/texts/pardo_ga1967.pdf

29 The 1948 draft World Constitution declares the four elements of life – Earth, water, air, energy – as common property of the human race (www.worldbeyond borders.org/chicagodraft.htm).

30 Originally, the intention was to declare all ocean space (its surface, water column, the seabed, and its living resources) common heritage, but it was soon recognized that this would be countered by power politics and conceptions of the oceans as crucial geopolitical infrastructure. By limiting the focus on the seabed and the ocean floor – identified as 'the Area' in the 1982 UNCLOS – it was envisaged that the principle of common heritage could gain important leverage within the UN system (Taylor 2011). Article 136–137 set out that 'all rights in the resources of the Area are vested in mankind as a whole'. Moreover, in order to ensure that the exploitation of the seabed and ocean floor would take place for the benefit of humanity, a specific authority was created: the International Seabed Authority. For more information on the authority see www.isa.org.jm/en/home.

31 The common heritage principle to manage the global commons as such was also of great symbolic significance in the debate about a New International Economic Order (Vogler 2012).

32 As noted by Agar (2012: 348), '… outer space and Antarctic space were both defined in a Cold War context as abstract international spaces, defined by legal treaties … and the use of which would privilege science'.

33 United Nations General Assembly Resolution 1962 (XVIII), Declaration of Legal Principles Governing the Activities of States in the Exploration and Use of Outer Space, 13 December 1963.

34 Formally the Treaty on Principles Governing the Activities of States in the Exploration and Use of Outer Space, including the Moon and Other Celestial Bodies; adopted by United Nations General Assembly Resolution 2222 (XXI), 19 December 1966.

35 Agreement on the Recue of Astronauts, the Return of Astronauts, and the Return of Objects Launched into Outer Space; adopted by the United Nations General Assembly Resolution 2345 (XXII), 19 December 1967.

36 Agreement Governing the Activities of States on the Moon and Other Celestial Bodies, available at: www.oosa.unvienna.org/oosa/en/SpaceLaw/gares/html/gares_34_0068.html; adopted by the United Nations General Assembly Resolution 34/68, 5 December 1979.

37 As the editors of this volume pointed out in their comments to this chapter, there is something deeply ironic about the fact that territories where life cannot be naturally sustained are labelled as spaces belonging to mankind as a whole.

38 Although these promises are not always fulfilled, as the saga of deep seabed exploitation attests. In practice, the narrow definition of 'the Area' in the 1982

UNCLOS (see footnote 30) meant that the common heritage status was assigned to a few mineral resources such as manganese nodules lying on the bottom of the ocean, or as described by a sceptic: 'ugly little rocks lying in the darkest depths of all creation' (Goodwin 1983: 74).

39   Although this is arguably changing with the debate on humanitarian intervention.
40   See for example the articles 6 and 7 of the Outer Space Treaty as well as the 1972 *Convention on International Liability for Damage Caused by Space Objects* (resolution 2777 (XXVI), annex) – adopted on 29 November 1971.
41   A fourth concept is the 'common concern of humankind' which has been used in the context of the protection of the climate and the ozone layer. See UN GA Resolution 43/53 (6 December 1988) on the 'Protection of global climate for present and future generations of mankind'. However, this is in fact a stripped version of the common heritage doctrine, more ambiguous and with vaguer legal implications. See also Shaw (2003: 455, n253); Schrijver and Prislan (2009).

Bibliography

Aalberts, Tanja E. and Werner, Wouter G. (2008) 'Sovereignty Beyond Borders: Sovereignty, Self-Defense and the Disciplining of States', in R. Adler-Nissen and T. Gammeltoft-Hansen (eds) *Sovereignty Games. Instrumentalising State Sovereignty in Europe and Beyond*. Houndmills: Palgrave, pp. 129–150.

Agar, Jon (2012) *Science in the Twentieth Century and Beyond*. Cambridge: Polity.

Allain, Jean (2007) 'The Nineteenth Century Law of the Sea and the British Abolition of Slave Trade', *British Yearbook of International Law*, 78(1): 342–388.

Anghie, Antony (2005) *Imperialism, Sovereignty and the Making of International Law*. Cambridge: Cambridge University Press.

Benton, Lauren (2010) *In Search for Sovereignty. Law and Geography in European Empires 1400–1900*. Cambridge: Cambridge University Press.

Brundtland Commission (1987), 'Our Common Future', report of the World Commission on Environment and Development (transmitted to the General Assembly as an annex to document A/42/427). Oslo and New York: United Nations.

Goodwin, Robert A. (1983) 'Common Sense vs the Common Heritage', in B. H. Oxman, D. D. Caron and C. L. O. Buderi (eds) *Law of the Sea: US Policy Dilemma*, San Francisco, CA: Institute for Contemporary Studies.

Grewe, Wilhelm G. (2000 [1984]) *The Epochs of International Law*, trans. M. Byers. Berlin: de Gruyter.

Grotius, Hugo (1916) *The Freedom of the Seas. Or the Right which Belongs to the Dutch to Take Part in the East Indian Trade*. Oxford: Oxford University Press.

Hardin, Garret (1968) 'The Tragedy of the Commons', *Science*, 162(3859): 1243–1248.

Jasper, Scott (ed.) (2010) *Securing Freedom in the Global Commons*. Stanford, CA: Stanford University Press.

Kraska, James (2011) *Maritime Power and the Law of the Sea: Expeditionary Operations in World Politics*. Oxford: Oxford University Press.

Mahan, Alfred Thayer (1918 [1890]) *The Influence of Sea Power upon History 1660–1783*. New York: Little, Brown.

Martinez, Jenny (2012) *The Slave Trade and the Origins of International Human Rights Law*. Oxford: Oxford University Press.

Mickelson, Karin (2014) 'The Maps of International Law: Perceptions of Nature in the Classification of Territory', *Leiden Journal of International Law*, 27(3): 621–639.

NATO (2011) 'NATO in the Global Commons: Global Perspectives', ACT Workshop report, 3 February. Washington, DC: Atlantic Council.

Oduntan, Gbenga (2003) 'The Never Ending Dispute: Legal Theories on the Spatial Demarcation Boundary Plane between Airspace and Outer Space', *Hertfordshire Law Journal*, 1(2): 64–84.

Ostrom, Elinor (1990) *Governing the Commons: The Evolution of Institutions for Collective Action*. Cambridge: Cambridge University Press.

Pardo, Arvid (1984) 'Ocean Space and Mankind (Third World Lecture 1984)', *Third World Quarterly*, 6(3): 559–572.

Posen, Barry R. (2003) 'Command of the Commons: The Military Foundation of US Hegemony', *International Security*, 28(1): 5–46.

Reich, Jerome (1965) 'The Slave Trade at the Congress of Vienna: A Study in English Public Opinion', *The Journal of Negro History*, 53(2): 129–143.

Sand, Peter H. (2004) 'Sovereignty Bounded: Public Trusteeship for Common Pool Resources', *Global Environmental Politics*, 4(1): 47–71.

Schmitt, Carl (2003) *The Nomos of the Earth in the International Law of the Jus Publicum Europeaeum*, trans. G. L. Ulmen. New York: Telos Press.

Schrijver, Nico and Prislan, Vid (2009) 'From Mare Liberum to the Global Commons: Building on the Grotian Heritage', *Grotiana*, 30: 168–206.

Selden, John (1635) *Mare Clausum: Seu De Dominio Maris Libri Duo*. London: n.p.

Shackelford, Scott J. (2009) 'The Tragedy of the Common Heritage of Mankind', *Stanford Environmental Law Journal*, 28(1): 109–169.

Shaw, Malcolm N. (2003) *International Law*. Fifth edition. Cambridge: Cambridge University Press.

Sloterdijk, Peter (2004) *Im Weltinnenraum des Kapitals: für eine philosophische Theorie der Globalisierung*. Frankfurt am Main: Suhrkamp.

Strandsbjerg, Jeppe (2010) *Territory, Globalisation and International Relations: The Cartographic Reality of Space*. Basingstoke: Palgrave.

Taylor, Prue (2011) 'Common Heritage of Mankind Principle', in K. Bosselmann, D. Fogeland J. B. Ruhl (eds), *The Encyclopedia of Sustainability. Vol. 3: The Law and Politics of Sustainability*. Great Barrington, MA: Berkshire Publishing, pp. 64–69.

White House, United States (2010), *National Space Policy of the United States of America*, Washington, DC, 28 June. Available at www.whitehouse.gov/sites/default/files/national_space_policy_6-28-10.pdf.

Vattel, Emerich de (1758) *The Law of Nations or the Principles of Natural Law*. Washington, DC: Carnegie Institution.

Vitoria, Franciscus de (1917 [1539]) *De Indis et de Ivre Belli Relectiones*. Washington, DC: Carnegie Institution.

Vogler, John (2012) 'Global Commons Revisited', *Global Policy*, 3(1): 61–71.

Werner, Wouter (2013) 'Mankind's Territory and the Limits of International Law-making', in R. Liivoja and J. Petman (eds) *International Law-making: Essays in Honour of Jan Klabbers*. Abingdon: Routledge, pp. 103–118.

Werner, Wouter G. (2004) 'State Sovereignty and International Legal Discourse', in I. F. Dekker and W. G. Werner (eds) *Governance and International Legal Theory*. Leiden: Martinus Nijhoff, pp. 125–157.

Wijk, Per Magnus (1982) 'Managing the Global Commons', *International Organization*, 36(3): 511–536.

5 Futures of Mankind

The emergence of the global future[1]

Jenny Andersson and Sibylle Duhautois

Introduction

Experiences of global interconnectedness, planetary and world order have existed throughout history, from historic notions of empire, Enlightenment understandings of political economy and global trade, to late nineteenth and early twentieth-century understandings of world federation, world movements and world citizens. Meanwhile, the post-war decades stand out as forging specific notions of world unity, in direct connection to emerging understandings of the possible global reach of human agency and subjectivity. Globality has been described as a phenomenon produced by science and technology, by new forms of assemblages of global data and expertise, and by new representations of planetary boundaries in the twentieth century (for instance Jasanoff 2001, Miller 2004, Edwards 2012). Such material, technological and scientific practices, giving visibility to the world, were matched by intellectual revelations of the interdependence of the world as both planetary whole and social system. A key work in globality studies, if there is such a thing, was Cosgrove's *Apollo's Eye* (2001), which proposed that the first photographic images of the world from the outside, enabled by the Apollo space program and ensuing satellite technology, marked a decisive break in human conceptions of the planet. The blue marble images of planet Earth nevertheless had important ideational precursors, for instance in the Spaceship Earth metaphors put forward by Richard Buckminster Fuller and Kenneth Boulding from the mid 1960s, to denote a closed, bounded system in which Man was both reckless cowboy and rational engineer (see Deudney and Mendenhall, this volume).

As suggested in the Spaceship Earth metaphor, understandings of planet and world behaviour were in fact reflections on humanity and human existence in a world understood as fundamentally shaped by human beings. Environmental historians have demonstrated the rise of planetary thinking in demography, ecologism and 'survivalism' (Robertson 2012). But such notions of Earth were paralleled, in the 1960s and 1970s, by notions of the world as an inherently social system, manmade artefact and ordered structure of nations, polarities and politics. In political science, sociology and the burgeoning field of International Relations, perceptions of the world system changed rapidly, in the 1960s and 1970s, from depictions carried by epistemological projects such as development economics and modernization theory, of the world as united by the same singular stage driven process, to ideas of a possibly chaotic, multipolar and dangerously interdependent system. The world, from the 1960s on, was understood as consisting of a complex multitude of actors, trends and problems that were difficult to oversee and control.

In this chapter we explore the connections between emerging post-war notions of world, humanity and future, as embedded in conceptions of 'common futures' and 'common problems' to all of Mankind. We propose that the idea of a shared, indeed global, world future came about as a result of activities in futures research, and ambitions in the 1960s and 1970s to create specific forms of expertise for the world future. Part of this expertise was the constitution of a wide repertoire of so-called 'world problems'. We tie our argument to developments in historical research and in particular the recent focus on transnationalism and global networks of activism and expertise. As argued by the historian Akira Iriye, transnational activism from the early twentieth century on can be understood as forging forms of 'global consciousness' as the intellectual equivalent of the material process of globalization. Emerging social movements such as the Red Cross responded to the idea of universal suffering in World War I with notions of the necessity to forge a global human community. The appearance, after World War I of key technologies such as aviation, radio, long distance telephones, strengthened ideas of the fundamental universality of Mankind (Iriye 2002: 8, 21). After World War II, the struggle against the atomic bomb took on global proportions (Evangelista 1999), and interwar dreams of forms of world government and world federation were reinvested with significance as part of an emerging conception that nuclear weapons united Mankind in a common destiny of threat and destruction (van Munster and Sylvest 2016).

Meanwhile, the creation of a global community was never a completed historic process. It remained something of a utopian dream. Certainly the idea that forms of human agency and subjectivity had to be reshaped on the global level in a wide range of arenas, ranging from the social sciences, to politics and religion, occupied a lot of post-war intellectual energy. The historian of international relations, Samuel Moyn, has recently proposed to view the struggle for human rights in the 1960s and 1970s as a 'substitute utopia', a deflection of utopian energy from exhausted political projects into ideas of humanity and human integrity as a sacred world 'covenant'. Moyn (2010: 121) asserts of the human rights struggle that 'human rights emerged as a minimalist, hardy utopia that could survive in a harsh climate', as notions of universalism were constantly circumscribed by the particularistic logic embedded in the negotiations of Cold War global politics. Evidently, the concept of globality needs caution. We are still referring to phenomena that were more globalizing and universalizing than they were in any real way global. Post-war organizations such as, for instance, Amnesty International, or indeed the World Futures Studies Federation which will be discussed here, were organized from the West and driven by Western agendas. They were distrustful of politics, and dreamed in fact of replacing politics with other forms of organization such as the structures of a decentralized world federation or even, global think tank. While they put forward claims to universal interests of humanity, they also tended to mirror, in their organization as well as in their arguments, fundamental power structures of the Cold War world. We need to ask, therefore, what kind of globality they expressed, the scope it embraced and the limits it encountered.

Nevertheless, we propose in this chapter that the idea of a common world future served as a source of mobilization and utopian energy in the immediate post-war decades. Many of the emerging social movements of the 1960s and 1970s, for instance the peace movement, the women's movement, and the environmental movement, were not at all new in the 1960s and 1970s, but their agendas changed in this period, as forms of activism were rearticulated as part of a global struggle against war, colonialism and the human destruction of the planet (Iriye 2002). In this they envisioned new forms of agency and new forms of awareness for an emerging global human subject, oftentimes referred to as 'Mankind'. The concept of Mankind was a reflection of global consciousness in two ways: first, the post-war idea that humanity was united by a common future was informed by understandings of planet and world as a matter of interdependency and systemic logic. Second, however, the concept Mankind referred to humanity as a new global actor that shared universal values, forms of consciousness and forms of potential agency. Such agency, in turn, could straddle a series of repertoires, between political engagement, social science interrogation and religious activism, all understood as acting on, in various ways, notions of global unity. Futurism and futures research, we propose, was one of the key areas in which this reflection on humanity was carried out, and the idea of the future itself is central to forms of globality in the post-war decades.

The future as world consciousness

An emergent literature has brought out a multifaceted history of forms of prediction and futurity, in particular pertaining to constitutions of global expertise and global governance in the Cold War era. Important strands in this literature have focused on understandings of futures as insecurity, threat, disaster and apocalypse, which gave rise to new forms of governmental expertise, risk detection and forms of surveillance post-1945 (Aradau and van Munster 2011). Indeed, some of the tools and methods of future research would be used in this way, mainly in the context of national governments. But the concern with the future also triggered important forms of global thinking, and central notions of the need to reshape political and scientific forms of action on the global level. Indeed, marking the immediate post-war period was a new concern with the world future, under the influence of ideas of impending apocalypse, outrage with world politics, and moral notions of the soullessness of modern civilization. While these concerns were articulated in a wide set of discourses, ranging from environmentalism to the struggle against the bomb or the Club of Rome's predictions of overshoot and collapse, they were also constitutive of the field of futurism and futures research, and futurism can be understood as carrying a fundamental reflection on the possibility of global consciousness (Andersson 2012).

Futurism began as an existential and moral interrogation into what being human meant in a world in which the forces of human creativity had resulted in the unfettered technology of thermonuclear power.[2] At the heart of this stood a set of interrogations into the awkward category of 'Man'. A set of writings, emerging in the decade after 1945, dealt indeed with the 'Condition of Man', with dissecting the conditions of human existence in an apocalyptic world.[3] In these writings, many of which were held together both by important elements of intertextuality as well as by specific actor relationships, Man appeared as a creature lost in time and space – indeed, as having lost a future and thereby a defining purpose of existence. Paradoxically this loss of future was taking place at a moment of human force, the very moment in world history when man appeared to have succeeded in mastering nature and universe with technologies of new planetary reach. The conundrum thus appeared as such: equipped finally with the material means with which to subject his environment and shape his destiny, Man seemed to have lost all ideas of common destiny and fate. It is not by chance that these writings gave a very specific place to the notion of the future. Man's Faustian failure to control the tools of his creation, science and technology, it was suggested, both by the American urban planner Lewis Mumford, who would become central to futurism, and by the political theorist Hannah Arendt, who also wrote, in 1961, *Between Past and Future*, had severed the cognitive connection between human lives and the history of human civilization, as well as crushed any hopes of grounded experience of the world in which he lived. Technology had operated a fundamental rupture in experiences of time, crippling the human capacity to actively imagine the future. The future as such had been set adrift, unfettered and empty to be filled with forms of aggression and false dreams of commercialism and automation.

Experiences of a rupture in the human experience of time were paralleled by ideas of spatial rupture. The atomic bomb was interpreted by a range of thinkers from 1945 on as a 'cosmic event' – in other words, as an event that surpassed the natural laws governing human existence and as introducing a measure of chaos and apocalypse into a human universe that had no natural boundaries anymore. This new chaotic universe needed a new mechanism of control, as exemplified in prevailing ideas from nuclear theorists and futurists of forms of world government, world consciousness and world federation. Less devastating spatial technologies than the Bomb were also understood as profoundly impacting on the conditions of existence. 'Long-range weapons' were described by Mumford as the introduction of a technological means of world arbitration, controlled by the detached power of the spatial engineer (Mumford 1944: 23). The Moon landing in 1969 was not unanimously hailed as the pushing of a new frontier. The 'probe', wrote Hannah Arendt of Apollo II, had not led to hopeful discoveries of other planetary worlds; it had rather raised the hope of physical escape from a devastated Earth (Arendt 1954: 260–275, 1958: 2).

The influence of Husserlian and Heideggerian existentialism and phenomenology on these reflections of the ominous free-floating state of Mankind is of course not accident but a matter of historic context (see Wolin 2007). Walter Benjamin's oft-cited image of the Angel of history blowing backwards into the future is still the perfect illustration of the experience of progress as systematic destruction of human futures that beset a range of Jewish and liberal thinkers after World War II. 'This storm is what we call progress' (Benjamin 2009: 10). While Benjamin's understanding of progress as destruction is well noted, much less noted is the way that the idea of a severed link between past and future was in fact widely shared among these intellectuals, and after 1945 in wider circles as well. To them, the destruction of the future was the crisis of Man, and the 'human condition' was an urgent call to the reshaping of more humane forms of the future. This was a key intellectual legacy as, in coming decades, the idea of the future came to stand as an organizing metaphor and image of a set of things that were wrong with the modern world and that would materialize as logical and catastrophic consequences of the continuation of the world present, unless forms of action were urgently taken (Andersson 2015).

The post-war concept of the future was thus fundamentally ambiguous. On the one hand, the future was understood as threatened by the innate destructive capacities of man; on the other, the capacity to possibly reimagine the future and reshape utopian aspiration was also put forward as the demarking characteristic of being human. The future was, as Hans Jonas would later put it, an imperative of human responsibility (Jonas 1979). From the 1950s on, the future figured both as a coming series of cumulative crises and disasters and, importantly, as a central strategic issue, as a matter of existential choice for a humanity which could choose to let its future fall apart or build a better future on the basis of a new global unity. In other words it was understood as a space both for the materialization of threats to humanity and as the *only* space of potential solutions, indeed as the one possible source of salvation. There was thus a fundamental utopianism in futurism, and in many ways that utopianism referred to the possibility of salvation by shaping new forms of action on the world level.

To futurists, saving the future of the world began as a process of reform of the human subject. This process of reform, clearly expressed in the writings of Lewis Mumford, meant to reforge human civilization around a constructive, peaceful and welfarist use of human rationality for the advancement, and not destruction, of Mankind. 'Man must be reformed at the core', a 'fundamental belief in the goodness of Man restored'. Mumford's monumental work, *The*

Condition of Man' had begun with his attempt to sketch, in 1944, a programme for human survival (Mumford 1944). It was based on his conclusion
that democratic societies paid a high price for their successful defence against
fascism. In terms similar to those proposed by Hannah Arendt, Günther
Anders or John Herz, Mumford saw democratic societies under conditions of
high technology as suffering from the same tendencies of totalitarianism as
Nazi Germany and Stalinist Russia. The totalitarian use of technology had
corrupted not only the German high culture of civilization but also the liberalism of the American republic. By unleashing the forces of destruction on
Hiroshima and then failing to step back from the horror produced, the US
had transformed itself into a de facto Nazi government intent on putting the
atomic bomb at the basis of its strive for global hegemony (Mumford 1946:
27). Survival thus depended on finding forms of resistance to such emerging
global domination.

Resistance, in turn, depended on the development of new forms of world
consciousness. Utopia is, wrote Mumford, the hope of a new 'world consciousness', a new sense of human unity on the global level (Mumford 1956: 236).
Developing a new world consciousness was an 'inward journey', one in which,
as Mumford saw it, the striving for domination of the outer limits of human existence would be replaced by an inward search for new principles of creativity,
salvation and responsibility. This inward journey would take place through a
process of radical imagination, of thinking differently the world and humanity's place in it, and only through this process of radical imagination could
new forms of global unity be imagined:

> The question is no longer whether this or that nation can survive. The
> question is whether mankind has enough imagination to mobilize, on
> behalf of peace and cooperation, forces men have hitherto conscripted
> only for war and destruction. Unless the crisis produces such a dynamic
> will, Man himself is lost.
>
> (Mumford 1946: 3)

Mankind, in these writings, emerged as a potential newborn human civilization, united by new forms of consciousness of the common challenges to the
world and imbued with a sense of future. Mumford's ideas of the need to save
the world future through a fundamental rethinking of Man had parallels in
works by other intellectuals of the time, such as the Dutch sociologist Fred
Polak and the German journalist Robert Jungk. From the early 1970s on,
they would all become central to the constitution of the field of futures studies
and instrumental in the creation of a World Federation for the Future, but in
the 1950s they each achieved renown for works that centred on the need to
restore the future as a central category of human action. While there is no
evidence of direct links between these actors at this point, the themes they
addressed were highly related: the idea of progress as operating a fundamental
rupture in time, the depiction of technology and automation as fundamental

obstacles for the human capacity to creatively imagine the future, the subordination of all human values to economic, scientific and social logics of rationality. In Jungk's *Tomorrow is Already Here* (1954, published in German as *Die Zukunft hast schon Begonnen*, 1952), the future is portrayed as dominated by the deterministic logics of technology. Mankind seems to have been pushed toward a particular future organized by the armaments race and leaving no place for an alternative use (or non-use) of the scientific discovery of the atom. Numerous atomic scientists such as Szilard saw the invention of the bomb and even its mere theoretical possibility as a threat to Mankind. They foresaw its dire consequences for the future and its world-altering capacity. But knowingly and willingly, mankind continued along the path of the bomb as though this road was inevitable. Technological progress has set in motion a determinism that can only be halted by a fundamental revival of the radical imagination. Such determinism represents a lack of freedom. 'In the "world without walls" which has increasingly come to be, the type of man on which America's greatness was based is becoming rarer and rarer: the strong, free man guided by his own conscience, constantly searching for something new' (Jungk 1954: 199).

To both Jungk and Fred Polak, the loss of creative capacity of imagining the future was understood as leading to devastating forms of apathy capable of triggering violence on a global scale. If Jungk's Mankind is rushing toward a future it has not fully chosen, Polak's Mankind in the book *The Image of the Future* (1961, published in Dutch in 1955) is going towards no future at all. Fred Polak was a Dutch-born Jew and, like Jungk, who was a resistance fighter, spent the war in exile. Polak's theory is that human civilization is driven by positive images of the future. No progress is possible without an optimistic idea of what is to come. Such optimism has to be about the very essence of humankind, its destiny and role in the world, and the influence that men have on their own lives. The key to social transformations lies in the human capacity to picture another and better world, radically different from the existing one but providing an ideal destination for humankind. Throughout history, some cultures have benefitted more than others from the strength of their images of the future. But for the first time, Mankind seems to have lost entirely the capacity to dream. 'We have lost the ability to see any further than the end of our collective nose' (Polak 1973: 195). In the absence of mobilizing images of the future, most of humanity is now weighed down by an accelerated time constantly overloading the present. We have become what Polak calls 'moment-ridden men' who cannot seek 'escape' in the future but are trapped in the present. To Polak this represents a violent crisis. Far from mere stagnation, it marks the destruction of human civilization, as the lack of mobilizing visions of the future spawns nihilism and hopelessness. Polak and Jungk arrive at the same conclusion as Mumford: that Mankind needs to be saved from his state of apathy by a fundamental radicalization of the future.

Possible paths discarded in the armaments race should be reopened and new optimistic images of the future forged. Those images, Polak agrees with

Jungk, should not be determined by external pressures such as technology or by following the track of one of the two superpowers (1973: 304), but they should be arrived at through new forms of democratic discussion. He encourages them to work on the issues of the future, to create new positive images of a possible world for tomorrow. This is urgent. For all three thinkers, the future is not a distant continent but rapidly closing in on humanity. Key trends are already in motion, creating a new situation of emergency.

Rather as in Mumford's thinking, utopia is the result of an inward journey into the human soul, but it is also the outer reflection of this inward soul search via the creation of world consciousness and forms of world government: the emphasis on global unity in futurists' thinking led to their belief that the future of humanity lay in forms of human organization at the level of the world. To Polak, rethinking the future meant moving images and conceptions of the future from the nation state to the universal level. The framework of the nation state together with the formation of geopolitical blocs in the Cold War world distorted the function of the images of the future: they had become stimulating not for Mankind but for *some specific men* at the expense of the others. 'The image of the future, at its best, has always been universal in character, a vision to serve and foster the growth of all mankind'. Indeed, any 'vision of the future which falls short of this universality will in the end leave the Earth a smoking ruin' (1973: 303).

Mankind

In these writings the idea of Mankind appeared as the symbol for a reborn human civilization united by a shared future consciousness. 'Mankind' as such was not a new concept at that time; it had much earlier origins. In the interwar period, references to Mankind were made by the early peace movement, and the concept was a signifier of the idea of world federation and world parliament, denoting understandings of a moral and judicial sacred covenant for humanity. But the meaning of the concept widened significantly after 1945, particularly in relation to the developing UN system. Whereas the Covenant of the League of Nations referred only to the members of the League, the UN Charter made reference to Mankind as the *totality* of human civilization, including coming generations that ought to be saved from the 'sorrow' experienced by the generations that had lived through two world wars (Preamble). As such, the concept of Mankind symbolized the hope of a unified post-conflict world, for which the peaceful values of human civilization needed to be reasserted. The preamble of the UNESCO's constitution, written in 1945, states that the organization was created 'for the purpose of advancing [...] the objectives of international peace and of the common welfare of Mankind' and the activities of the organization would be heavily tainted by conceptions of common human legacy and destiny. However, reflections on how to recreate a peaceful human civilization went far beyond the UN system and marked a range of transnational activities. The Russell-Einstein manifesto (1955) that inspired the Pugwash conferences began, 'We have to learn to think in a new way'. And ended:

> There lies before us, if we choose, continual progress in happiness, knowledge, and wisdom. Shall we, instead, choose death, because we cannot forget our quarrels? We appeal as human beings to human beings: Remember your humanity, and forget the rest. If you can do so, the way lies open to a new Paradise; if you cannot, there lies before you the risk of universal death.
>
> (Russell-Einstein Manifesto 1955)

Similar notions of the need to reshape forms of scientific, religious or political engagement as forces of global unity came for instance from different ecu-menical initiatives around the World Federation and World Council of Churches, or from the so-called Council for the Study of Mankind, a Protes-tant and Quaker organization. One of its members, the American futurist Warren Wagar wrote. 'Man of today is neither intellectually nor spiritually prepared for the Mankind age' (Wagar 1971: viii).

Mankind had to be *created*. In environmental discourse from the 1940s on, 'Mankind' was the signifier of the idea of the human species, of humanity as a population that might follow the same cycles of overpopulation and crash noted by Fairfield Osborn or William Vogt in relation to other species (Robertson 2012). In our sociopolitical context, Mankind emerges as the sig-nifier of a nascent global humanity that can be and needs to be brought to consciousness of its condition in order to emerge. In particular, a significant amount of transnational activity would focus, after 1945, on the question of human values and the question of how a new universal destiny of humanity could be shaped. Culture, science and particularly social science would emerge as privileged arenas for this reflection, which focused on the problems of 'world values' and 'world problems'. The post-war social sciences, as exemplified for instance by the creation of the International Sociological Association and other transnational organizations, functioned as a concrete arena of transnational circulation (Guilhot and Heilbron 2008). But they were also understood as a form of active intervention in the shaping of global subjectivity, by mapping and charting emerging global human values. The new survey and interview techniques that had been pioneered in the applied sociology of Parsons and Lazarsfeld became central to this activity, promoted in particular by UNESCO's International Social Sciences Council. From the mid-1960s, a series of works on the future of the world emerged, many of them with direct connection to the UNESCO, the International Social Sciences Council and the wider UN system. UNESCO also pioneered futures studies and futures research, in the hope of finding a new universal science of Mankind (UNESCO archives DDG 2/34 / PSP). The future thus appeared as a kind of heir to UNESCO's initial attempt, begun in 1946, to write a universal history of Mankind (Maurel 2010, Raj 2013).

The first of these future-oriented studies were attempts to systematically collect people's conscious or unconscious visions of the future, in order to study and explicate the potential existence of a world public opinion on major future issues. This had a potentially subversive purpose, mirroring conceptions of the need to use new forms of global imagination as a radical force put forward by Mumford and others. Studying the images of the future that might be hiding in the global public, it was thought, would be a way of highlighting the discrepancy between the futures that actually dominated world developments and those that were in fact desired or dreamed of by world citizens. The most emblematic product of this activity probably is the big project on 'Images of a Disarmed World' and 'Images of the World in Year 2000', carried out by the Vienna European Coordination Centre for Research and Documentation in the Social Sciences, a centre created in 1963 by the International Social Science Council in order to coordinate international comparative research in areas of interest to the UNESCO. In 1964 and 1965 some 5,000 persons were surveyed in France, Norway and Poland about their attitudes to disarmament and about how they imagined a possible future disarmed world. The project was part of UNESCO's attempts, from 1960 on, to promote a public opinion in favour of disarmament, among other things by furthering scientific studies that emphasized the positive consequences of disarmament for the solving of a set of other world issues. For this purpose, UNESCO mobilized, through its decentralized system of NGOs and affiliated forms of expertise, parts of the international peace movement and the burgeoning field of futures research. Within the peace movement there was already the idea that solving world problems depended on promoting strong positive visions of the future. For instance, that was the conclusion reached by the Women's International League for Peace and Freedom (WILPF), in which Elise Boulding, who had translated Fred Polak's book in 1961, was active.[4] 'Images of a Disarmed World' consisted of a questionnaire, in which the succession of questions was intended to shed light on the impending global threats that shaped Mankind's capacity to imagine the future. After answering the question, 'In your mind what is the greatest danger man is facing *right now?*' – with 'nuclear weapons' and 'world war' as top suggested answers – the interviewees were encouraged to depict 'the world situation [as it] will be ... in five years and in twenty years'. But Mankind was not regarded as definitively trapped in a future mechanically resulting from the difficult present situation. On the contrary, the long term was depicted as a field that remains open and which can be influenced by human action. Thus, the interviewees were asked not only about what they thought would happen but also about what they would like to see happening and about what, according to them, would be the best way to reach such a desirable future situation.[5]

The focus on disarmament futures paved the way for a much larger inquiry into images of world futures in the second phase of the study. In the course of 1966 it was decided that 'Images of a Disarmed World' would be 'expanded considerably so as to include any dimension of the future' (Ornauer et al. 1976). New polls were conducted, in 14 countries and under the leadership of the Norwegian peace researcher and systems theorist Johan Galtung. 'Images of the World in the Year 2000' was a study of international opinion on various subjects, from the future state of religion to the possible consequences of automation, demographic prospects and international relations developments. The study asked people in detail how they felt about the year 2000 (Ornauer et al. 1976: 639). The shift in emphasis from disarmament as the primordial global issue to a much wider interest in images and attitudes pertaining to the future, stressed the global focus. 'Images of a Disarmed World' was already asking people about the future of the world, asking questions of opinions about 'what man would become', and seeking to map, also, preferences around forms of world organization and world government.[6] But 'Images of the World in the Year 2000' was a virtual global opinion poll. In 1964, the emphasis was on collecting opinions on each side of the East–West divide, in a reflection that mirrored the idea that the division of Europe symbolized the world struggle for the future and that Europe was the quintessential battleground of the Cold War. The second phase of the survey remained profoundly European, including countries such as Czechoslovakia and Yugoslavia (both countries understood in the 1960s as borderline countries between East and West and possible sources of change to the communist system), but non-European countries (India and Japan, beacons of modernization but also symbols of different paths) were also included in the study. Altogether, research institutes and individuals in about 30 countries were contacted. The goal was now clearly to broaden the scope of the project so that a 'word public opinion' could be depicted as realistically as possible. Such a common world opinion on the future was also derived, with some effort, from the results. In the analysis of the results, the researchers stressed commonality and shared outlook – indeed, 'a striking identity of views on most of the questions asked' (*UNESCO Courier* August/September 1967: 7). In actual fact the raw data did not necessarily indicate what the researchers took as proof of the existence of 'a general opinion regarding attitudes towards the world of tomorrow' (*UNESCO Courier* August/September 1967: 7).

'Images of the World in the Year 2000' was, in other words, an active intervention in an imagined global community, mobilized in the name of a common future. The interlinkages between peace research and the similarly new science of futures research are significant. As demonstrated by this example, early studies into the conditions for disarmament functioned in fact as vehicles for a more general interest in world futures and for the elaboration of methods, in particular the global value survey, that would then be used, with much larger scope, in the coming years, in order to detect and define so-called 'world problems'. It is also not by chance that several actors of peace research were key actors in the development of the field of futures research.

The main researcher of 'Images of the World in the Year 2000', Johan Galtung, was a sociologist who had studied with Lazarsfeld and Parsons at Columbia. In 1959, Galtung founded the Institute for Peace Research Oslo, PRIO, and in a series of writings in the late 1960s and early 1970s he outlined a theory of multipolar world order and alternative world futures as organized around the nonaligned countries. For Galtung, systematic work on the future was a way of opening up disregarded alternatives to world order and forging value change. This interest in the future as a particular world consciousness led him in coming years to distinctly New Age conceptions of transcendental imagination and to conceptions of peace and conflict research as a global process of delivery which could be orchestrated by futures expertise (Andersson 2015). Galtung was however also central to the development of futures studies in the period from the late 1960s as a particular kind of scientific expertise for the shaping of world futures. It was also predominantly through Galtung's efforts that prospective studies or futures studies would become utilized within the framework of the UN system as a particular tool for envisioning and creating world futures.

Galtung was emblematic of a second generation of futurists, who, equipped with the tools of social science – in particular the new quantitative interest in value and survey studies, modelling, and systems theory, actively sought to promote forms of global futures consciousness. In 1967, Galtung organized, with Robert Jungk, the First International Future Research Conference under the auspices of PRIO. The proceedings of the Conference were published two years later under the label *Mankind 2000*, and Mankind 2000 was also the name of the organization created at the same time with the explicit purpose of promoting a common future for all Mankind. The ambition of the conference was to set the new methods of futures research, interview techniques, forms of forecasting, prognosis and modelling as the basis of a democratization of the world future. The global future was, several futurists contended, orchestrated from the 'ivory tower of a think tank', in other words, from, as it were, the American RAND Corporation, the predictive models of which were central to the shaping of Cold War world order (Galtung in *Mankind 2000*, 1969: 109).

Mankind 2000 also intended to articulate the future as a global concern, in several respects. First, it was intended to overcome the bipolarity of both the Cold War struggle, and the existing forms of protests against it. In fact the Mankind 2000 'project' had been thought up by Robert Jungk in the context of his work with the peace movement. The international peace movement, split between liberal or nonaligned peace movements and the Soviet-dominated World Peace Council, mirrored the struggles of the Cold War world (Wittner 1993). Mankind 2000 was Jungk's by identifying the future as a unifying issue that might bring together what he clearly hoped would be a new social movement on a planetary scale, which the peace movement could unite under and join. Second, parallel to several other activities that took shape at the same time, most prominently the Club of Rome, Mankind 2000 sought to stress the existence of common, world-encompassing problems that not only surpassed national boundaries but also defied ideas of convergence between the systems or stage-driven trajectory of global modernization and allowed for divergent world futures (Gilman 2003). Third, it meant specifically to create forms of collaboration between futurists, many of whom were trapped behind the Iron Curtain but had methodological and theoretical insights into methods of prognostication.

These methods were understood as capable of having an active bearing on the world future. At the conference, futurists were described as a new kind of modern-day utopians, ready to invent better futures, and as 'men and women who think that man is not the victim but the molder of his destiny' and believe that 'this confidence in the future and opposition to the darkness of our times may finally prevail' (*Mankind 2000*, 1969: Preface). The Oslo conference emphasized the methods of futures research as methods that would move away from technocratic forms of long-term planning and introduce participatory techniques – such as the future workshop developed by Jungk or a global future exhibit – as ways of mobilizing global public futures. Democratizing futures research would, in the futurists' view, multiply the possible representations of the future, hence increase the number of alternatives available to the world. As John McHale, one of the most influential American futurists and present in Oslo, wrote: 'we need more and more diverse, "alternatives" futures – not less. The future belongs to all men' (*Mankind 2000*, 1969: 256). The concept of Mankind was indeed a recurrent notion in most of the contributions of the participants. 'Whether there will be a future of humanity depends on our ability to convert mankind … into an effective social unit' (*Mankind 2000*, 1969: 66). Essential to such a unit was the creation of new forms of international cooperation around the study of the future and the creation of 'completely independent, national, international and supranational research-institutes ("civilian think-factories"), specially devoted to the coordinated study of the future' (*Mankind 2000*, 1969: 328). Such independent forms of future research would be a way of surmounting the propagandistic war of future visions and 'war of forecasts' of the Cold War (*Mankind 2000*, 1969: 280). In an era of polarization, only the idea of a common future could offer an exit from conflict.

Thus, world problems with a long-term dimension were understood as constituting a space for dialogue between East and West and for opening up new notions of the world that might transcend bipolarity. The eventual creation of a World Futures Studies Federation, in 1973, reflecting much more widely held ideas of federation as a solution to problems of world government, also embodied these hopes for the development of new forms of global future understanding. Through such a decentralized federation, based on the idea of the UNESCO system, without hierarchical structure and encompassing the globe, possibly with the support of new communication technologies such a tele-satellite system or a channel for the future, futurists would be able to promote a new global future consciousness.

The constitution of world problems

Through the organization of the Mankind 2000 conference and a number of world conferences on futures research that would follow, futurism was transformed from a matter of philosophical and intellectual reflection into a scientific activity drawing on new methods of social science as well as alternative forms of communication such as exhibited images and objects that sought to project an array of possible world futures. The final section of this chapter examines the way that futures research from the late 1960s and early 1970s onwards was directly involved in the constitution of what was referred to as 'world problems', problems conceptualized as common to humanity and having to do with systemic and long-term trends in world developments.

The 'problem catalogue' of the world expanded hugely in the years from the mid-1960s on. Ideas of 'world problems' or 'common problems of Mankind' gave birth to a wide range of activities within various institutional frameworks. While conceptions of common world futures had begun, in the immediate post-war period, with observations concerning the bomb and with the growing debate on disarmament, they developed, in the activities of these organizations, into much wider reflection on a series of problems that would either have comparable or common effect in large parts of the world or were actively created through trends in an interconnected world system. Disarmament, famine control, automation, value change (the 'loss of values'), overpopulation, energy needs and pollution were all understood as such global issues (despite the fact that, at that time, value change was a Western issue while population growth was conceptualized as a Third World problem). Several of the organizations that had emerged post-1945 focused on one specific world problem and developed their reflections into veritable lists or catalogues of world trends. For example, the Pugwash movement extended its focus on controlling the bomb to a wider interrogation of a number of world problems, including 'Problems of Developing Nations', 'Environmental Problems' and 'World Resources and Population Problems' (*Bulletin of Atomic Scientists* 1973: 22–29). The Club of Rome, which published its famous report based on the World Models, *The Limits to Growth* in 1972, also created a register or inventory of world future problems called the 'World Problematique'. It was produced by panels of young people across the globe, with the idea that these 'future generations' were best positioned to rank the urgency of problems facing humanity. At the end of the 1960s, the most frequently quoted items on this, never stable, list were the atomic issue and the problems linked to overpopulation, but the Club of Rome listed up to 49 'continuous critical problems' (Ozbekhan 1970: 14).

The constitution of these world problems was dependent on forms of trend extrapolation, forecasting and prediction which, from the late 1960s on, aided by computer modelling, could deal with multifactor causality, feedback loops and systemic interdependence. Indeed, global issues were only visible through the prism of the 'long term', through projections of their anticipated development and their interaction with other issues in a systemic whole. Underlying the description of world problems was forms of systems analysis, which by the late 1960s projected the world as constituted in the complex interplay between human values and technology, between dynamic and non-dynamic factors, between natural and social boundaries. Systems analysis allowed for understandings of 'the Problem' as universal. Even problems that might have local expression, for instance hunger, were in fact larger expressions of global unity. Former RAND systems theorist, Club of Rome modeller and futurist Hasan Ozbekhan wrote, 'We are now living in a single system, and the problem is always system-wide' (Ozbekhan, *Mankind 2000*, 1969: 129). As all long-term problems are part of a world system, all problems pertaining to the future needed to be handled as part of an emerging world state. Thus, already in 1970, a report from the Club of Rome contended that world problems were not 'a number of separate and discrete problems' but rather a 'predicament systemic in character', a 'problematique [that had] transcended discrete categories of events' (Ozbekhan 1970: 11). This switch from lists of problems that could be indirectly connected to each other to a comprehensive narrative encompassing all the troubles facing Mankind was a direct product of the application of systems theory – in particular by the UN from the mid-1970s. UNESCO's resolutions on disarmament are indicative of the gradual adoption of such a systemic approach to world problems. Until 1974, disarmament was connected to other 'long-term' 'world problems' by a kind of budgetary relation within the organization. UNESCO sought to encourage disarmament on the understanding that it would free economic resources that could then be directed at the struggle against other world problems such as illiteracy (UNESCO archives, document 12C/Resolutions, 1962: 45). This viewpoint was also promoted by the UN, according to which:

> the Disarmament Decade proclaimed by the General Assembly of the United Nations in … December 1969 should contribute, through a reduction of armaments under effective international control, to the channelling of the resources thus freed to the promotion of the well-being of humanity, by intensifying the drive against hunger, sickness, ignorance, illiteracy and the other evils of underdevelopment, thus promoting social progress and the full development of man's capabilities.
> (UNESCO archives, document 18C/Resolutions, 1974: 109)

In other words, world problems were understood as having a fundamental functional interdependence in a global system of evolving global resources, priorities and human values. In order to have some input into this highly complex matter, UNESCO in particular began actively working with futurists.

This collaboration can be traced back to the late 1960s. It was UNESCO's *International Social Science Journal* that produced some of the first scientific renderings of futures research (vol. XXI, 4, 1969). In 1973, the World Futures

Studies Federation (WFSF) was created in the UNESCO headquarters and affiliated to the organization with a 'mutual information' status. A lot of the input on futures research for UNESCO would come from the Federation. The same year, UNESCO participated in the creation of the United Nations University, an institution dedicated to 'research, advanced training and dissemination of knowledge concerning major global problems' in which many futurists – for example, Galtung, Elise Boulding and Eleonora Masini – were involved (UNESCO archives, 1977 UNU activity report to UNESCO, p. 6). Within the context of the UN University, these futurists – and in particular Galtung – would work in the coming years with tools of futures research, trying to shape forms of future consciousness but also and importantly teaching the tools of futures research, the forecasting, extrapolation and envisioning techniques that they saw as the chief instruments for the creation of world future consciousness.

The organizational logic behind UNESCO's interest in futures research was motivated by the idea that futures studies, forms of forecasting and long-range planning (labelled *forward studies* within the organization) were instrumental in helping it orientate its activities 'towards the highest aspirations of humanity' (UNESCO archives, Doc 78 EX/Decisions). From 1968, UNESCO started using statistical indicators, long-range forecasting and systems analysis to project trends in the development of world problems. When a 'preprogramming office' was created in UNESCO in 1971, a task force on indicators was constituted in order to provide 'an analytical description of major world problems in the fields of Unesco's competence', i.e. education, science, social sciences, humanities and culture, and communication. The preprogramming office director was the Moroccan Mehdi Elmandjra, who was also a prominent member of the WFSF. The identification of long-term trends and world problems would then be transformed into the long-term objectives from which UNESCO's programmes derived (UNESCO archives, DDG 2/34 / PSP).

Expertise on the future was solicited not only with respect to the definition of world problems but also in order to define programmatic priorities for world futures. As such, the focus on long-term issues and future problems of global scale would also become a diplomatic way of neutralizing sensitive issues and using expertise as an alternative to clashes of interest and ideology within an organization that itself reflected prevailing divisions of the world. The organizational focus on 'long-term world problems' was another way to unite human effort on the global level, but in a seemingly apolitical, diplomatic and expert-driven undertaking. This emphasis on the concreteness of global future issues as supposedly non-ideological problems can also be found in the United Nations University documents, according to which the organization's objective is to 'enable experts from the whole world to tackle together specific and concrete world problems' (UNESCO archives: 1977 UNU activity report to UNESCO, p. 4).[7]

In practical terms, however, discourses on Mankind's long-term problems could hardly be neutral. The rhetorical strength that came from depicting an issue as a 'world problem' was soon discovered and denounced. Thus, during the 1983 UNESCO General Conference, when the USSR deployed the term 'global problems of Mankind' to describe the nuclear issue, opponents such as the Chinese delegation asserted that this vision of the problem was not universal (UNESCO General Conference proceedings, 1983, p. 428). In other words, if the future emerged, in this context, as a universal problem, posited as a possible suprapolitical category capable of bringing humanity together, the same world future was also reduced to a series of problems that required, for their solution, apolitical forms of expertise. The future travelled, between the 1950s and the 1970s, from a source of reenchantment and human reform to a problem of world management.

Concluding remarks

While 'world problems' could appear as a more neutral, more pragmatic way to deal with Mankind's future, they were not deprived of values discussion, political quarrels or philosophical concerns regarding the role of humanity. In fact, in the development of futures research and through the course of these decades we see a repetitive tension between two conceptions of the world's future: one contemplates a given globality and world entity that should be dealt with in the most neutral and efficient way, whereas the other emphasizes globality as a superior value, as the space wherein lies the hope for the world. Between these two conceptions there is a certain change in emphasis over time. The world future underwent a remarkable slimming down from the political, philosophical and existential reflections of 1950s futurism to the constitution of lists and repertoires of world problems in the 1970s. The very idea of global issues, in the context of the Cold War, was contentious. Indeed, the concept of universalism meant different things to the West and to the USSR, not to mention to the emerging South. In this context, the recourse to expertise emerged as a possible space for dialogue. Through this insistence on non-ideological expertise, however, much of the radicality of earlier ideas of the future as a space where universal interests of Mankind could be articulated and defended evaporated. Futurists, from the immediate post-war years on, argued that the focus on 'world problems' was an effective way to deal with Mankind's fate, as long as all humanity could decide on how to address them. As futurists advocated global management of the future and of world problems in the interest of Mankind, they dreamed of new forms of world organization that would transcend world politics and create forms of engagement and activism that would set the interests of Mankind first and proceed to order the world according to these. Social science was, to them, a key arena for this. But the many attempts to incarnate such proto forms of world government – the 'World Forum' created by the Club of Rome to deal with the world problematique or indeed the global think tank of the WFSF itself – arguably did not fulfill this role but rather developed over time into forms of global consultancy (Ozbekhan 1970). Nor did such organizational attempts succeed in democratizing representations of the global future. The WFSF made substantial efforts to attract contributions from futurists all over the world but never escaped the fact that it was dominated by a crowd of Western intellectuals and activists.

Notes

1 We acknowledge funding from the European Research Council within the framework of a Starting Investigator Grant to Andersson.
2 As such we want to set it apart from two other activities, namely futurism as the nihilistic and technotopian art form associated with the First World War and futures research in a more explicit Cold War setting associated with the RAND Corporation and predictions of nuclear holocaust. For the latter see Andersson (2012).
3 Most notably Hannah Arendt, *The Human Condition*, 1958, and Lewis Mumford, *The Condition of Man*, 1944.
4 Bussey and Tims 1965: 241, ISSC archives, ISSC/7/1.8 Vienna Center Projects, Remarks on the research study on Peace Research conducted by Prof. J. Stoetzel, July 1964. Ingrid Eide, a Norwegian peace activist who took part to the 'Images of a Disarmed World Project', was also active in WILPF. At the time she was also known as Ingrid Galtung as she was married to Johan Galtung.
5 Question 17: 'How would you like to see the world organized after total disarmament?' and question 23: 'In case there should be disarmament, what do you personally think would be the most effective idea right now?'
6 *UNESCO Courier* August/September 1967, question 5, for instance, is about the greatest danger *man* is facing. ISSC archives, ISSC/7/1.8 Norwegian questionnaire, question 17 'How would you like to see the world organized after total disarmament?' The suggested answers prioritise options according to which the world would be as it is now or more unified politically, the first proposition being 'a world government'.
7 Translated from the French: 'permettre à des savants du monde entier d'affronter en commun certains problèmes mondiaux spécifiques et concrets'.

References

Andersson, Jenny (2012) 'The Great Future Debate and the Struggle for the World', *American Historical Review*, 117(5): 1411–1431.

Andersson, Jenny (2015) 'Midwives of the Future: Futurism, Futures Studies and the Radical Imagination', in J. Andersson and E. Rindzeviciute (eds) *Forging the Future: Transnational Perspectives on Science and Politics during the Cold War*. New York: Routledge.

Appadurai, Arjun (2013) *The Future as Cultural Fact: Essays on the Global Condition*. New York: Verso.

Aradau, Claudia and Rens van Munster (2011) *Politics of Catastrophe: Geneaologies of the Unknown*. New York: Routledge.

Arendt, Hannah (1954) 'The Conquest of Space and the Stature of Man', in Hannah Arendt, *Between Past and Future*. New York: Penguin Classics, pp. 260–275.

Arendt, Hannah (1998 [1958]) *The Human Condition*. Chicago, IL: University of Chicago Press.

Benjamin, Walter (2009) *On the Concept of History*. New York: Classic Books.

Bulletin of Atomic Scientists (1973) 'Pugwash: Raison d'être', February, 22–29.

Bussey, Gertrude and Margaret Tims (1965) *Women's International League for Peace and Freedom, 1915–1965: A Record of Fifty Years' Work*. London: Allen & Unwin.

Cosgrove, Denis (2001) *Apollo's Eye: a Cartographic Genealogy of the Earth in the Western Imagination*. Baltimore, MD: Johns Hopkins University Press.

Edwards, Paul N. (2012) *A Vast Machine: Computer Models, Climate Data, and the Politics of Global Warming*. Cambridge, MA: MIT Press.

Evangelista, Matthew (1999) *Unarmed Forces: The Transnational Movement to End the Cold War*. Ithaca, NY: Cornell University Press.

Galtung, Johan (1969) 'On Futures Research and its Role in the World', in Johan Galtung and Robert Jungk (eds) *Mankind 2000*, Oslo: PRIO, pp. 103–117.

Galtung, Johan and Robert Jungk (eds) (1969) *Mankind 2000*. Oslo: PRIO.

Gilman, Nils (2003) *Mandarins of the Future*. Baltimore, MD: Johns Hopkins University Press.

Guilhot, Nicolas and Johan Heilbron (2008) 'Towards a Transnational History of the Social Sciences', *Journal of the History of the Behavioural Sciences*, 44(2): 146–160.

Iriye, Akira (2002) *Global Community: The Role of International Organizations in the Making of the Contemporary World*. Berkeley, CA: University of California Press.

Jasanoff, Sheila (2001) 'Image and Imagination: The Formation of Global Environmental Consciousness', in C. A. Miller and P. N. Edwards (eds) *Changing the Atmosphere: Expert Knowledge and Environmental Governance*. Cambridge, MA: MIT Press, pp. 309–337.

Jonas, Hans (1979) *Das Prinzip Verantwortung*. Frankfurt am Main: Insel Verlag.

Jungk, Robert (1954) *Tomorrow is Already Here*. New York: Simon & Schuster.

Maurel, Chloé (2010) 'L'Histoire de l'Humanité de l'UNESCO (1945–2000)', *Revue d'Histoire des Sciences Humaines*, 22 (June): 161–198.

Miller, Clark (2004) 'Climate Science and the Making of a Global Political Order', in S. Jasanoff (ed.) *States of Knowledge: The Coproduction of Science and Social Order*. Abingdon: Routledge, pp. 46–67.

Moyn, Samuel (2010) *The Last Utopia: Human Rights in History*. Cambridge, MA: Belknap Press of Harvard University Press.

Mumford, Lewis (1944) *The Condition of Man*. London: Secker & Warburg.

Mumford, Lewis (1946), 'Gentlemen: You Are Mad!', *The Saturday Review*, 9 (2 March), 5–6.

Mumford, Lewis (1956) *The Transformations of Man*. New York: Harper & Row.

Ornauer, Helmut et al. (1976) *Images of the World in the Year 2000: A Comparative Ten Nation Study*. Atlantic Highlands, NJ: Humanities Press.

Ozbekhan, Hasan (1969) 'The Role of Goals and Planning in the Solution of the World Food Problem', in Johan Galtung and Robert Jungk (eds) *Mankind 2000*. Oslo: PRIO, pp. 117–150.

Ozbekhan, Hasan (for the Club of Rome) (1970) *The Predicament of Mankind: Quest for Structured Responses to Growing World-wide Complexities and Uncertainties – a Proposal*. Philadelphia, PA: University of Pennsylvania.

Polak, Fred (1973 [1955/1961]) *The Image of the Future*. Amsterdam: Elsevier.

Raj, Kapil (2013) 'Beyond Postcolonialism and Postpositivism: Circulation and the Global History of Science', *Isis*, 104(2): 337–347.

Robertson, Thomas (2012) 'Total War and the Environment: Fairfield Osborn, William Vogt, and the Birth of Global Ecology', *Environmental History*, 17(2) 1–29.

Russell, Bertrand and Albert Einstein (1955) 'The Russell-Einstein Manifesto', 9 July. Available at http://pugwash.org/1955/07/09/london-launch-of-the-russell-einstein-manifesto/.

van Munster, Rens and Casper Sylvest (2016) *Nuclear Realism: Global Political Thought during the Thermonuclear Revolution*. Abingdon: Routledge.

Wagar, W. Warren (ed.) (1971) *History and the Idea of Mankind*. Albuquerque, NM: University of New Mexico Press.

Wittner, Lawrence S. (1993) *One World or None: A History of the World Nuclear Disarmament Movement through 1953*. Stanford, CA: Stanford University Press.

Wolin, Richard (2007) *Heidegger's Children: Hannah Arendt, Hans Jonas, Hans Kollwitz, Hebert Marcuse*. Princeton, NJ: Princeton University Press.

6 Anthropocene incitements

Toward a politics and ethics of ex-orbitant planetarity

Nigel Clark

Introduction

Earth system scientist Will Steffen and his multi-disciplinary co-authors have recently cautioned that our species may be on 'a one-way trip to an uncertain future in a new, but very different, state of the Earth System' (Steffen et al. 2011: 757). There is nothing especially novel about the idea that humankind is transforming the Earth as a whole – an intuition that might be seen as the logical corollary of the quest for universal knowledge, progress and improvement that has defined western – later global – modernity. Along the way there have been a number of attempts to come up with a unifying concept to convey a sense of human impact on a planetary scale – including Italian geologist Antonio Stopanni's positing of an 'anthropozoic era' in the 1870s and Russian geochemist Vladimir Vernadsky's notion of a human-dominated 'noosphere' as a stage in the Earth's evolution, couched in the 1920s and 1930s (Crutzen 2002; Zalasiewicz et al. 2011). But as ethical philosopher Clive Hamilton and historian of science Jacques Grinevald insist, only fully developed Earth system thinking with an understanding of the planetary body as a single, complex dynamical system can offer a clear formulation of an Earth with the potential to shift in its totality from one operating state to another. And only by way of such an integrated perspective can we grasp the full gravity of the 'rift in the history of planet Earth' being opened by the aggregated impact of the human species (Hamilton and Grinevald 2015: 9).

With its synthesizing vision, Earth systems science is now drawing the agency of our own species and the dynamism of Earth processes into a unified conceptual framework. As sustainability theorist Johan Rockström and his collaborators explain:

> The Earth System is defined as the integrated biophysical and socio-economic processes and interactions (cycles) among the atmosphere, hydrosphere, cryosphere, biosphere, geosphere, and anthroposphere (human enterprise) ... . Thus, humans and their activities are fully part of the Earth System, interacting with other components.
>
> (2009: 32)

The ascendant term for the world that is being engendered by this co-production of human and other components of the Earth system is the Anthropocene. The Anthropocene hypothesis proposes that the cumulative influence of a range of human socio-material activities on Earth processes has reached such a level that it amounts to a shift out of the current geological epoch – the 10,000–12,000 year-old interglacial known as the Holocene that follows the end of the last Pleistocene glaciation – and into a novel geological period (Crutzen 2002; Zalasiewicz et al. 2011). First proposed by marine scientist Eugene Stoermer in the 1980s then championed by Nobel Prize-winning atmospheric chemist Paul Crutzen in the early 2000s, the Anthropocene idea has caught on with remarkable speed. Fast becoming a bridging concept between the natural sciences, social sciences and arts and humanities, as well as enjoying a lively uptake into popular culture, the Anthropocene – as an epoch – is also in the running for official inclusion in the Geological Time Scale.

Since 2008, the Anthropocene Working Group has been gathering evidence to support the claim for an epochal shift to present to the International Commission on Stratigraphy – with a planned submission date of late 2016. As working group chair Jan Zalasiewicz and his colleagues remind us: 'The Geological Time Scale is held dear by geologists and it is not amended lightly' (2010: 2228). To attain formal recognition, in the words of the working group, 'the "geological signal" currently being produced in strata now forming must be sufficiently large, clear and distinctive' (Subcommission on Quaternary Stratigraphy, 2015). Not only must this 'footprint' be an effectively permanent addition to the lithic composition of Earth, it also needs to be geosynchronous – that is, distributed right across the planet's surface at the approximately the same time.

Many decisions about the status and timing of geological periods have been and still are hotly contested. Even amidst this fractious discursive field, the Anthropocene offers exceptional grounds for dissensus. Because the formative processes of the proposed epoch are current and ongoing, researchers cannot simply work from existing rocks, fossils and other 'solid' evidence. They must orientate themselves to the lithographic signals that may or may not be discernible to a hypothetical observer far in the future. As sociologist Bronislaw Szerszynski points out to fellow social science and humanities scholars: 'it is important to realize that the truth of the Anthropocene is less about what humanity is doing, than the *traces* that humanity will leave behind' (2012: 169). From the perspective of Earth scientists themselves, however, the provocation may work the other way round. Stratigraphers, paleontologists and other geoscientists find themselves in the novel predicament of attending to 'what humanity is doing' right now in order to predict which of these activities are the best candidates for long term 'fossilization'.

From this peculiar situation certain political problems or incitements are beginning to materialize, though these are not necessarily entirely novel questions. And neither are they self-evident ones. After reviewing the gradual uptake of environmental issues by researchers in international relations and cognate fields of political inquiry, Clive Hamilton, Christophe Bonneuil and François Gemenne conclude that 'political theory, stuck in the Holocene, has been slow to recognise the Anthropocene and what it means' (2015: 9). In important ways, this is quite understandable. In most social science and humanities disciplines sustained attention has rarely been afforded to geologic forces and processes, so the question of why it might now matter that humankind could be joining this neglected domain is by no means an obvious or straightforward one. To put it another way, we might ask why exactly it is politically or ethically significant that humans – or part thereof – are being acknowledged as geologic agents, when geological agency per se has so often been assumed to be devoid of ethico-political valence or purchase (see Clark 2011: 7–11; 2013: 2827–9).

But Hamilton and his co-authors' call to think politics with or through geological epochs – to allow the Earth its own historicization – is itself indicative of shifting assumptions, as is Hamilton's own urging that 'social scientists must become geophysicists' (2015: 35–6). If there is indeed something of a 'geologic turn' underway in social, cultural and philosophical thought and practice, it is one that cannot be decoupled from the inverse movements of the natural sciences. For as the 'Anthropocene' denomination indicates, a concern with human agency is gravitating toward the core of certain fields of Earth science. And this is more than a matter of engaging empirically with social processes and dynamics. Following in the footsteps of many prominent climate scientists, geoscientists are becoming increasingly aware and reflexive about the political significance of their own research. As Zalasiewicz et al. deliberate:

> The Anthropocene might be used as encouragement to slow carbon emissions and biodiversity loss, for instance; perhaps as evidence in legislation on conservation measures; or, in the assessment of compensation claims for environmental damage. It has the capacity to become the most politicized unit, by far, of the Geological Time Scales and therefore to take formal geological classification into uncharted waters.
>
> (2010: 2231)

Some social thinkers have been driven to expose what they see as critical shortfalls in the discourse of Anthropocene science – including the framing of humankind as an undifferentiated whole, insufficient attention to the social relations and dynamics of capital, or intimations of teleological thinking. Such rejoinders may be justified, though ultimately they leave social or political thought itself geologically immune and unperturbed. In this chapter, I take the Anthropocene idea as an incitement to try and think the political *through* the Earth and its dynamical processes. If this means asking what might be new in the current ascent of the idea of humans as geologic or geophysical agents, it also invites the question of how the nascent understanding of a human–planet conjuncture stands in relation to earlier depictions of the interface between global humanity and the physical Earth.

Both the proposition that human activities the world over have become interwoven into a single nexus and the notion that Earth as a whole is responsive to this planet-scaled social system seem to resonate closely with ideas about globality that cystallized in the immediate post-war era. If it was already apparent to historian and technology theorist Lewis Mumford in 1948 that 'every nation or group, however isolated in appearance, is part of an infinitely complicated and involved ecological partnership of planetary dimensions' (cited in van Munster and Sylvest, 2014: 540), it looks to have taken another half century for the sciences to consummate the union of global humanity and planetary ecology in a single, fully resolved formulation. Concordant with the timing of early expressions of global socio-political and ecological thought, the current frontrunner for the moment at which our species attains full geophysical agency is the post-World War II burst of globalization and economic growth that Anthropocene exponents refer to as the 'Great Acceleration' – a juncture now seen as more likely to meet the demand for a geosynchronous footprint in the stratigraphic column than the previously favoured late eighteenth to early nineteenth-century Industrial Revolution (Steffen et al. 2011: 743). While the post-war boom offers numerous examples of socio-economic and technological developments ascending into exponentiality, the conspicuousness of its potential signal in the compositional layering of the Earth's crust is enhanced by the contemporaneous presence of radionuclides deposited by atmospheric nuclear weapons deployment and testing (Zalasiewicz et al. 2011: 2230).

All of which might suggest that the advent of the Anthropocene represents the apotheosis of post-war global thinking: the moment at which the work of assembling the planet into a single, integrated entity culminates in the full synchronization of social and planetary dynamics and in the coming of a new epochal self-consciousness. But such a reading, I would argue, covers only part of the picture and misses much of what is most provocative about the Anthropocene. The Anthropocene hypothesis does indeed emerge out of the geosciences' increasingly unitary and systemic conception of the planetary body, just as it channels the experience and the thematizations of intensifying social globalization. But I propose that in the very process of advancing the understanding of planetary dynamics, it also breaks with the grammar and imagery of the 'whole Earth'. The emerging motifs of the Anthropocene – thresholds in the Earth system, the fossil trace of humankind in future geological strata, an Earth evacuated of human presence – each in their own way open fracture lines in the imaginary of global unity and holism. More than this, these tropes render the very process of representing the globe enigmatic and paradoxical.

To start to get a sense of where the Anthropocene thematic might be taking constructions of globality, I turn to the specificities of the different scientific approaches to studying Earth processes that are now collaborating in the new storying of the planet. For many commentators, it is Earth system science – with its focus on planet-scaled interdependencies, dense feedback loops, and structural couplings – that is the key to the Anthropocene narrative. I suggest, however, that it is just as important to reconsider the ontological promptings of the more 'orthodox' geological sciences: to conceive of planetarity not only with reference to the two-way or reciprocal relations advanced by systems thinking but also in terms of the structural hierarchies and asymmetries that come into relief when we take seriously the Earth's compositional layering or stratification. After looking at the new forms of political thinking that are convening around the threat of violating thresholds in the Earth system, I turn to the questions posed to political thought and action by the confrontation with deep geological time and the 'inhuman' forces of Earth and cosmos.

Science and politics of planetary thresholds

If, as we have seen, the Anthropocene hypothesis can be said to hinge on a new scientific understanding of the way that the major Earth processes work together as an evolving, dynamically interactive system, we need to be mindful that it has taken over half a century of intensive research in the geosciences to identify and track the mechanisms through which the planet's various subcomponents mesh into this functional whole. Sharp observers have noted the irony that it took a humanity divided as never before – the great post-war rift of competing super powers – to nurture such a vision of planetary oneness. Cold War military planning, maintains Joseph Masco, 'encapsulated the Earth in military, command, control, and surveillance systems', but in the process 'it also created new understandings of the Earth, sea, and sky, and of the biosphere itself as an integrated ecological space' (2010: 29).

The confirmation of the theory of global plate tectonics in the 1960s offered the first comprehensive and unified model of the 'solid' Earth: one which demonstrated how the planet's major geological features were an expression of the incessant mobility of Earth's crust. Over subsequent decades, such an understanding of the dynamics of the lithosphere was extended to the planet's hydrosphere, atmosphere, crysophere and, later, biosphere. At the same time, major research projects identified the cycles and reservoirs of the Earth's main chemical components (Westbroek 1992: Ch. 4; Davis, 1996). Increasingly, these discoveries impinged upon and informed each other, and in the process previously distinct disciplines and sub-disciplines of geoscience began to gel. Out of this convergence gradually emerged a conception of a planetary body whose constituent elements appeared fully interdependent, a system imbued with dynamical properties that could not be divined from its parts alone. Prior to these developments, physical geographer Dennis Wood elaborates, the standard view was that:

> Things … *touched*. They sort of pushed each other around. But there was
> none of the sense of interpenetration, of multiple causation, of feedback,

of mutual interdependencies, of ... *the structural coupling* that is the essential characteristic of our situation as we understand it today.

(2004: 69–70)

Less sanguine commentators have pointed out that, for all the coherence and dynamism of the newly disclosed systemic Earth, much of the 'gradualism' that had prevailed in the geological sciences since the late eighteenth century remained unperturbed (Davis 1996: 53–5). Periodic outbursts of seismicity or volcanicity aside, this was still a planet that mostly evolved conservatively: its major chemical reservoirs and circuits were deeply entrained, its continental plates inched along, its strata accreted over millions of years. At the more modest scales at which the ecological sciences tended to operate, however, changes of a different pace were coming onto the agenda. In a variety of real-world systems ranging from eutrophying lakes to the algal colonization of coral reefs, field ecologists were noting that major transitions often seemed to be abrupt rather than cumulative and gradual (Scheffer et al. 2001). Ecosystems appeared to absorb stresses or shocks up to a point, but once that limit was crossed, the system in its entirety would lurch into rapid, irreversible change.

This sense that 'sudden, drastic switches to a contrasting state' (Scheffer et al. 2001: 591) were the norm in many ecosystems found resonance with the observations of other complex systems of varying kinds and scales. An interest in deciphering such shared dynamics formed the core of the interdisciplinary field of complexity studies that came of age in the 1980s. While an understanding that systems composed of many interacting parts exhibited similar dynamical behaviours had at this point been developing for several decades, previous research had tended to focus on the processes that promoted stability or allowed for systems to re-establish equilibrium after perturbation (Urry 2005: 5). But what captivated a new generation of complexity researchers were the 'non-linear' dynamics through which a system could transform itself into a novel state – leading to a new regard for the positive feedback loops through which pressures or perturbations, beyond a certain threshold, amplified themselves as they reverberated through the system.

In retrospect, we can see that toward the end of the twentieth century, Earth science and complexity studies were fast closing in on each other – propelled not by the imperatives of the Cold War arms race but by the new concern with anthropogenic climate change. Arguably, what finally unhinged geoscience from the vestiges of gradualism was the unexpected discovery of abrupt climatic change. Analyzing polar ice cores and related proxies of past climate, climatologists found compelling evidence that throughout the Pleistocene, temperature changes of up to 15 degrees Fahrenheit had frequently occurred in less than a decade (Broecker 1987; Alley 2000: 115–22). In this way, the idea of a threshold beyond which lay a runaway, cascading and irreversible shift to a new systemic state quickly jumped scales to the planetary level.

Given that by the turn of the twenty-first century, geophysical thinking was already well advanced in its integration of the sub-components of the Earth system, it is unsurprising that the idea of global climate being nudged into an alternative state by human impacts was soon extended beyond climate to encompass the Earth system in its entirety. For as Hamilton sums up: 'disturbing the climate inevitably means disturbing all components of the Earth system' (2015: 34). By the same logic, awareness of the need to prevent anthropogenic activity from pushing climate into a danger zone of potentially abrupt climate change was shortly extrapolated to the other major components of the Earth system.

The idea of putting in place forms of 'protection' for a range of vital Earth systems was set out in an influential multi-authored, interdisplinary paper entitled 'Planetary Boundaries: Exploring the Safe Operating Space for Humanity' – which explicitly linked this imperative to the transition from the Holocene to the Anthropocene (Rockström et al. 2009). As Rockström and his colleagues proposed, while thresholds themselves inhere in Earth systems and are thus essentially non-negotiable, the process of identifying and agreeing upon 'safe' boundaries or guardrails around these thresholds is a profoundly political one – calling for collective negotiation. Though as it stands, they lament, 'Current governance and management paradigms are often oblivious to or lack a mandate to act upon these planetary risks' (Rockström et al. 2009: 32). Already in 2005, before the Anthropocene idea had gained wide currency, political scientist Frank Biermann was advancing the concept of 'Earth system governance' as a way of highlighting the political challenges posed by the possible violation of planetary thresholds.

Though the failure of collective efforts to prevent global warming reaching 'dangerous levels' is only too obvious, and the lack of political mainstreaming of boundary risks more generally needs to be noted, commentators such as Hamilton, Bonneuil and Gemenne (2015) make a compelling case that planetary threshold shifts are an emergent object of contention with considerable significance for our worldviews and our politics. And yet, if there is something about conceiving of Earth in terms of its potential to flip between operating states that is historically unprecedented, then it is striking just how familiar most of the political responses to date seem to be. When Biermann proclaims that 'the extent of the potential impacts of Earth system transformation will require continually evolving norms of global solidarity' (2014: 40), he could well be conversing with the post-war theorists of the thermonuclear predicament.

Though the literature reveals little sense of continuity with this earlier tradition of theorizing planetary crisis, key themes of 1940s and 1950s global thinking resonate strongly in claims by Earth system governance theorists that the mutual dependence of states disclosed by threshold threats prescribes a need for a new or strengthened transnational political architectures. 'First and foremost, Earth system transformation increases the *interdependence of states*', asserts Biermann (2014: 49 author's italics). And still more insistently: 'it appears questionable whether full national sovereignty can be upheld for the most essential environmental standards that are needed to protect the planetary boundaries' (Biermann 2012: 8), leading to the conclusion that 'a World Environment Organization is needed as a new powerful agent' (Biermann 2014: 119). Or as Wijkman and Rockström counsel: 'The ideal would be a strong and reformed United Nations, or a whole new world organization whose task to is to act in the interests of us all' (2012: 174).

Like some of their predecessors in the immediate post-war period, political thinkers of the Earth system crisis dwell on the issue of injustice at the global scale and probe the tensions between top down and bottom up governance (see Wijkman and Rockström 2012: 184; see also van Munster and Sylvest 2014: 541–2). While the principal proposals – including strengthened international treaty-making and novel transnational organizations – involve alliances of nation-state actors, there is expected to be significant contribution from non-state actors at various scales, to address what Biermann et al. refer to as 'the problem of multilevel, or multilayered, governance' (2010: 281). But, arguably, where the resonance of the more radical theorists of post-war thermonuclear crisis is at its strongest is less in the details than in the overarching aspiration to bring global humankind and an endangered planet into a radical new alignment. And this is where the Anthropocene concept – the 'coupled ecosphere–anthroposphere complex' – seems at once to raise the stakes of imperilment and to bring the desired synchronization of humanity and planet to a new intensity. For with the coming of age of Earth systems theory, what had earlier been a grand intuition of global ecological and socio-political interconnectivity has evolved into a sophisticated, empirically substantiated understanding of the dynamics of structural couplings, feedbacks and interconnectivity.

In one sense, the pronounced echo of 1940s and 1950s global political thought in current Earth system governance thinking is a tribute to the prescience and enduring purchase of the former (see Craig, this volume). But we might also ask whether this unintentional recycling of five or six decades-old themes and ideals under supposedly very different conditions suggests that the political and ontological provocations of the 'new understanding of *being as geological*' of our species (Yusoff, 2013; 780) have really been taken to heart. In particular, I want to argue that the tropes of mutuality, interdependence and interconnectivity foregrounded in Earth system political thought represent a rather selective appropriation of contemporary geoscience. Reciprocal or two-way relations, though vital to understanding certain planetary dynamics, are far from the only modes of relating that feature in contemporary scientific accounts of Earth. What might the implications be, I now ask, of picking up on the incitements of some of the other aspects of Anthropocene science? This is a question that also puts to test some of the axioms of critical social and political thought itself.

Beyond interdependence: the asymmetries of geology

Whether they are conceived in terms of agonism and contestation or solidarity and co-operation, contemporary social thought has a marked predilection for two-way or reciprocal relations. In much critical thinking, the very fact that worlds are composed out of relationships is taken as the condition of being able to order or assemble realities otherwise – and generally these relations are presupposed to be inter-active or multi-directional. An important accomplice to such premises has been a certain reception of post-structural theory: a reading which assumes that all binaries are problematic, and believes that the best way of overcoming them is to show how some of the content relegated to one side of the division is also to be found on the other side. Especially in progressive thinking around the so-called culture–nature duality, a strong sense of co-enactment or mutual entanglement is now the order of the day (Clark, 2011: 44–50). In short, when notions of *relationality* are advanced in critical social and political thought, what is usually being affirmed is a preference – at once ontological and political – for *inter-relationality* (see Barnett 2005: 6–9).

Symptomatically, when Biermann speaks of deferred or long-term changes in the Earth system, he proclaims that 'intergenerational interdependence is at the core' (2014: 38). The significance of the *inter* in interdependence here invites interrogation, however, for if there is one thing that characterizes the inheritance by generations to come of changes triggered in present, it is the essential non-reciprocity or radical asymmetry of this relationship. The crack this reveals in the ontopolitical allegiance to relational symmetry and reciprocality, I would argue, deepens into an abyss if we prise further into the incitements of geological time and geophysical forcefulness.

For humanist thought, perhaps the most troubling aspect of the discipline of geology's findings for over two centuries has been its disclosure of an Earth whose long and eventful history admits of a human presence only in the eyeblink of its closing moments. The vast bulk of this geo-story precludes any 'coupled ecosphere–anthroposphere complex' simply because it contains no trace of the human. What is important to recognise is that the Anthropocene hypothesis is grounded at least as much in the understanding of these abyssal inhuman domains as it is in any sense of Earth system–social system co-coupling. As stratigrapher, paleontologist and Anthropocene working-group chair Jan Zalasiewicz depicts – in his popular writing – the probable legacy of our species in the rocks of Earth:

> It is less than ten thousand years in duration, this interval, and so just one per cent of one million years, which is itself just the small change of geological time. Seemingly with the stratigraphic thickness of a piece of cigarette paper, it will be caught between the ancient past and the substantial future.
>
> (2008: 89)

Other strata in which humans do not feature, Zalasiewicz notes, may be anywhere up to ten kilometres thick (2008: 56). The processes that generate this lithic layering, he impresses upon us, are unique amongst the planets that comprise our solar system: 'The Earth, by comparison with these neighbour-ing planetary bodies, is a treasury of strata, a gigantic machine for producing strata' (2008: 17). While it is the interplay of biological life, air, water, ice and rock that compose new strata, it is Earth's exceptionally mobile plate tec-tonics that propel this process. And in turn, it is the circulation of viscous rock deep within Earth that drives tectonic plate motion – all ultimately powered by the internal heat of the planet's core (Zalasiewicz 2008: 51, 62).

While the exact mechanics are still a matter of debate, it is worth stressing that the deep-seated driving forces of stratal formation are almost entirely impervious to the interactions that animate Earth's surficial layers, just as the massive influx of solar energy that fuels the biosphere will rain down on the planet with no regard to whatever terrestrial life makes of it. In short, rela-tions of mutual dependence, reciprocity and feedback are not the first or last word in the shaping of our planet. Indeed, the region in which the tight structural couplings foregrounded by Earth system scientists actually operate might best be seen as a slender envelope, a critial but membraneous interzone where the overwhelmingly *non-reciprocated* forces of the inner Earth and the sun converge.

It is only relatively recently that social and philosphical thinkers have begun to return in a sustained way to the ontological promptings of the profoundly *inhuman* geology that so perturbed and inspired their late eighteenth–early nineteenth-century predecessors. As philosopher Iain Hamilton Grant (2011) would have it, it is geology that offers thought in general the starkest model of relationships that are non-correlative: those that are radically asymmater-ial, strongly hierarchical, and dependent rather than interdependent. What he refers to as the 'geology lesson' is the idea that everything that exists is in some sense dependent on the conditions that came before it. Existence – or the universe – in this way, is predominantly structured by 'lines of serial dependency, stratum upon stratum' (Grant 2011: 44). Critical social, philoso-phical and political thinkers, it would seem, have shied away from affirming such subtending relations because they mistake them for being determinative or foundational: that is, they assume that identifying originary conditions impo-ses a restriction or a preconceived direction on what is to follow. But as Grant and fellow 'non-correlationist' thinkers insist, the lesson of geology is that antecedent or subtending conditions are always in excess of whatever forms and productions they give rise to. In other words, when new things emerge out of a pre-existing stratum, they only realize some of the manifold possibilities that inhere in their substrate (Grant 2011; see also Land 2011: 110–11).

In regard to Earth, as geographer Kai Bosworth recognizes, the implication of such an avowal of subtending stratal relations is that vital constructive and destructive processes must be seen to *exceed any logic of interconnectivity*:

> Ecological or geologic dangers, threats or catastrophes impinge upon us not due to a *lack* of understanding or thought by humans, but due to a

surplus of potentiality exhibited by the Earth. In order for this surplus to exist, it must *not* be essentially connected to every other part of the Earth system.

(2013: fn 4)

I am not implying that Earth systems thinkers have in any way skipped the 'geology lesson'. They are well aware of the brevity of the anthropic 'moment' within the greater span of Earth history. The idea that the surge of our own species is sudden, brief and belated is, after all, the fulcrum of the Anthropocene hypothesis. So too do many Earth systems scientists offer intriguing insights into the way that the coupled interactions they position at the crux of planetary systemicity are themselves nested within the larger dynamical systems of the cosmos (see Smolin 1997; Clark 2005). But in the always already political climate in which Earth systems theory has germinated, it seems to be accepted that putting the stress on social system-physical system *inter*-dependence provides the surest path to political pertinence. And this is an assumption with which socio-political thinkers, on account of their predilection for reciprocal relations and their long-standing suspicion of recourse to fully inhuman domains, have been largely complicit.

There are however social scientists and humanities scholars whose engagements with the geosciences – and reflexivity over their own disciplinary precepts – have led them to their own versions of the 'geology lesson'. So although Hamilton foregrounds the structural couplings that precipitate threshold shifts in the Earth system, he also knows when to back away from any presuppositon of symmetry or co-dependence. 'Our task now,' he declares, 'is to do what we can to pacify, or at least not aggravate further, *something vastly more powerful than we are*' (Hamilton 2014: 8 my italics). It is historian Dipesh Chakrabarty, perhaps more than any of his humanist compatriots, who has acknowledged the import of the Earth sciences' antecedent or subtending conditions and begun to probe what they might mean for rethinking the political. From the path-breaking 'Climate of History' (2009) paper onwards, Chakrabarty has been trying to convince fellow progressive thinkers that the crisis of human-induced climate change compels us to think beyond the time spans in which our familiar political categories and investments have purchase and to front up to the unequivocally inhuman reaches of Earth history. Conversing with paleoclimatology and other fields of geoscience, he reminds us that – however momentous the current (and deeply uneven) human imprint on climate might be – the issue of climate change cannot but implicate us in cycles, rhythms and periodicities that vastly exceed human tenure on the Earth (2014: 2–3). Anthropogenic climate change, Chakrabarty insists, makes little sense if it is orphaned from the inherent propensity of planetary climate to ebb and shift. 'Our current warming,' he avers, 'is an instance of planetary warming that has happened both on this planet and on other planets, humans or no humans, and with different consequences. It just so happens that the current warming of the Earth is of human doing' (2014: 22).

Some years ago cultural theorist Gayatri Chakravorty Spivak drew attention to the implication of human social life in biological and geological processes. Scouting the borderlands where '"history" moves into "geology"' (1999: 69, fn 86), she noted how such a move revealed limits on the human ability to 'make history in a deliberate way' (1995: 171). Chakrabarty extends and develops this logic in the context of the changes headlined by the Anthropocene. Taking the very convergence of human and Earth history at the current juncture as an initial impetus, he asks what it means that these two histories diverge radically if we extend our gaze far beyond the present. Resonating with the way that Zalasiewicz contextualizes the human stratum as a slender province sandwiched 'between the ancient past and the substantial future', Chakrabarty takes climate change and the Anthropocene problematic as a means of disclosing the yawning asynchrony between the human-centredness of the '"global" of globalization literature' and the much more-than-human scale of planetary dynamics (2014: 22). And this incongruity, he suggests, has profound implications for the way we think about politics. Citing climatologist David Archer, Chakrabarty writes: 'Archer goes to the heart of the problem here when he acknowledges that the million-year timescale of the planet's carbon cycle is "irrelevant for political considerations of climate change on human time scales"' (2014: 3).

Thinking in terms of the inherently dynamic and catastrophic nature of our planet, in this way, we are thrown up against the very limits of the political, the bounds of what can be negotiated or might be done differently. As literary theorist Claire Colebrook puts it in a related context, in countenancing a materiality that bears no trace whatsoever of human activity, the world of collective action and praxis confronts the 'monstrously impolitic' (2011: 11). For Spivak, for Chakrabarty, for Colebrook, by no means is the positing of such limit or threshold to the political a renunciation of responsibility or of the possibility of justice. But what it does start to do is to unsettle that laudable ambition of post-war global thinking to align human globality with the space-time of Earth. The dream of forging global unity, of 'creating one world and one humanity' (Mumford, 1954 cited in van Munster and Sylvest, 2014: 542), begins to unravel: not simply because humankind is shot through with inequality and difference, as has long been recognized, but because Earth in its very physicality convulses with differential and other-worlding forces.

Elaborating on the issue of what it might mean to allow these inassimilable – perhaps unimaginable – dimensions of the geologic to perturb the contours and categories of critical sociopolitical thought, Chakrabarty explains: 'I call these gaps or openings in the landscape of our thoughts rifts because they are like faultlines on a seemingly continuous surface; we have to keep crossing or straddling them as we think or speak of climate change' (2014: 3). In the final section, I pick up on this notion of 'rifts' in the spherical unity of Earth in both their literal and figural senses. Gesturing back to the ways in which global oneness has been represented and imagined in the post-war era, I consider how the experiences of a more fractious, multiple and 'ex-orbitant' globality might be expressed, and open the question of how ethics and politics might begin to measure up to the excesses of the Anthropocene.

Toward a politics and ethics of ex-orbitant planetarity

The irony of the post-war construction of globality, as we have seen, is that a divided and conflictual socio-political landscape produced the evidence that enabled Earth to be envisioned anew as a single, integrated entity. But we have also caught wind of a subsequent irony. From out of the core of the scientific construction of the planet as a unified system – from the very understanding of the tight coupling of its components, the seething complexity of its interconnections, the power and density of its feedback loops – an Earth began to materialise that had the potential to transform itself into whole new configurations. An Earth, in other words, that is not at one with itself. And in turn, this planetary rifting – this emergent non-self-identical image of Earth – has consequences for how we might think about the otherness or alterity within the human species and the potential to negotiate our own differences.

In ways that are as yet inchoate and unresolved, I have been suggesting, the post-1945 image of 'whole Earth' is disintegrating, fracturing, multiplying. As Zalasiewicz sums up it: 'the Earth seems to be less one planet, rather a number of different Earths that have succeeded each other in time, each with very different chemical, physical and biological states' (cited in Hamilton, 2014: 6). The idea of an Earth system with multiple possible states – at once linked and separated by an effectively imperceptible threshold – has been pivotal to this shift. But we should not overlook the onto-existential perturbations of a much older, but still evolving, geological science: the vision of a planet rent by great vertical subdivisions, each stratum an archive of once flourishing life forms permanently consigned to stone. And we would do well to remember that over two centuries ago, Immanuel Kant responded to the emerging geological evidence of a 'sequence of different world epochs' by brooding: 'How many such revolutions (including, certainly, many ancient organic beings no longer alive on the surface of the Earth) preceded the existence of man, and how many ... are still in prospect, is hidden from our enquiring gaze' (1993: 66–7).

If stratigraphy has long confronted its audiences with a succession of almost entirely inhuman worlds, so too is it now the site of speculation about a stratum defined by human residues – with all that this entails about imagining our own irreversible mineralization. While the image of the human reduced to a fossil trace in the stratigraphic column is another budding Anthropocene motif, we should keep in mind the presaging of this apparition in the thermonuclear anxieties of the post-war period. The connection is more than analogical, for it is one of the architects of the Anthropocene hypothesis, Paul Crutzen, who first proposed that aerosols and gases produced by nuclear explosion and fire would 'change the heat and radiative balance and dynamics of the Earth and the atmosphere' (Crutzen and Birks, 1982: 123). In this way, the concept of nuclear winter already motioned towards a sense that human impacts might transform the functioning of Earth at a systemic level, just as the research carried out in the Cold War 'nuclear era' had previously helped assemble this very systemicity.

Where the posited threshold transitions of the Anthropocene diverge most markedly from the earlier thematic of thermonuclear holocaust is in the much more clearly articulated role of Earth's own complex dynamics in their trajectory. But the social science reception of the abrupt climate change, Earth system threshold and Anthropocene theses may not have been helped by the fact that the idea of human geologic agency and the concept of a multi-state Earth turned up in our conceptual in-boxes more or less simultaneously. It might have been better for our own clarity of critical thinking had we absorbed and processed these two huge incitements separately, for they are by no means mutually implicated. As Chakrabarty and his geoscientist counterparts have underlined, there is little that our species could do that would make any great difference to the planet if the Earth system did not have its own inherent capacity for climate change or state-shifting. In this sense, it is important that social scientists and humanities scholars recognise that, even in the absence of human-induced climate change, even without anthropic disturbance of the reigning Earth system regime, this would still be a planet whose innate changeability poses fearsome challenges to human habitation and imposes stark limits on our capacities for collective action. For, as climatologist Richard Alley sums up the state of our incumbent geologic epoch, quite apart from any consideration of human 'forcing' of the Earth system, 'The current stable interval is among the longest in the record. Nature is thus likely to end our friendly climate, perhaps quite soon' (2000: 4).

Indeed, if we begin to think our human being and becoming *through* the geophysical, rather than just thinking critically or socio-politically *about* unstable Earth systems, then our various agencies, capabilities and potentialities might themselves be seen as conditioned by the long experience of living with planetary volatility (Clark 2011). In a quite literal sense, to take up the figure of the rift from Chakrabarty and from Hamilton and Grinevald, we humans might see ourselves as creatures of a shifting, convulsive and cosmically exposed Earth. As far as we know, the genus *Homo* emerged along a rift valley, the site of the largest and most enduring example on the planet of the fracturing that occurs when a landmass overlies a major upwelling or 'superplume' of the molten rock that makes up Earth's mantle (King and Bailey 2006; Clark 2012). Paleoclimatologists also stress the formative role of increased aridity in East Africa, the effect of regional tectonic uplift, orbital forcing (changes in the tilt of the Earth's axis and orbit) and global climate changes brought about by reductions in global carbon dioxide levels (Maslin and Christensen 2007). Planetary fracturing and ex-orbitance, it would appear, run deep in our becoming. As anthropologist Yves Coppens describes the emergence of the earliest humans: 'We are partly the fruit of an astronomic event, helped by a tectonic one, which produced a dramatic drought in periequatorial eastern Africa' (1999: 17). If the viciously see-sawing climatic fluctuations of the Pleistocene helped shape us into the species we became, they also contributed to the culling of our genus from multiple branches down to a single species, a reminder that what we now experience as human unity is itself the jittery and contingent expression of a cataclysmic Earth history (Gunaratnam and Clark 2012).

Just like any other species, we bear in our physiological make-up, our behaviour patterns, our own variation, the traces of the planetary instability our kind has endured. In this regard, critical thought about human difference may still be catching up with the shocks and the stimuli of a swiftly evolving Earth science, still struggling to come to terms with the implications of a planet that has not for many millions of years been anywhere near as stable as it has been for the last 10,000 years. What is fast becoming apparent is that an earlier imaginary of a naturally unified planet that is artificially rifted by human discord is losing its purchase. In so many ways, the extra-orbital whole-Earth photographs turn out to have been deceptive. Not only did the static 'blue marble' image show little of the dynamic interconnectivity of Earth's subsystems, the layers of active accretion that underpinned the planet's radiant surface or the multiplicity lurking behind oneness, it could not even hint at the possibility that human difference or alterity might itself express something of the differential forces proper to Earth itself.

'Both the Anthropocene and the scholarship that tries to grasp it are less than one and more than many,' observe Swanson, Nubandt and Tsing, riffing off an old anthropological slogan (2015: 151). If the question of how to depict Earth's strange new convolution of multiplicity and unity is a tricky one, perhaps even more so is the challenge of representing a humanity that is deeply divided both by sociopolitical and physical differentials – and yet at risk of being thrown together by the very event of its extinction. Unsurprisingly, the iconography of the Anthropocene is beset by paradox: thresholds whose precise co-ordinates will only be identified by their catastrophic violation, a human geologic stratum for which there will be no human witnesses, a posthuman planet gradually effacing the traces of the very being that is beginning to imagine this destiny.

No amount of scientific knowledge will bridge these rifts or aporias in our current experience of the Earth. For with the coming of the Anthropocene, and indeed, with the opening up of geological time more generally, literary theorist Timothy Morton argues, we confront 'an abyss whose reality becomes increasingly uncanny, not less, the more scientific instruments are able to probe it' (2012: 233). Tellingly, one of the most searching and poignant literary expressions of the current planetary predicament, Cormac McCarthy's *The Road*, evokes the concurrent disappearance of a physical world and a language to describe it: 'The world shrinking down about a raw core of parsible entities. The names of things following those things into oblivion. Colors. The name of birds. Things to eat' (2006: 293).

For all their good intentions, efforts to instate protection for planetary boundaries, to render the Earth system governable, or even more optimistially, to map out a 'good Anthropocene', still seem to be in thrall to the dream of synchronizing global humanity and planetarity that characterizes the 'high globality' of the post-war era (see Deudney and Mendenhall, this volume). But an Earth that is both open to the perturbations of the cosmos and replete with its own capacities for self-transformation has more in common with philosopher Jacques Derrida's sense of the 'non-contemporaneity with itself of the living present' (1994: xix): a logic he himself, late in life, had begun to extend to 'the fragile destiny of the planet' (2005: 117). Any politics and ethics that would work *through* rather than *about* the dynamism of Earth will need to accept that the passage across systemic thresholds lies not only ahead of us but also in our past; the idea that all of us who have made it through to the present have already, in our lines of descent, made it across a great many planetary rifts. And we will need to recognise that any ability to negotiate the schisms that will keep opening in the stratified, mobile and ex-orbitant body of the Earth is not only a matter of the skills we might wish to cultivate, but is also the very condition of our capacity to be together and to act collectively.

If politics is itself enabled, triggered, aggravated and sometimes undone by the geophysical processes that subtend human existence, then the political is condemned to being experimental – in the material as well as the discursive or institutional sense (Clark, 2014). Earth systems governance theorist Victor Galaz and his colleagues seem to be moving in promising directions when they propose that 'dealing with ecological surprise and cascading effects of environmental change, requires multilevel ad hoc responses, where a high degree of flexibility and experimentation is allowed' (2012: 4). Although closing with 'allowed' here hints that the full import of what it might mean to be doing the work of improvisation and re-assembly in the midst of an opening planetary rift may still be sinking in. Wherever there is experimentation there is the risk of failure, of falling short, or of excessive success, meaning that a big part of any politics and ethics of an ex-orbitant planetarity will be how we choose to engage with others whose experiments have not delivered what they hoped for (see Masco, this volume). It is hard to imagine a collective response to abrupt and cascading change in the Earth system that is not also a reply to proliferating ethical demands and an ongoing work of mourning.

Finally, there is nothing in the reimagining of the world in-and-through its geophysical fracturing and multiplying that subtracts in any way from the quest for global justice that animated the most critical and sensitive ethico-political thought of the immediate post-war period. Although, in the spirit of Lewis Mumford's reflection that 'If politics means anything today, it must become "the art of the impossible"' (1954 cited in van Munster and Sylvest, 2014: 539), we might expect to see acknowledgment of the interminability or unattainability of any such task. Writing half a century after Mumford's diagnosis, Gayatri Chakravorty Spivak – beholding a globe ever-more fractured by social and environmental fault lines – will affirm 'the internationality of ecological justice in that impossible, undivided world of which one must dream, in view of the impossibility of which one must work, obsessively' (1999: 382).

References

Alley, Richard (2000) *The Two-Mile Time Machine: Ice Cores, Abrupt Climate Change, and Our Future*. Princeton, NJ: Princeton University Press.

Barnett, Clive (2005) 'Ways of Relating: Hospitality and the Acknowledgement of Otherness', *Progress in Human Geography*, 29(1): 5–21.

Biermann, Frank (2012) 'Planetary Boundaries and Earth System Governance: Exploring the Links', *Ecological Economics*, 81 (September): 4–9.

Biermann, Frank (2014) *Earth System Governance: World Politics in the Anthropocene*. Cambridge, MA: MIT Press.

Biermann, Frank, Michele Betsill, Joyeeta Gupta, Norichika Kanie, Louis Lebel, Diana Liverman, Heike Schroeder, Bernd Siebenhüner and Ruben Zondervan (2010) 'Earth System Governance: A Research Framework', *International Environmental Agreements*, 10(4): 277–298.

Bosworth, Kai (2013) 'Notes Towards a Geological Uprising by way of a Dark Feminism', *Society and Space*. Available at http://societyandspace.com/reviews/reviews-archive/woodard-2013-kai-bosworth (accessed 27 January 2015).

Broecker, Wallace (1987), 'Unpleasant Surprises in the Greenhouse', *Nature*, 328 (9 July): 123–126.

Chakrabarty, Dipesh (2009) 'The Climate of History: Four Theses', *Critical Inquiry*, 35(2): 197–222.

Chakrabarty, Dipesh (2014) 'Climate and Capital: On Conjoined Histories', *Critical Inquiry*, 41(1): 1–23.

Clark, Nigel (2005) 'Ex-orbitant Globality', *Theory, Culture & Society*, 22(5): 165–185.

Clark, Nigel (2011) *Inhuman Nature: Sociable Life on a Dynamic Planet*. London: Sage.

Clark, Nigel (2012) 'Rock, Life, Fire: Speculative Geophysics and the Anthropocene', *Oxford Literary Review*, 34(2): 259–276.

Clark, Nigel (2013) 'Geoengineering and Geologic Politics', *Environment and Planning A*, 45(12): 2825–2832.

Clark, Nigel (2014) 'Geo-Politics and the Disaster of the Anthropocene', *The Sociological Review*, 62(S1): 19–37.

Colebrook, Claire (2011) 'Matter without Bodies', *Derrida Today*, 4(1): 1–20.

Coppens, Yves (1999) 'Introduction', in Timothy Bromage and Schrenk Friedemann (eds) *African Biogeography, Climate Change and Human Evolution* New York and Oxford: Oxford University Press, pp. 13–18.

Crutzen, Paul (2002) 'Geology of Mankind', *Nature*, 415(6867): 3–23.

Crutzen, Paul and John Birks (1982) 'The Atmosphere after a Nuclear War: Twilight at Noon', *Ambio*, 2(2–3): 115–125.

Davis, Mike (1996), 'Cosmic Dancers on History's Stage? The Permanent Revolution in the Earth Sciences', *New Left Review*, 217 (May/June): 48–84.

Derrida, Jacques (1994) *Spectres of Marx: The State of the Debt, the Work of Mourning, and the New International*. New York: Routledge.

Derrida, Jacques (2005) *Rogues: Two Essays on Reason*. Stanford, CA: Stanford University Press.

Galaz, Victor, Frank Biermann, Beatrice Crona, Derk Loorbach, Carl Folke, Per Olsson, Måns Nilsson, Jeremy Persson, Åsa Allouche and Gunilla Reischl (2012) "Planetary Boundaries": Exploring the Challenges for Global Environmental Governance', *Current Opinion in Environmental Sustainability*, 4(1): 80–87.

Grant, Iain Hamilton (2011) 'Mining Conditions: A Response to Harman', in Levi Bryant, Nick Srnicek and Graham Harman (eds) *The Speculative Turn: Continental Materialism and Realism*. Melbourne: re.press: 41–46.

Gunaratnam, Yasmin and Nigel Clark (2012) 'Deep Race: Climate Change and Planetary Humanism', *Darkmatter*, 9(1). Available at www.darkmatter101.org/site/2012/07/02/pre-race-post-race-climate-change-and-planetary-humanism/ (accessed 12 October 2015).

Hamilton, Clive (2014) 'Can Humans Survive the Anthropocene?' Available at http://clivehamilton.com/can-humans-survive-the-anthropocene/ (accessed 4 October 2015).

Hamilton, Clive (2015) 'Human Destiny in the Anthropocene', in Clive Hamilton, Christophe Bonneuil and Francois Gemenne (eds) *The Anthropocene and the Environmental Crisis: Rethinking Modernity in a New Epoch*. Abingdon: Routledge, pp. 32–43.

Hamilton, Clive and Jacques Grinevald (2015) 'Was the Anthropocene Anticipated?' *The Anthropocene Review*, 2(1): 1–14.

Hamilton, Clive, Christophe Bonneuil and Francois Gemenne (2015) 'Thinking the Anthropocene' in Clive Hamilton, Christophe Bonneuil and Francois Gemenne (eds) *The Anthropocene and the Environmental Crisis: Rethinking Modernity in a New Epoch*. Abingdon: Routledge.

Kant, Immanuel (1993 [1938]) *Opus Postumum*. Cambridge: Cambridge University Press.

King, Geoffrey and Bailey, Geoff (2006) 'Tectonics and Human Evolution', *Antiquity*, 80(308): 265–286.

Land, Nick (2011) *Fanged Noumena: Collected Writings 1987–2007*. Falmouth: Urbanomic.

McCarthy, Cormac (2006) *The Road*. London: Picador.

Masco, Joseph (2010) 'Bad Weather: On Planetary Crisis', *Social Studies of Science*, 40(1): 7–40.

Maslin, Mark and Beth Christensen (2007) 'Tectonics, Orbital Forcing, Global Climate Change, and Human Evolution in Africa', *Journal of Human Evolution*, 53(5): 443–464.

Morton, Timothy (2012), 'Ecology without the Present', *The Oxford Literary Review*, 34(2): 229–238.

van Munster, Rens and Casper Sylvest (2014) 'Reclaiming Nuclear Politics? Nuclear Realism, the H-bomb and Globality', *Security Dialogue*, 45(6): 530–547.

Rockström, J., W. Steffen, K. Noone, F. S. Chapin III, E. Lambin, T. Lenton, M. Scheffer, C. Folke, H. Schellnhuber, B. Nykvist, C. de Wit, T. Hughes, S. van der Leeuw, H. Rodhe, S. Sörlin, P. Snyder, R. Costanza, U. Svedin, M. Falkenmark, L. Karlberg, R. Corell, V. Fabry, J. Hansen, B. Walker, D. Liverman, K. Richardson, P. Crutzen and J. Foley (2009) 'Planetary Boundaries: Exploring the Safe Operating Space for Humanity', *Ecology and Society*, 14(2): 32.

Scheffer, M., S. Carpenter, J. A. Foley, C. Folkes and B. Walker (2001), 'Catastrophic Shifts in Ecosystems', *Nature*, 413 (11 October): 591–596.

Smolin, Lee (1997) *The Life of the Cosmos*. London: Weidenfeld and Nicolson.

Spivak, Gayatri Chakravorty (1995) 'Acting Bits/Identity Talk', in K. Appiah and H. L. Gates, Jr (eds) *Identities*, Chicago, IL: University of Chicago Press, pp. 147–180.

Spivak, Gayatri Chakravorty (1999) *A Critique of Postcolonial Reason: Toward a History of the Vanishing Present*. Cambridge, MA: Harvard University Press.

Steffen, W., A. Persson, L. Deutsch, J. Zalasiewicz, M. Williams, K. Richardson, C. Crumley, P. Crutzen, C. Folke, L. Gordon, M. Molina, V. Ramanathan, J. Rockström, M. Scheffer, H. J. Schellnhuber and U. Svedin (2011) 'The Anthropocene: From Global Change to Planetary Stewardship', *Ambio*, 40(7): 739–761.

Subcommission on Quaternary Stratigraphy (2015) 'Anthropocene Working Group'. Available at http://quaternary.stratigraphy.org/workinggroups/anthropocene/ (accessed 4 October 2015).

Swanson, Heather, Nils Bubandt and Anna Tsing (2015) 'Less Than One But More Than Many: Anthropocene as Science Fiction and Scholarship-in-the-Making', *Environment and Society: Advances in Research*, 6(1): 149–166

Szerszynski, Bronislaw (2012), 'The End of the End of Nature: The Anthropocene and the Fate of the Human', *The Oxford Literary Review*, 34(2): 165–184.

Urry, John (2005) 'The Complexity Turn', *Theory, Culture and Society*, 22(5): 1–14.

Westbroek, Pieter (1992), *Life as a Geological Force: Dynamics of the Earth*. New York: W. W. Norton.

Wijkman, Anders and Rockström, Johan (2012) *Bankrupting Nature: Denying our Planetary Boundaries*. Abingdon: Routledge.

Wood, Denis (2004) *Five Billion Years of Global Change: A History of the Land*. New York: The Guilford Press.

Yusoff, Kathryn (2013) 'Geologic Life: Prehistory, Climate, Futures in the Anthropocene', *Environment and Planning D: Society & Space*, 31(5): 779–795.

Zalasiewicz, Jan (2008) *The Earth after Us*. Oxford: Oxford University Press.

Zalasiewicz, J., M. Williams, W. Steffen, and P. Crutzen (2010) 'The New World of the "Anthropocene"', *Environmental Science and Technology*, 44(7): 2228–2231.

Zalasiewicz, J., M. Williams, R. Fortey, A. Smith, T. Barry, A. Coe, P. Bown, P. Rawson, A. Gale, P. Gibbard, J. Gregory, M. Hounslow, A. Kerr, P. Pearson, R. Knox, J. Powell, C. Water, J. Marshall, M. Oates and P. Stone (2011) 'Stratigraphy of the Anthropocene', *Philosophical Transactions of the Royal Society A*, 369(1938): 1036–1055.

7 Climatic globalities

Assembling the problems of global climate change

Samuel Randalls

Introduction

In 1989, Al Gore stated that 'we are witnessing an unprecedented and massive collision between our civilization and the Earth' (Gore 1989). Not only is our way of life at risk from emerging environmental threats and the conflicts they might engender; these threats are themselves the result of anthropogenic planetary changes. This interwoven story of humans and the global environment is a classic example of what we might call a form of planetary thinking or a condition of globality. Indeed, much of the literature on climate change assumes that a global environmental threat needs to be matched by global political tools and policies.

The one-world quality of environmental reasoning re-asserts the attractiveness of globalization (as process) and appeals to thinking globally. Globalization is classically thought of in terms of the growing expansion of international governance, increasingly mobile economic networks and the development of technologies that enable time-space compression. Globality, however, is often defined as a condition, a way of thinking on a planetary scale that is beyond globalization. While often signified in a singular form, a planetary condition of interconnectedness between natural and social systems can be deconstructed to reveal multiple political constitutions and contestations (van Munster and Sylvest, this volume). As Tsing (2000: 353) writes more broadly: 'globalisms themselves need to be interrogated as an interconnected, but not homogeneous, set of projects.' Globality is only possible within a particular historical conjunction of ideas that enable global spaces to emerge as objects of political concern (Bartelson 2010).[1]

One notable absence in accounts of globality is that they often assume a human globality that neglects the centrality of the planet's physical, chemical and natural systems (van Munster and Sylvest, this volume). By contrast, debates about the Anthropocene have foregrounded attention to the human role in shaping the Earth's environments as well as the vulnerability of humans to natural forces. Popularized from the work of Crutzen (2002), Steffen et al. (2007) and Ruddiman (2005), the Anthropocene has since become a shorthand for people discussing a new-found connection, an almost dialectical relationship, between humans and environmental processes that considers both the precarity of the planet as well as that of life on the planet (Clark 2010, 2014; this volume). Yet this vision of radical interconnectedness, a new argument for globality, is predicated on a great deal of debate about what exactly this means in practice and whether Anthropocene thinking (or the Anthropocenic gaze, Wahlberg 2014) is radically different from thinking globally, carefully or resiliently, or indeed whether it simply invokes a reformed 'natural-scientific universalism' (Baucom 2012).

The issue of climate change is a privileged analytical entry point for interrogating the connection between globality and the Anthropocene in more detail. While discourses of climate change have refocused attention on human-environment interconnectedness, they do not simply embrace an Anthropocenic view. Rather, they have engendered many different types of global thinking of which 'Anthropocenic globality' is only one. Hence, this chapter argues that there is a multiplicity of global climate problems at stake, from concerns about rising anthropogenic emissions increases to claims for justice and equity; from protecting national security to calls for a new cultural renaissance with nature to live within the Anthropocene. Each of these problem-frames enacts 'global climate change' in a different way and calls for a wide array of interventions with diverse, sometimes overlapping and sometimes contradictory consequences.

From this I draw a simple conclusion: climate change is not a singular problem. Climate change is enacted as a problem through different assemblies of practices, sciences, interventions, policies and ideas. Even given the tight coupling of science and policy in many climate change debates, these are not all referring to the same ontological reality to be managed, but rather have different goals and new entities in sight.[2] To develop the multiple climatic globalities argument, I first briefly review some of the ways we might discuss the assembling of the problems of climate change (Blok 2014) and the conceptual tools that may be of value. I then go on to deploy two separate analytical cuts. First, I consider how in the post-war period energy efficiency has been put forward as a solution to both global cooling (1970s) and global warming (1990s). Interestingly, the solution comes to legitimize very different worldviews within its enactment of a global climate. Second, I consider different proposed solutions to global warming and show how these emerge from different climatic artefacts, policies, practices and performances. The chapter concludes by offering some reflections on how to politically engage multiple climatic globalities.

Assembling climate change

Hulme (2009) and Malone (2009) have done extensive and very productive work in exploring the different ways in which climate change is framed as an issue. Malone (2009) for instance shows that the majority of climate change framings coalesce around the broad idea that more modernization will help solve this environmental issue, even if this does not diminish the continued vitality in other networks of more ethical, political, justice or even sceptically based discourses. It can be very tempting to relate these different discourses as merely different views of essentially the same problem. A brief look at the history of modern environmentalism, however, suggests that we need to go beyond accounts of a singular global climate condition. Some scholars have pinned environmentalism to a counter-cultural movement, originating particularly in the 1960s with the popularity of tracts like Rachel Carson's *Silent Spring* and the revival of ecotheological discourse (Anker 2013). Others instead argued that Cold War military politics and technologies have shaped the development of global environmental science (Hamblin 2013; Masco 2010).

Climate globalities can be both militarized and countercultural in origin exactly because they are not representative of a singular global climate condition. They express and engender multiple competing agendas, which are held together in a way that sometimes has greater friction and sometimes less so. Diverse assemblings of environmental concerns involve different practices and ways of living and have different political implications. Once we accept that global environmental issues, and climate change specifically, are multiply constituted through diverse scientific-political assemblages, the focus on trying to find the best solution (which view is the right one and how can we communicate it and act on it) shifts to asking a series of profound questions about how the assemblages are formed and partake in the politics of globality: In whose interests are globalities made? What kinds of practices are they enacted through/with? What kinds of materials, technologies, ecologies, and philosophies do they draw on? And what are the frictions created between these different networks?

To study the assembling of environmental issues and to draw out the multiple politics of globality, I draw inspiration from two bodies of literature. The first comes from Annemarie Mol's (2002; 2008) work exploring the multiplicity of the body in practice. Here I draw from Mol's (2002) work on the body in medical practice, which suggests that the variety of practices regarding atherosclerosis remakes the body and disease not as a singular entity neither as pluralist bodies. Mol (2002) rather suggests 'the body multiple' – more than one, less than many. She delinks the question of what to do from the question of what is real and argues that this 'politics-of-what' must 'assume that the end points of trials, the goals sought for, are political in character' (Mol 2002: 175). Politics opens up questions rather than solving them through facts or argument.

Lahsen's (2009) ethnographic engagement with scientists and policymakers in different ministries in Brazil shows how Mol's argument about 'the body multiple' can be used to understand how climate science is multiply constituted in these political environments in very different ways. For example, the Ministry of Science and Technology remained much more sceptical of the 'European' science on the Amazon being a carbon sink that appeared to legitimate the emergence of financial mechanisms to avoid deforestation, while those close to the large-scale biosphere-atmospheric experiment in the Amazon – including the media, the IPCC and the United Nations Framework Convention on Climate Change (UNFCCC) negotiating teams, and the majority of the Brazilian government – supported the scientists' idea of the Amazon as a great carbon sink. While part of this is about the interplay of local and international politics, the interesting point is that the science of what the Amazon is (a carbon sink or not) is tied together with these political reasonings – to use Sheila Jasanoff's (2006) language one can say these are co-produced. Lahsen's (2009) conclusion can be extended more broadly to embrace many aspects of climate change science; witness the debates between paleoclimatologists and contemporary climate modellers, the different communities within the IPCC (Hulme and Mahony 2010) or the recent friction about the uncertainties in the latest IPCC's assessment report (Maslin and Austin 2012). Scientists, in other words, do not unite around a singular climatic or Anthropocenic globality.[3]

The second inspiration comes from Marieke de Goede's (2012) use of assemblage theory in her account of terrorist financing. Here, de Goede argues that terrorist finance is an interweaving of 'culture, material praxis and calculative technology', which come together to 'make government possible' (de Goede 2012: 31). Applying her insights to studying climate change, we cannot simply separate out a real climate that is represented discursively in multiple ways. We need to trace the connections over disparate times and spaces, materials and discourses – the 'circulating references' (Latour 1987) – around which climate change assemblages are gathered and enacted. There is thus a certain constitutive or performative element of these assemblages in the diverse ways they materialize climate change. As I will argue, different ways of assembling climate change create their own definitions of the climate change that is imagined as being at risk or incomplete and in need of a solution.

Benson's (2012) exploration of the Argos satellite-based environmentally monitoring and surveillance system helps to illustrate this point. He shows that while the technological infrastructure provides a singular platform, it enables a multiplicity of visions, uses and practices with the data. This is because Argos needs customers (scientific and government primarily) to grow the commercial value of its market. The prioritization of challenges to be dealt with in the system changes over time as it is shaped by interest groups representing the most valuable customers – in most recent years, actors interested in climate change. Thus, within the space of this technology there is no uniform user or policy that emerges from this. Indeed, one can argue this more broadly about climate modelling, as the 'infrastructural globalism' involved in making global data and making data global are deployed in a wide diversity of ways by policymakers (Edwards 2010). Fixations on climate targets are counterposed with fears that models can never deliver *one* answer, not to mention the ways in which climate models have reshaped and been reshaped by changing expectations and modelling in weather forecasting too.

Even if a global imagination of the Anthropocene is advanced, a singular politics does not emerge.

Multiple climatic globalities 1: agreeing solutions

If the Anthropocene is said to re-awaken attention to the historical importance of human–environment relations, it is useful to consider how solutions to the problems of human impacts are woven together in different time periods to different concerns. This is an important way of getting at the question of the politics of globality and challenging the singularity that a global environmental ethic is often said to invoke. One oft-noted historical feature of climate change debates is the interest in and discussion of global cooling futures, particularly in the 1960s and 1970s. The popular fascination with the potential arrival of a new ice age was captured in popular books such as Calder's (1974) *The Weather Machine* and global cooling influenced attitudes to global atmospheric changes in important ways (see Figure 7.1).

Climate change could reduce food availability, enhance floods or droughts or failures in monsoons, threatening everyday life and likely leading to large political unrest. This was sometimes tinged with a Cold War fear that perhaps the Soviets (or the Americans) might be deliberately engineering the environment. Climate became endowed with cultural power, an idea that would reshape and reformulate a wide array of other discourses (Ross 1991).

Figure 7.1 Calder's projection of a new ice age
Source: The Impact Team 1977: 23.

Many responses to global cooling focused on the potential need to increase CO_2 emissions in the atmosphere, an argument that traces historically back to for example Svante Arrhenius in the late nineteenth century, who suggested that the planet might need heating up to save humanity (Fleming 1998). More industrial civilization could be just the answer to the climatic crisis. But as insecurity arose about the direction of future climate changes, cooling as well as warming rhetoric could be deployed to argue for the same kind of solutions. In other words, solutions could be multiply deployed to both warming and cooling.

A good example of this can be found in a 1977 book published under the auspices of The Impact Team and bound with two CIA reports as appendices. The underriding fear in *The Weather Conspiracy* (The Impact Team 1977) was of the dawning of a new ice age that would be hastened if society did not rapidly move to low carbon pathways. While the book tried to avoid radical views towards warming or cooling (see Figure 7.2), it erred on the side of making policy changes precisely as a precautionary measure in the event of an oncoming ice age describing the climate of the 1940s to 1970s as unprecedented and abnormally good for civilization and likely to be swiftly followed by cooling.

The proposed solution for the report's authors was energy efficiency. To prevent future climatic changes, individuals should take simple solutions to reduce their energy consumption and thus reduce the future risks from environmental changes. Readers are advised to consider fuel-efficient cars and driving strategies, as well as car-pooling; at home, readers should install insulation, thermostat controls and lower energy light bulbs, take showers rather than baths, and they should lead the way on recycling and reducing waste. As the report states 'Each of us can, and should, save energy in other

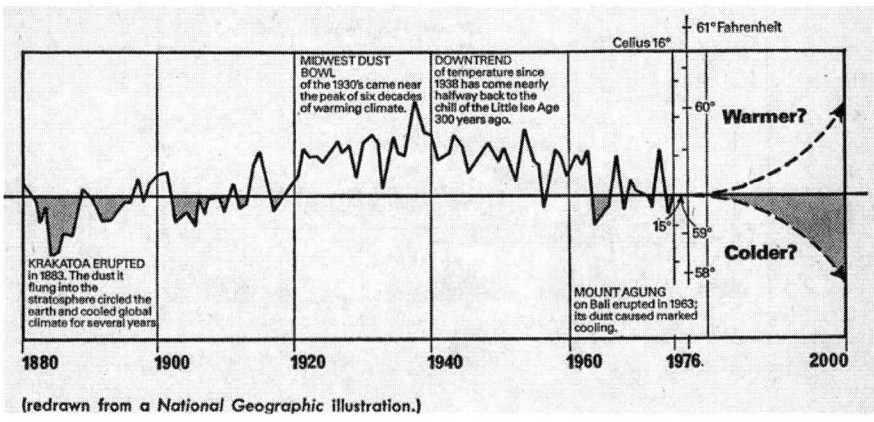

Figure 7.2 Warmer or colder?
Source: The Impact Team 1977: 62.

ways every day' (The Impact Team 1977: 139). All of this occurs in the name of protecting civilization from global climatic changes. Interestingly, the end of the report incorporated an open list of organizations to contact if the reader wished 'to become a crusader' (Impact Team 1977: 141) for the cause. Fighting global climate change was a war against history, in this case the history of ice ages (and so prior the Anthropocene).

I could draw from a very extensive range of literature to equally show how the same energy efficiency and reduced consumption solutions equally go to support the 'fight' against global warming and that the idea of a crusade, war or fight against climate change is undiminished (Hulme 2009). In the case of global warming, however, the same policies are wrapped up into a rather different vision of the climate at risk – one that is warmer on average rather than cooler, and one in which the next ice age is rather less a concern than the rapidly rising temperatures that may trigger extreme events. Interestingly, in the case of warming discourses, the normal climate is frequently judged to be pre-industrial temperature since that is what international climate policy is compared to (how many degrees of warming above pre-industrial temperature), while for cooling discourses it was preventing normal weather (ice ages) in the interest of preserving our abnormally warm conditions.

Al Gore's 'An Inconvenient Truth' is representative of the concern with rising temperatures, as his presentation of solutions (energy efficient cars, renewable energy, energy efficiency, carbon capture and storage, cycling and public transportation solutions) is couched in the language of ecological modernization and green growth (Luke 2008). Gore likewise sets this out as a moral challenge and it is consistent with his earlier 1989 warning that climate change would be dealt with internationally at a point when countries became concerned about their future security. Gore's climate warriors then adopt the same policies as the crusaders of The Impact Team, but for an entirely different climatic goal: the prevention of global warming in the Anthropocene.

Policies and science on climate change are not tied together so tightly that they cannot be unwoven and rewoven in various different ways. Reducing energy consumption works whether the goal is to prevent cooling or warming – there is a unity around the practice, even while the at-risk planetary status differs. The climatic goal is vastly different (prevent warming or cooling), although both share a desire to preserve a good climate for humanity to flourish.

Multiple climatic globalities 2: disagreeing solutions

Similar solutions can be attached to different end goals, hence the politics of globality is not singular, but multiple. If we turn the analysis now to proposed solutions to global warming, we will also see another set of multiple globalities at work. If global warming, as climate change, is the predominant problem today amidst a catalogue of human impacts on the environment, it is not a singular problem for which people simply propose different kinds of solutions. Rather, there are a number of different climate change assemblages or groups of practices of 'solutions' that enact particular problem-solution formations, that variously overlap or conflict with other formations. It is through these frictions that the multiple politics of globality become visible.

Blok (2014) argues that there are 'multiple climatic problems' and presents a series of problematizations; interdependent areas in which a problem becomes delineated and made potentially resolvable, but which do not encompass nor accrue to a form of totalizing climate change governance. This has important implications for how we think about the emergence of an idiom of global stewardship within an Anthropocenic imagination. Here I explore three sites in brief (individual behavioural change, market led actions and climate security) in relation to the good outcome envisioned in these assemblages.

Climate change has been highlighted as a global economic issue in reports that show the economic advantage of investing money now in carbon emissions reduction to prevent future high costs from climate damages (Stern 2007). This constructs a global economic entity that is vulnerable to climate change, but also a global climate vulnerable to the output of the economy. A simple cost-benefit equation, however, does not work in the economic interests of all countries involved in the climate policy negotiations. Some benefit and others lose from future climate change scenarios, with the increase in global temperature up to 2 degrees Celsius considered to be economically optimal or at least not detrimental to global GDP because of the opening up of large grain areas in Russia and North America. This poses a problem for those arguing that carbon dioxide emissions should be reduced to the lowest possible level as it is not in the global economic interest to do so (Randalls 2011a). For global climatic governance, the national economy (as GDP) has to be reshaped into a global entity to then be managed efficiently, with common parlance including terms like 'cost-effectiveness', 'internalizing externalities' and the 'market as the ideal information processor'.

Carbon markets have been the dominant solution to this economic problem. They assemble sets of calculations and models of carbon emissions within a financial trading environment (MacKenzie 2009) where the ticker price for the credits becomes a source of profit as much as of concerted efforts to reduce emissions. Paterson and Stripple (2012) deploy the term 'virtuous carbon' to emphasize the ways in which virtuality and morality are entwined in carbon markets such that the moral goodness of carbon trading to 'save the planet' outweighs specific critiques of market failures. But the reshaping of national economies goes beyond carbon markets, as climate change has become a hook to tie to a variety of economic interests. Janković and Bowman (2013) have argued that many businesses now require the continual proliferation of fears and concerns about climate change to continue stimulating and incentivizing the growth of the climate business sector. Indeed, they suggest that 'it seems green investment is becoming not so much a solution but an end in itself' (Janković and Bowman 2013: 252). Likewise, Funk (2014) has traced a diverse set of ways in which businesses are trying to profit from the new interest in climate change solutions including insurance, adaptation technologies and flood defence.

In other words, assembling a business case around climate change requires a continual reminder of business performance and growth in environmental investment that relies less on an external referent – 'an environmental ontology of climate crisis' (Janković and Bowman 2013: 252) – than its own internal, capitalistic logics. As such, this global assemblage draws legitimacy from climate science (as meta-discourse, rather than in specific pronouncements), but does not require the practices of green investment to simply be solutions to climate change. Rather they also have their own logic, which is about growing the economic value and performance of environmental business (see Figure 7.3). So in these practices, climate change is cast as a climate that is stable for economic activity, whether this is by assembling a global optimal climate or an optimal business environment to profit from the environmental changes.

These practices actively shape an economic and environmental globality. To take a rather different example, for some commentators a global issue like climate change is a collective problem and therefore needs to be 'brought home' to encourage cultural and moral change. Responsibility for consumption and self-governance encourages multi-scalar thinking captured in the slogan 'think globally, act locally'. It also expands the scope of action to all humankind as drivers of consumption. As a Conservative member of the UK parliament put it: 'You can't blame dying forests on slick entrepreneurs and acid rain on Yuppees. Industry exists to meet the demands of the community.'[4] Individualization takes many different forms, but there are some commonalities. One common approach is towards encouraging people to change behaviours in non-didactic ways. This is perhaps best exemplified in the term 'nudge', which Thaler and Sunstein's (2009) use to describe 'libertarian paternalist' interventions. These change the choice architecture through intervening in practices or product displays that make it an easier decision to buy 'better' products. Labels on products to represent calculative or technical assessments of calories, carbon, ethical trading standards and so on have become a key intervention to shape the globally responsible citizen. The combination of choice and calculation is at the heart of this. In personal carbon allowance proposals, for example, as Parag and Strickland (2009) point out, they use the word 'budgeting' to confirm similarities with financial budgetary management. Carbon can simply be organized and managed like finance, diet, alcohol units or other parts of people's everyday lives. There is also an affective engagement particularly in terms of what Isin (2004) discusses as the neurotic register. Citizens are to be concerned enough to worry about their personal footprints as well as act calculatively to manage the risks.

Another shared argument is that household technological changes are tied to moral changes. Common interventions would be choosing more efficient transportation, insulation, turning down thermostats and choosing locally produced foods. These technologies and practices however are not just about

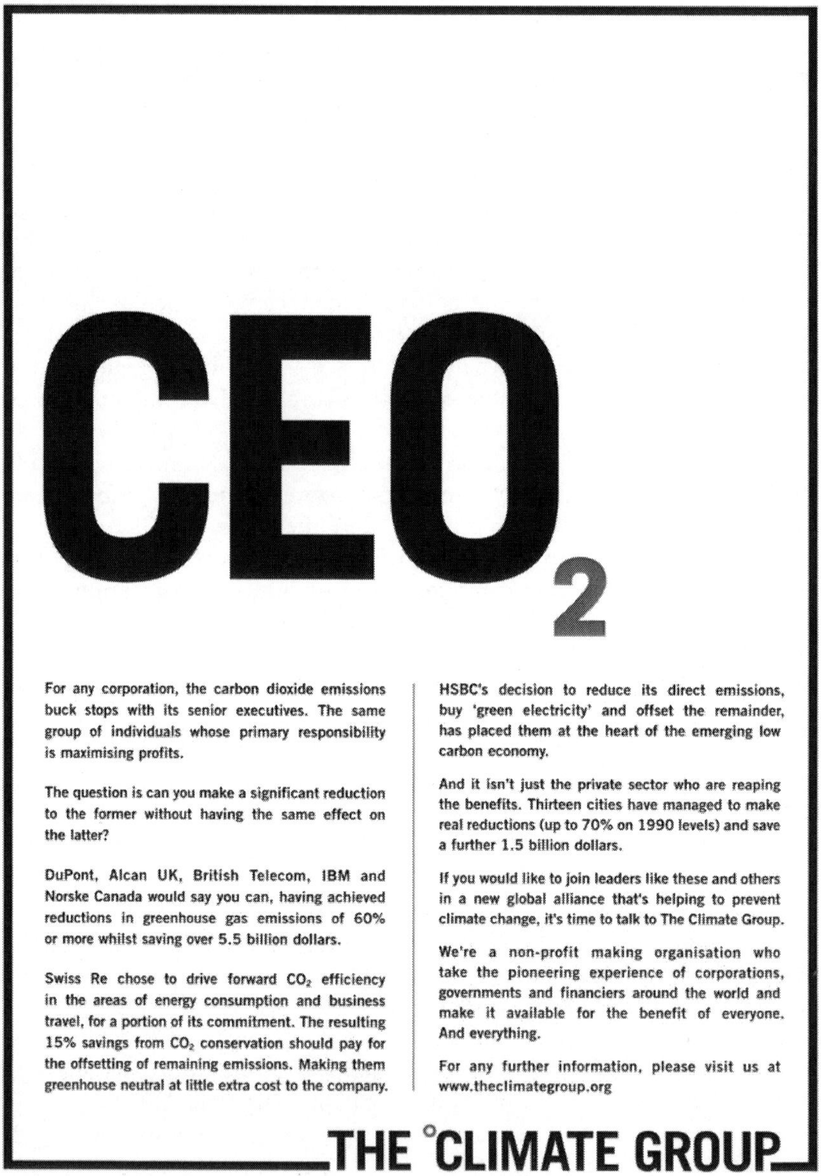

Figure 7.3 The carbon market
Source: 'Low-Carbon Leaders' supplement, *Environmental Finance* 2005.

reducing emissions. They have a more complex role in our lifestyles as they produce a climate-concerned subject that is to manage climate change (Hargreaves 2014), not least to reduce feelings of planetary guilt. As Mol (2008: 58) writes: 'technologies do not subject themselves to what we wish them to do, but interfere with who we are.' A focus on individual behavioural change enacts practices that in purporting to govern climate change are equally as much about encouraging new ways of living (see Figure 7.4).

It is not just a neutral threat of climate change in which behavioural change is one of many options to resolve the problem, but rather that climate change is modelled and counted by establishing 'carbon equivalency' as the commodity that is to be managed to save the planet. Climate change is enacted as a problem of carbon management, legitimating interventions into better governing the use of carbon in people's lives. The desired outcome of this politics of globality is the rational carbon consumer, who will enable the reduction of carbon dioxide emissions to prevent climate change. In this image, a global citizenship is at stake, where the consumer is constituted as a responsible steward of the Earth that carefully manages the accelerated human impacts on the environment in the Anthropocene. Taking care is shaped and represented as an ideal modality for living safely in the Anthropocene, albeit it is frequently reduced to an individualized, behavioural signal that misses the kinds of ethical reconfigurations that others have associated with global citizenship.

The final example concerns the enactment of climate change as a global security risk through an assembling of security officials, risk models and the legitimating power of rhetoric of threat and fear. For all this seeming authority, however, Oels (2014) suggests that there has been rather less in the way of dramatic interventions than might be expected from climate change as an exceptional state. That said, the security assembling of climate change is important, not least given the desire to intervene directly in terms of geo-engineering (Masco, this volume) or the desire to monitor or govern potentially 'dangerous' populations. Indeed, these security practices precisely govern through an interconnected globality in which risks appear from a globally induced cause and with global consequences. Governments are not only anticipating potential worst-case scenarios but also actively imagining a phantasmagoria that becomes real (de Goede and Randalls 2009) as displayed in images, films and discourses about climate change. US and German security reports have explored the kinds of risks that might be developing as a result of climate change (see Figure 7.5). Particular places and populations become risky: the North African and Middle-Eastern water-deprived regions that might foster Islamic radicalism or the Bangladeshi migrants fleeing rising waters into neighbouring India.

Climate threats are defined through scientific analysis and modelling, but these are not without political assumptions. For example in climate-health research, Southeast Asian countries, unlike European ones, are predicted to have significant deaths from malnutrition, primarily because of a modelled

Figure 7.4 The making of climate-concerned subjects
Source: 'Confronting Climate Risk' supplement, *Environmental Finance* 2007.

assumption that the European Union will supply food to all its member states whereas the Southeast Asian countries will be less co-operative with each other (Randalls 2011b).

These lists, model outputs and maps become performative, particularly as models are increasingly used to adjudicate the success of policy goals. Interventions to prevent the radicalization or migration of the climatically vulnerable

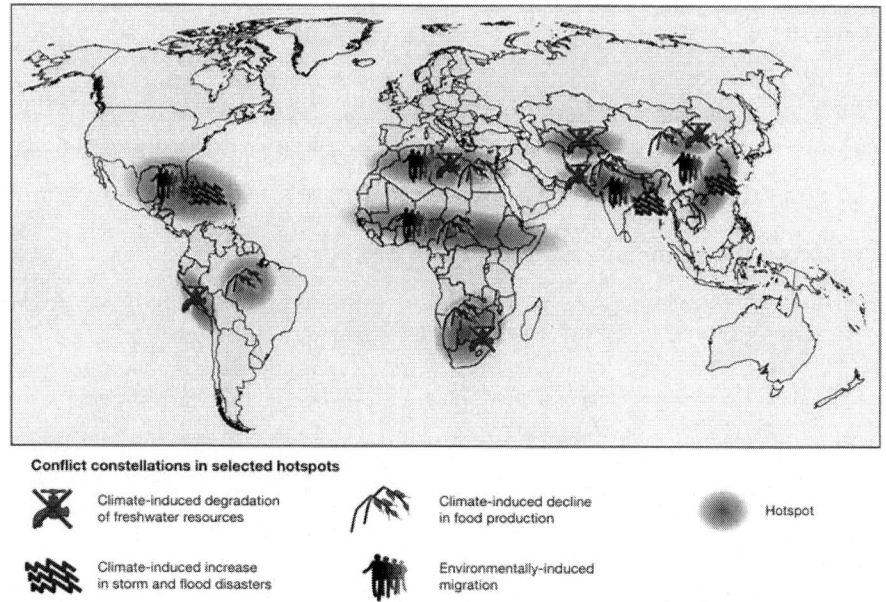

Conflict constellations in selected hotspots

Climate-induced degradation
of freshwater resources

Climate-induced decline
in food production

Hotspot

Climate-induced increase
in storm and flood disasters

Environmentally-induced
migration

Figure 7.5 The climate-security nexus
Source: Diagram from an Advisory Council report on climate security risks published through the German government (WBGU 2007). Reproduced with permission from the WBGU.

are combined with invocations to enhance food and water security to prevent these outcomes and forestall deaths. Yamane (2009) highlights how sub-sistence farmers in Sri Lanka are defined through agro-ecological maps as particularly vulnerable to the risks of climate change and in need of developing export-led agriculture to reduce their vulnerability. This may work acceptably when the cash flows in, but acts to hinder the back-up subsistence economy that also had supported these farmers through previous years of poor weather. Ironically, interventions to target the security risks of climate change engender the same kinds of vulnerabilities that they are supposed to be protecting against.

The climate-security assemblages not only have an effect on lives, they enact new categories ('the climate migrant', 'the vulnerable', 'the potential climate-induced terrorist') that then redefine a whole set of lives in specific ways (Baldwin 2013). At the same time, climate change becomes dangerous or threatening ontologically in a way that will affect Western lifestyles or national interests (Kurz et al. 2010). The 'good' outcome is a world secured from climate change (impacts), but that does not necessarily mean interventions to prevent climate change. An alternative can be compensation through insurance mechanisms (Stripple 2012), while a securitized climatic globality prioritizes a particular way of exploring environmental risks and their human consequences with a focus on intervention (whether in the human or material environment) to deal directly with risky populations and protect the rest of the world. People's ways of life are to be constrained by the interventions to secure the privileged individuals ability to continue the right to choose. In this context, the assemblage climate change enacts a highly divided and unequal form of globality.

Frictions and alignments in climatic globalities

One objection that might be raised at this point is that surely these various approaches can and do align. In other words they are different *representations* of the same problem (that of global climate change). It is of course quite probable that different climate assemblages can work together, but in other cases they will come into conflict. Kurz et al. (2010) have shown that 'maintaining our lifestyles' is one of the most dominant discourses dominating the popular literature related to climate change, but it is doubtful whether everyone on the planet is or can be gathered around such an invocation.

Nevertheless, a good example of this politics of globality can be gleaned from Funk's (2014) recent book *Windfall* exploring the ways in which financial profit and security discourse can align. Climate migration interventions work both to securitize the risks of a dry Sahara for increasing attempts of people to cross to Europe, while at the same time governments invest money and expertise in trying to make the Sahara productive through forestry projects or by developing large solar energy schemes. Perhaps the best instance of lifestyle management can be seen in the rapidly growing green land grabs where entrepreneurs from countries deemed vulnerable to climate change buy land elsewhere in the world to ensure the continuation of their food supply in a future climate-constrained world. China pursued land deals worldwide (indeed, its attempt to extract three million acres in Madagascar is considered a factor in the political coup there), Qatar sought land in Kenya; Kuwait in Cambodia – and so on (these are all detailed in Funk 2014).

Making money aligns with an expropriation of land and a rather fragmented global geography of climate-change winners and losers that traverses borders in a new globality of connections. On the one hand, a stable global economy, particularly for oil-producing countries, depends on the securitized practices that enable the way of life for those in richer countries to continue as before. Yet this image of a climate globality seems rather disconnected from the 'think globally, act locally' slogans of classical environmentalism on the other. Likewise, the profit–security linkage is distinctly at odds with global policy-making focused on reducing CO_2 emissions. At a fundamental level, these futures being enacted are in a tense relationship with each other. They create 'friction' (Mol 2002), which is in part how we know they are enacting very different climate globalities.

It is not just that these different practices conflict as they reshape geopolitical borders and economic activities. They also conflict in their fundamental vision of what the ontological problem of climate change is about, as well as in their political attempt to secure a future given this ontology (some are more empowered than others). In other words, a stable economic climate might not be the same as a stable climate or a secure climate or a climate in which humans engage in a careful acceptance of precarity (Clark 2010; Hird 2010). Different problem framings assemble a global imagination of climate risk through different expertise, models, imaginations, concerns and idealized solutions. These are partly related to power. For example, the vision of security prompts attention to particular risky areas regardless of whether that vulnerability is caused by human-induced or natural climatic changes (or climate at all), while for climate change adaptation financing, vulnerability to climate change is reworked into interventions to make populations economically productive in generating GDP as a strategy to resolve these new climate risks. Concurrently, the global economy (as the ontological entity at risk) is claimed to be vulnerable to the risks from global climate change, but at the same time environmentalist campaigners argue that the capitalist economy is the ultimate cause of climate change (the planet as ontological entity at risk).

For some, climate change cannot be solved without recourse to justice and equity, a claim that in turn lies rather unheeded in the argument that the planet does not care where CO_2 emissions are reduced as it is the global circulation of molecules that matters. Different global imaginaries assemble climate change in specific ways and envisage particular interventions to resolve what they perceive to be the core problem and ontological entity at risk with/through/from/of climate change, interventions that overlap and contradict in various ways with other imaginaries of the problem at stake. A just solution may not solve the risks of climate change to the global capitalist economy, while an economically optimal solution may not reduce CO_2 emissions, and reducing CO_2 can be done without specific heed to justice or economic concerns.

Much also depends on the strength of the networks being built around these climate problems (Blok 2014), as some have more allies than others. Thus, the argument needs to take account of the importance of power, as certain types of ideas, technologies and practices coalesce into concrete enactments of climate change while others are excluded, not enacted. What is fundamentally obscured in a 'one globality' argument is that each of these assemblages of practices makes claims about the nature of the outcome to be achieved, which in turn is irreducibly tied to ontological and political-philosophical commitments about the good life. Practices compete to define climate change in different ways such that no simple reductive resolution is possible.

Taking the Anthropocene as a given starting point may stand in the way of our need to carefully articulate what kinds of entities, things, people and ecologies are at play in the various enactments of planetary concern, thinking globally or assembling climatic globalities. It is important to see these diverse practices as enacting and performing different climatic globalities and to see these as ontological, epistemological and political-philosophical claims. Claims to engineer an optimal climate for production and consumption should be taken just as seriously as claims that thinking globally might open up new ethical and political arrangements. These are not mere ideas that float detached from material implications or from powerful organizing bodies like neoliberal think tanks.

Conclusions

While it can be tempting to think of the interconnected natural and social systems invoked by the concept of the Anthropocene as enabling a closer interaction and recognition of human–environmental relations, I have argued that it would be unwise to simply view this as the emergence of a new, universal planetary globality. Even in the case of a purportedly global environmental risk like climate change, there are a wide variety of ways in which climate change is enacted or assembled through different practices, models, technologies and discourses. Through the examples of energy efficiency in global cooling and warming debates and the different ways in which contemporary climate change is invoked as a security, economic and individual behavioural issue, I have suggested that these different practices assemble rather different climatic globalities in practice. These globalities are neither completely separate nor simply different representations of the same object. They have diverse political effects and constitute in different ways the 'goods' to be achieved and the 'bads' to be avoided. As Tsing (2000: 351) suggests, we need to 'reverse this [singular] globalist thinking to turn concerns about the global back into researchable questions' that incorporate 'critical distance' in our evaluations of global visions.

If the idea of a global climate change problem to be solved is so dominant (as Hulme 2009, suggests), what might be gained from thinking about climatic globalities as multiple rather than as one totalizing globality? As Mol (2002: 184) puts it: 'Presenting the *body multiple* as the reality we live with is not a solution to a problem, but a way of changing a host of intellectual reflexes.' This is why a multiple politics of globality is crucial. Exploring the diverse assemblings of climatic and Anthropocenic globalities resists buying into singular claims about environmental change that can only be discussed on their own terms. For example, one common climate policy formulation simply states that from an agreement about a global mean temperature target and resultant emissions target, it is simply a case of putting into place policies designed to reduce emissions to meet that goal. This, however, ignores many important questions that one could ask about the kind of lives to be lived and whether or not this policy ideal is embraced by other climate change practices, such as those embedded in security or behavioural change frames.

In other words, a singular climate change global problem framing in which climate becomes a resolvable technical issue circumscribes the kinds of debates that are crucial for thinking through the planetary implications of a renewed focus on climate (Clark 2010; this volume). Planetary thinking must necessarily be multiple, laying bare the ways in which globalities are assembled through different ideas, artefacts, images and practices. Rather than end up as an enthusiast or critic, as occurred with some of the globalization literature, the requirement to empirically analyse the multiple ways in which planetary globalities are assembled generates the political grounds to assess which of these assemblages to support or contest, engage with or resist.

Notes

1 The emergence of planetary images from space, often held up as a key condition for the emergence of globality (Poole, 2008), are only relevant within a particular cultural and moral reasoning that hints at the value of such a global view (Jasanoff, 2004).
2 I will use the term 'global warming' at various points where I wish to emphasize that I am referring to are global warming inspired climate change literatures as opposed to global cooling ones. In other places, I will simply use the term 'climate change' to designate all types of climatic change.
3 A similar multiplicity emerges in the dating of the Anthropocene. For Ruddiman (2005) the Anthropocene has emerged over thousands of years of human history, while Crutzen and Steffen (2003) date its emergence to the development of the steam engine in the late eighteenth century but also suggest that the accelerated human impacts since 1950 are central to the Anthropocene.
4 Speech by Conservative MP Peter Brooke in October 1988, short transcript; copy held by the author.

References

Anker, Peder (2013) 'The call for a new ecotheology in Norway', *Journal for the Study of Religion, Nature and Culture*, 7(2): 187–207.

Baldwin, Andrew (2013) 'Racialisation and the figure of the climate change migrant', *Environment and Planning: A*, 45(6): 1474–1490.

Bartelson, Jens (2010) 'The social construction of globality', *International Political Sociology*, 4(3): 219–235.

Baucom, Ian (2012) 'The human shore: postcolonial studies in an age of natural science', *History of the Present*, 2(1): 1–23.

Benson, Etienne (2012) 'One infrastructure, many global visions: the commercialization and diversification of Argos, a satellite-based environmental surveillance system', *Social Studies of Science*, 42(6): 843–868.

Blok, Anders (2014) 'Experimenting on climate governmentality with actor-network theory', in: Johannes Stripple and Harriet Bulkeley (eds) *Governing the Climate: New Approaches to Rationality, Power and Politics*. Cambridge: Cambridge University Press, pp. 42–58.

Calder, Nigel (1974) *The Weather Machine and the Threat of Ice*. London: BBC.

Clark, Nigel (2010) 'Volatile worlds, vulnerable bodies: confronting abrupt climate change', *Theory, Culture and Society*, 27(2–3): 31–53.

Clark, Nigel (2014) 'Geo-politics and the disaster of the Anthropocene', *The Sociological Review*, 62(S1): 19–37.

Clark, Nigel and Nick Stevenson (2003) 'Care in the time of catastrophe: citizenship, community and the ecological imagination', *Journal of Human Rights*, 2(2): 235–246.

Crutzen, Paul (2002) 'Geology of mankind', *Nature*, 415 (3 January): 23.

Crutzen, Paul and Will Steffen (2003) 'How long have we been in the Anthropocene era?', *Climatic Change*, 61(3): 251–257.

Edwards, Paul (2010) *A Vast Machine: Computer Models, Climate Data, and the Politics of Global Warming*. Cambridge, MA: MIT Press.

Fleming, James Rodger (1998) *Historical Perspectives on Climate Change*. New York: Oxford University Press.

Funk, McKenzie (2014) *Windfall: The Booming Business of Global Warming*. New York: Penguin.

de Goede, Marieke (2012) *Speculative Security: The Politics of Pursuing Terrorist Monies*. Minneapolis: University of Minnesota Press.

de Goede, Marieke and Samuel Randalls (2009) 'Precaution, pre-emption: arts and technologies of the actionable future', *Environment and Planning: D*, 27(5): 859–878.

Gore, Al (1989) 'The global environment: a national security issue', in Ruth DeFries and Thomas Malone (eds) *Global Change and Our Common Future*. Washington, DC: National Academy Press, pp. 177–186.

Hamblin, Jacob Darwin (2013) *Arming Mother Nature: The Birth of Catastrophic Environmentalism*. New York: Oxford University Press.

Hargreaves, Tom (2014) 'Smart meters and the governance of energy use in the household', in Johannes Stripple and Harriet Bulkeley (eds) *Governing the climate: New Approaches to Rationality, Power and Politics*. Cambridge: Cambridge University Press, pp. 127–143.

Hird, Myra (2010) 'Indifferent globality: Gaia, symbiosis and "other worldliness"', *Theory, Culture and Society*, 27(2–3): 54–72.

Hulme, Mike (2009) *Why We Disagree about Climate Change*. Cambridge: Cambridge University Press.

Hulme, Mike and Martin Mahony (2010) 'Climate change: what do we know about the IPCC?', *Progress in Physical Geography*, 34(5): 705–718.

Isin, Engin (2004) 'The neurotic citizen', *Citizenship Studies*, 8(3) 217–235.

Janković, Vladimir and Andrew Bowman (2013) 'After the green gold rush: the construction of climate change as a market transition', *Economy and Society*, 43(2): 233–259.

Jasanoff, Sheila (2004) 'Heaven and Earth: the politics of environmental images', in Sheila Jasanoff and Marybeth Long Martello (eds) *Earthly Politics: Local and Global in Environmental Governance*. Cambridge, MA: MIT Press, pp. 31–52.

Jasanoff, Sheila (2006) 'The idiom of co-production', in Sheila Jasanoff (ed.) *States of Knowledge: The Co-production of Science and Social Order*. Abingdon: Routledge, pp. 1–12.

Kurz, Tim, Martha Augoustinos and Shona Crabb (2010) 'Contesting the "national interest" and maintaining "our lifestyle": a discursive analysis of political rhetoric around climate change', *British Journal of Social Psychology*, 49(3): 601–625.

Lahsen, Myanna (2009) 'A science-policy interface in the global south: the politics of carbon sinks and science in Brazil', *Climatic Change*, 97(3): 339–372.

Latour, Bruno (1987) *Science in Action: How to Follow Scientists and Engineers through Society*. Cambridge, MA: Harvard University Press.

Luke, Timothy (2008) 'The politics of true convenience or inconvenient truth: struggles over how to sustain capitalism, democracy, and ecology in the 21st century', *Environment and Planning: A*, 40(8): 1811–1824.

MacKenzie, Donald (2009) 'Making things the same: gases, emission rights and the politics of carbon markets', *Accounting, Organizations and Society*, 34(3–4): 440–455.

Malone, Elizabeth (2009) *Debating Climate Change: Pathways through Argument to Agreement*. London: Earthscan.

Masco, Joseph (2010) 'Bad weather: on planetary crisis', *Social Studies of Science*, 40(1): 7–40.

Maslin, Mark and Patrick Austin (2012) 'Climate models at their limit?', *Nature*, 486 (14 June): 183–184.

Mol, Annemarie (2002) *The Body Multiple: Ontology in Medical Practice*. Durham, NC: Duke University Press.

Mol, Annemarie (2008) *The Logic of Care: Health and the Problem of Patient Choice*. Abingdon: Routledge.

Oels, Angela (2014) 'Climate security as governmentality: from mitigation to resilience', in Johannes Stripple and Harriet Bulkeley (eds) *Governing the Climate: New Approaches to Rationality, Power and Politics*. Cambridge: Cambridge University Press, pp. 197–217.

Parag, Yael and Deborah Strickland (2009) 'Personal carbon budgeting: what people need to know, learn and have in order to manage and live within a carbon budget, and the policies that could support them?', Working paper UKERC/WP/DR/2009/ 014. UK Energy Research Centre, London.

Paterson, Matthew and Johannes Stripple, (2010) 'MySpace: governing individuals' carbon emissions', *Environment and Planning: D*, 28(2): 341–362.

Paterson, Matthew and Johannes Stripple (2012) 'Virtuous carbon', *Environmental Politics*, 21(4): 563–582.

Poole, Robert (2008) *Earthrise: How Man First Saw the Earth*. New Haven, CT: Yale University Press.

Randalls, Samuel (2011a) 'Optimal climate change: economics and climate science policy histories (from heuristic to normative)', *Osiris*, 26(1): 224–242.

Randalls, Samuel (2011b) 'Climate change pathology', *Environment and Planning: A*, 43(6): 1242–1247.

Ross, Andrew (1991) *Strange Weather: Culture, Science and Technology in the Age of Limits*. London: Verso.

Ruddiman, William (2005) *Plows, Plagues and Petroleum: How Humans Took Control of Climate*. Princeton, NJ: Princeton University Press.

Steffen, Will, Paul Crutzen and John McNeill (2007) 'The Anthropocene: are humans now overwhelming the great forces of nature?', *Ambio*, 36(8): 614–621.

Stern, Nicholas (2007) *Stern Review on the Economics of Climate Change*. Cambridge: Cambridge University Press.

Stripple, Johannes (2012) 'The subject of security in a warming world', *Brown Journal of World Affairs*, 18(2): 181–194.

Thaler, Richard and Cass Sunstein (2009) *Nudge: Improving Decisions about Health, Wealth and Happiness*. New York: Penguin.

The Impact Team (1977) *The Weather Conspiracy: The Coming of the New Ice Age*. New York: Heron House Publishing.

Tsing, Anna (2000) 'The global situation', *Cultural Anthropology*, 15(3): 327–360.

Wahlberg, Ayo (2014) 'Human activity between nature and society: The negotiation of infertility in China', in Kirsten Hastrup (ed) *Anthropology and Nature*. New York: Routledge, pp. 184–195.

WBGU (German Advisory Council on Global Change) (2007) *World in Transition: Climate Change as a Security Risk. Summary for Policy-makers*. Berlin: WBGU.

Yamane, Akiko (2009) 'Climate change and hazardscape of Sri Lanka', *Environment and Planning: A*, 41(10): 2396–2416.

8 Envisioning 'global security'?

The Earth viewed from outer space as a motif in security discourses

Columba Peoples

Introduction

Outer space-based technologies, most notably satellite systems, are increasingly crucial to contemporary understandings of our global condition. Images and data beamed back from satellites are used to monitor Earth from afar (meteorology and environmental monitoring being but two examples), and satellite technologies also form a vital component of modern mapping techniques and global communication infrastructures. While some scholars have evaluated the politics of Earth observation at a general level (for excellent examples, see Brannon 2013; Deibert 2003; Litfin 1998, 1999), though, the role of space technologies in constituting understandings of 'global security' remains relatively understudied. Where the role of space technologies and practices of Earth monitoring are considered in relation to security, the story is often told as one in which images of Earth from space have generally failed to deliver a substantive degree of 'global' security consciousness. Reflecting in the late 1950s on the security dilemmas of the nuclear era and the future of international politics, as noted in the introduction to this volume, John Herz (1959: 317) pointed to the need for a 'comprehensive view of ... the world and mankind as a whole', a "world's eye view", a *Gesamtschau* ... '. By 1983, Daniel Deudney could confidently assert that 'The first photograph of humanity's home, the Earth floating in the void of space, alone and fragile, has changed forever how we think about our species' interaction with the natural world and how we manage our population, resources and environment'; but, equally, that 'Curiously, this new way of looking at ourselves has yet to significantly affect thinking about security' (1983: 5). If anything, some argue, rather than generating a sustainable conception of 'whole-Earth security' and a 'geopolitics of peace' as advocated by Deudney, developments in space-based technologies have simply allowed for more entrenched militarism and statist geopolitics:

> Today, [outer] space is filled with satellites offering near perfect resolution on the surface of the Earth and able to transmit that data with great speed and precision to computers and cell phones, as well as early

warning systems, missiles and drones. What we cannot seem to do is find an exterior viewpoint on war itself – a perspective that would allow an assessment not only of the reality of conflict but also of the motivations, fantasies and desires that support and enable it. Indeed expert systems of all sorts – military, economic, political and industrial – all seem unable to learn from failure and instead in the face of crisis simply retrench and remobilize longstanding and obviously failed logics.

(Masco 2012: 1107)

The technical capacity for a 'world's eye view', it appears, has thus not been sufficient in itself to inspire an accompanying degree of 'global' security consciousness at a macro level or scale (Buzan and Wæver 2009).

The diverse ways in which the image, or rather images plural, of Earth viewed from space have been employed and deployed within extant discourses of 'security' (self-identified as such) have much to tell us as to why this might be the case. Earth viewed from space functions as a recurrent motif, in different ways, within discourses on 'global security', and suggests the possibility of envisioning (in a literal, pictorial sense) security at a global scale as facilitated by the advent of space-based imaging and sensing technologies. This does not, however, necessarily mean that the possibilities for viewing Earth from space lead directly to a unitary, corresponding, or monolithic view of global security. As is explored in the chapter via three distinct case studies, views of Earth from space are employed to underpin substantially different understandings of what global security might mean. In the iconography of US defence agencies historically, the view of Earth from space is used to denote military mastery of the globe and to make the claim that global security is synonymous with the extension of American power. More recent use of the motif in programmes such as the European Union's 'Copernicus' Earth Observation Programme try to articulate a broader conception of global security that encompasses the remote sensing and monitoring of environmental issues, surveillance of borders and of population flows, and management of crises. Other examples, such as the non-governmental GlobalSecurity. org, employ the motif less to denote the possibilities for envisioning the globe as a whole but instead for new capacities to 'zoom in' on security issues from space in order to create better public understanding of a range of the current context of 'global security'. In terms of the broader theme of this edited collection, each of the case studies suggests differing and even contending understandings of 'globality' even if they are all functionally dependent on and invoke the 'infrastructural globalism' (Edwards 2010: 23) of satellite systems and accompanying technologies of geosurveillance. The uses of the motif – in these case studies at least – suggest that rather than necessarily correlating to a unified vision of global security, images of Earth from space are now part of 'the conceptual resources necessary for both territorial demarcation and national identity construction' (Bartelson 2010: 220; cf. Walker 2010).

'Powers of planetary scope': Earth viewed from outer space

Although contemporary use of satellites and their related Geographic Information Systems (GIS) – not to mention applications such as Global Positioning Systems (GPS) and Google Earth – may be seen at the 'cutting edge' of modern techniques of geosurveillance (Crampton 2010: 112), for scholars such as John Agnew such systems represent only the most recent outgrowth of a particularly 'modern' tendency:

> [From the Renaissance on,] quantification of the world into precise bits and pieces (by latitude and longitude for example) was possible only because of the visualization of the world as a whole. Powers of 'planetary scope' could henceforth be deployed to control sea lanes and routes of circulation. In this way, global space was 'hierarchized' and ordered into zones of greater and lesser significance in which different activities and behaviours were appropriate. Technical systems for ordering the Earth's surface, therefore, were important elements in the development of the modern geopolitical imagination.
>
> (Agnew 2003: 21)

Jens Bartelson has gone so far as to argue that idea of the world as 'one single and homogenous socio-political space' (2010: 220), emanating from Renaissance cosmological beliefs as well as processes of geographical and scientific discovery, created the conditions for the emergence of modern international relations: 'Conceptualizing the world as a spherical object was precondition of the subsequent division of that globe into distinct portions by means of geometrical methods, but also for the subjections of these to exclusive sovereignty claims' and a 'blend of cosmological and communitarian beliefs [that] provided crucial justifications for further global expansion by European states' (Bartelson 2010: 223, 227). For Agnew, such efforts at quantification and visualization of the world as a whole are a necessary condition of thinking about (modern) 'world' politics:

> the 'modern' world is defined by the imaginative ability to transcend the spatial limits imposed by everyday life and contemplate the world conceived and grasped as a picture [...] [S]eeing the world-as-a-picture, as an ordered, structured whole, separates the self who is viewing from the world itself. The observer stands outside of terrestrial space, so to speak, and frames the world as apart from and prior to the places and people it contains.
>
> (Agnew 2003: 15)

On this reading, contemporary technologies and practices of outer space-based geosurveillance represent the apex of a much longer historical trajectory. From the heyday of space exploration in the 1960s and early 1970s up to the present use of satellites and Earth remote sensing to undergird global communications, mapping and environmental monitoring, space technologies are often credited with creating and sustaining a 'picture' of the world that did not exist prior to their development and applications. Images of Earth taken from outer space are frequently cited, used and re-used in attempts to characterise the Earth as a single or unitary 'global' space. As the seminal work of Denis Cosgrove (1994) argues, two images in particular, 'Earthrise' (denoted by NASA as AS8-14-2383) and 'Whole Earth' or the 'Blue Marble' (denoted NASA AS17-148-22727) (see Figures 8.1 and 8.2) have retained particularly lasting prominence and significance in this regard (see also Poole 2008). The photos were taken by US astronauts aboard the *Apollo 8* mission to orbit the moon in 1968 in the case of Earthrise and from *Apollo 17* in 1972, the last American mission to the moon to date, using hand-held 70mm Hasselblad cameras in both instances.

Figure 8.1 NASA AS8-14-2383 ('Earthrise')

Figure 8.2 NASA AS17-148-22727 ('The Blue Marble')

Yet, as Cosgrove discusses at length, the 'Earthrise' and 'Blue Marble' images did not appear *de novo*. They are, he contends, both symptomatic and now a key underpinning of what he elsewhere terms as the 'Apollonian Perspective' (Cosgrove 2001) – invoking the American missions' self-identification with the Greek deity: 'As a sun-god he circled the Earth, his dispassionate vision encompassing the pathetic doings of mortals' (Cosgrove 1994: 273). The perspective taken in the images are thus akin to the kind of 'god-trick' ('of seeing everything from nowhere', as Donna Haraway (1988: 581) famously puts it), that for Cosgrove – in terms that echo Agnew's historicization of 'powers of planetary scope' – extend an already pre-existing 'habit' of 'distanced, objective and penetrating' observation of 'the globe':

> implicit in Ptolemeic cartography's positioning of the observer at sufficient distance to see the spheres of the Earth ... The fifteenth century rediscovery of this mode of territorial mapping marks the beginnings of European modernity ... The habits of simultaneously gazing upon the

world and mastering it are increasingly synonymous in the lavishly deco-
rated globes, atlases and world maps that were designed to satisfy the
lusts of Baroque princes … By the eighteenth century, the intellectual
mastery of globes … was an accomplishment expected of the educated
European bourgeoisie, male and female alike.

(Cosgrove 1994: 271, 272)

The 'Earthrise' and 'Blue Marble' images, on this reading, joined an already
established cultural practice of 'gazing' (Cosgrove 2006: 9) upon the globe –
or rather globes – from afar. Paul N. Edwards (2010: 2–3) likewise argues that
'Long before the astronauts stared down in awe from outer space, notions of
a "global Earth" had begun to emerge in language, ideology, technology and
practice' with an 'overdetermined semiotic web' already prepared by '(among
other things) the post-World War II "One World" movement; the United
Nations; the 1957–58 International Geophysical Year; … the Earth-orbiting
satellites Sputnik, Telstar, and TIROS …'. Such images of Earth viewed from
space have become not only cultural objects of lasting significance but also
sites of contested 'visions' in their own right, an integral part of a longer
'history of competing globalisms' (Lazier 2011: 608). As is often noted, the
use of the 'Blue Marble' image on the dust jacket of James Lovelock's *Gaia:
A New Look at Life on Earth* indelibly linked it to Lovelock's thesis of Earth
as a unitary system or biosphere (see Lovelock 1989). However, that association is not exclusive, and both the 'Earthrise' and 'Blue Marble' images have
routinely been employed in countervailing and contested ways. Cosgrove
notes, variously, that the 'Earthrise' image came to be used in promotional
materials by TRW Engines Inc. with surrounding text lauding the technology
that made the *Apollo 8* mission possible, used to signify a kind of 'secular
mastery of the world through spatial control' (1994: 287–88); while the 'Blue
Marble' came to adorn, amongst other things, the cover of the *Whole Earth
Catalog* – which focused on promoting 'grassroots' political activism (and is
still used on the website chronicling the now defunct catalogue's history
today) as a signifier of '[a] quasi-spiritual interconnectedness and the vulnerability of terrestrial life' (Whole Earth Catalog 2014) – as well as the cover of
subsequent work by the publication's editor, Stewart Brand (see Brand 2009).

US defence agencies: the iconography of 'full spectrum dominance'

While the 'Earthrise' and 'Blue Marble' images might be well be regarded as
'iconic', Cosgrove's account suggests a need for critical awareness of the conditions in which they are produced and then reproduced intertextually, the
pre-existing cultural and historical frameworks that they come to be understood in relation to, and the contending political agendas that have subsequently attempted to offer definitive interpretations of the significance of the
images. In particular, debate persists as to the extent to which the dissemination of the 'Earthrise' and 'Blue Marble' images can actually be credited with

stimulating either a novel sense of 'global consciousness' or an enhanced environmental sensibility. Sheila Jasanoff, although crediting 'The picture of the Earth hanging in space' as 'a fitting emblem of western environmentalism's transnational ambitions', also notes the fact that:

> The image confronts Americans today at every turn, from the revolving globe used as a background for so many televised, and now networked, news programs to the logo that wordlessly asserts the global reach of credit cards, airlines, automobile manufacturers, telephone companies, bookstores, academic programs, and virtually every other product or service that travels.
>
> (Jasanov 2001: 310)

Although the extent and experience of that ubiquity (Jasanoff 2001: 310; Lazier 2011: 606) is not solely limited to American viewers and consumers, such views of the Earth pictured from space likewise 'confronts' us (in Jasanoff's terms) as a recurrent motif in the promotion of US national security, albeit pictured at a global scale. The emblems of multiple US defence agencies (Figure 8.3) provides an immediate case in point, incorporating a view of Earth from space in (among others) the emblems of the US Strategic Command, the Defense Intelligence Agency and the National Geospatial-Intelligence Agency.

Strategic Command's long-standing emblem depicts an artistic rendering of Earth viewed from space, with continental North America clearly identifiable. 'The globe, as viewed from space, symbolizes the Earth as being the origin and control point for all space vehicles and represents the command's span of operation', as the Command's own explanation of the emblem tells us. 'Encompassing the globe are orbital paths crossed diagonally, each bearing two polestars, detailed white, representing the Command's satellite platforms and their worldwide coverage in accomplishing the intelligence, surveillance,

Figure 8.3 US defence agencies' emblems
Note: from left to right – Strategic Command, Defense Intelligence Agency and National Geospatial-Intelligence Agency.

reconnaissance, communications, early warning and navigation missions' (United States Strategic Command 2014). Strategic Command's appropriation of the Earth viewed from space motif (or rather its explanation of its use of that motif) thus interweaves a claim about the 'global' purview of the US with references to the satellite infrastructure that makes that purview possible. Overlaying that backdrop a range of supplementary icons are explained in heraldic terms: a metal gauntlet ('a symbol of strength, power and loyalty') grasps three lightning bolts ('lethality and speed') and an olive branch ('a constant reminder of the command's mission of securing peace'). The seal of the Defense Intelligence Agency maintains the practice of viewing Earth from space, again as an artist's representation but this time in a fuller 'downward' view as if from above the North Pole, where two additional 'red atomic ellipses symbolise the scientific and technical aspects of intelligence today and of the future'. Behind the 'globe' stands a 'flaming torch and its gold colour represent knowledge, i.e. intelligence "lighting" the way of the "known" light blue-green world against the darkness or unknown symbolized by the dark background – the "area of truth" still sought by the worldwide mission of the agency' (Defense Intelligence Agency 2014).

The emblem of the National Geospatial-Intelligence Agency (NGA) as on the agency's homepage is less ornate in terms of use of icons and symbols, depicting as it does a partial view of Earth set in the darkness of space. North and South America are in view as is, beyond that, a blazing sun. As distinct from the US Strategic Command and Defense Intelligence Agency, the NGA emblem includes cloud cover, perhaps indicative of an attempt to present the emblem as a more 'realistic' comparison to photographic images of Earth from space as an accompaniment to the NGIA motto that stands alongside the emblem: 'Know the Earth ... Show the Way ... Understand the World'. Immediately below its mission is set out as being to 'provide timely, relevant, and accurate geospatial intelligence in support of national security' (National Geospatial-Intelligence Agency 2014a).

Whereas the emblems of the US Strategic Command and Defense Intelligence Agency require a degree of assisted symbology or heraldic interpretation, the NGA's logo eschews the use of icons instead relying on additional explanatory text to frame the image within in terms of its overall purpose. When the resolution and size of the NGA's emblem is increased, the viewer notices that in fact the Earth presented is partially criss-crossed by grid lines, indicating that the tendency to overlay the image of Earth viewed from space has not been entirely done away with in this instance. Elsewhere, though, there are instances where US defence agencies rely even more on the framing of images of Earth viewed from space than they do iconography to assert the 'global' significance of American defence and national security interests. Chief among these is a recent promotional campaign by the US Missile Defence Agency (MDA) (see Figure 8.4). The MDA's emblem, unlike its previously discussed counterparts, opts for a much more stylized variant of the Earth from space motif (see logo on bottom right), with an orb encompassed by the representation of the red looping trail of an interceptor missile and, as explained by the MDA's Richard Lehner, 'a flash (not a star) denoting a missile intercept' (quoted in Malcolm 2010). More broadly, though, the Earth viewed from space functions as the literal backdrop for an explanation of the MDA's promotion of missile defence. The MDAs downloadable wallpaper (Figure 8.4) shows an image of Earth from space, and the image, though digitally rendered, is essentially a variation of the familiar 'Earthrise' and 'Blue Marble' pictures, but composed in such a way as to depict the continental US at the heart of the image beneath a partially obscured sun. Notably, the image features very few other adornments, save for the identifying text and logo of the MDA, and its central banner text: 'Lead one of the greatest technological achievements of our time.' Here, as Cosgrove noted of TRW's use of the 'Earthrise' photo in its advertising, Earth viewed from space is framed not within the context of environmental fragility but instead in reference to an assumed spirit of technological excellence and secular mastery (cf. Peoples 2010).

Figure 8.4 US Missile Defense Agency 'wallpaper'
Source: Missile Defense Agency.

GMES/Copernicus: A broader view of global security?

In the iconography of US defence agencies, then, it could be argued that the motif of Earth viewed from space is frequently used to signify 'powers of planetary scope' as in Agnew's double sense of that term: an aspiration towards command of the globe and a supporting ability to view any part of it from space (that is, the desired scope or extent of US power), enabled by satellite and geosurveillance infrastructure (the technological scope(s) through which the Earth can be viewed). These figurative representations of Earth viewed from space also explicitly allude to the fact that historically, to paraphrase Neil Smith, the political economy and context of our contemporary capacities for viewing Earth from space is 'heavily underwritten by a military agenda' (Smith 1992: 259). As well as the military dimensions of ostensibly civilian space exploration such as the *Apollo* missions (see Sheehan 2007: 20–54), during the Cold War era satellite overflights and innovation in space and satellite technologies were driven in large part by the superpowers' desire to monitor and observe each other's nuclear arsenals, as well as monitoring nuclear weapons testing globally (Masco 2010). And as John Cloud (2001: 233) details extensively, the Cold War produced a scientific and technical infrastructure that aspired to be accurate enough to 'both wage and preclude nuclear war', with systems such as the US Department of Defense WGS (World Geodetic System), which uses a combination of surface gravity and satellite data to provide the 'reference frame upon which all geospatial intelligence is based' (National Geospatial-Intelligence Agency 2014b), the CORONA satellite photo-reconnaissance system (the precursor to modern Earth imaging and remote sensing satellites), MGIS (Military Geographic Intelligence Systems) and its later offshoot of civilian GIS, or Geographic Information Systems, and GPS (Global Positioning Systems) all emanating from the US Cold War defence infrastructure (Cloud 2001). The emblematic uses of Earth viewed from space by US defence agencies effectively celebrates the development and legacy of this 'closed world' military technological infrastructure of 'real time' global monitoring and surveillance (Edwards 1996: 75).

Other uses of the Earth-viewed-from-space motif, however, allude to a distinct agenda of 'global' security that ostensibly seeks to take a greater distance from the military applications and significance of viewing Earth from outer space. A prime example in this respect is GMES, the European Union's programme for 'Global Monitoring for Environment and Security' (GMES), recently rebranded (in 2012) as 'Copernicus: The Earth Observation Programme' (for an overview and discussion see Lamy and Saint-Martin 2014). The name change, the European Commission argues, 'pay[s] homage to a great European scientist and observer', and specifically to Nicolaus Copernicus' theory of the heliocentric universe (European Commission 2012). In grandiose terms the, the announcement of the name change seeks to align the programme's purposes and significance with Copernicus' 'establishment' of the fact (see Bartelson 2010: 225) that the Earth constitutes a single planetary 'sphere' with a common centre of gravity:

> He [Copernicus] opened man to an infinite universe, previously limited by the rotation of the planets and the sun around the Earth, and created a world without borders. Humanity was able to benefit from his insight and set in motion the spirit of scientific research which allowed us to have a better understanding of the world we live in.
>
> (European Commission 2012)

Although the name has changed, 'environmental and security issues' remain at the core of the 'Copernicus' agenda, as they did in its previous incarnation as GMES, and the basic combination of technologies – 'Earth observation and *in situ* sensors such as ground stations, air-borne and sea-borne stations' – likewise remains the same. The new programme even continues to use the same introductory video used previously (Copernicus: The Earth Observation Programme 2011).

'Copernicus'/GMES situates 'security' as being one amongst a spectrum of issues that also includes 'land, marine, atmosphere, climate change, emergency management [and security]'. The introductory video for the programme thus makes allusion to the 'improvement of the security of European citizens', in relation to maritime and border surveillance in particular, set alongside images of deforestation, hurricane winds, power stations belching out smoke, desertification and splintering ice sheets. Interspersed with these images of planetary crisis (the narrator identifies them as such) are computer generated images of satellites observing the Earth from above, of scientists in white lab coats working with microscopes, and the shoots of healthy green plants and fields of crops. Edited together as a montage, the video repeats the same editorial technique multiple times: namely, it begins from a computer-generated shot of Earth viewed from space, almost always including a piece of satellite hardware; which then transitions to a more 'earthly' image of a sunrise, a city landscape, or a decimated forest; and then to a scientist at work, a logger cutting down a tree, or a polar bear floundering at the edge of an ice-sheet. In the ten-second sequence from which the stills are taken, the Earth as observed from above by satellite transitions to become the base of a glass under running water, which in turn then morphs into a laboratory (florence) flask over a Bunsen burner. The view then 'zooms out' again to a view of Earth from space, encircled by a single satellite and its orbital ellipse; which in turn becomes a 'virtual globe' overlayed with climatic data, a representation of global warming as it is followed by an image of the Earth surrounded by flame.

'Copernicus', the European Space Agency (2013) argues, 'is set to make a step change in the way we care for the planet by providing reliable, timely and accurate services to manage the environment, understand and mitigate the effects of climate change and help respond to crises'. But although the objectives of the programme are articulated in terms of planetary crises and the role of Earth observation technologies – satellite technologies in particular – in observing, understanding and responding to those crises, proponents of GMES/Copernicus stop far short of speaking of an agenda for 'planetary' or 'whole Earth' security. Monitoring and maintaining 'border security' remain as a discrete objective of the programme, which serves to suggest that 'security' objectives are different to and separate from the wider agenda of 'planetary care'. Equally, some have suggested that the distinction between GMES/Copernicus and the EU's defence and (military) security agenda is more porous than its promotion as an 'Earth Observation Programme' implies (Oikonomou 2012: 104; Slijper 2009: 72). Although the 'powers of planetary scope' envisaged for 'Copernicus' may be framed ostensibly within a comprehensive environmental agenda that seeks to maintain and enhance the lives of people within and beyond the EU, the prospective management and use of the system remains very much 'top-down' in its focus: 'The main uses of Copernicus are policy makers and public authorities who need the information to develop environmental legislation and policies or to take critical decisions in the event of an emergency, such as a natural disaster or a humanitarian crisis' (Copernicus: The Earth Observation Programme 2013). In this light the virtuous framing of the Copernicus programme as an effort to create global environmental security (European Commission 2012), which initially seems to contrast with the overt militarism and national security focus of US defence iconography, comes to look more partial and particularistic. Its imagery of global planetary and environmental crisis, such as in video sequence in Figure 8.5, are invoked as a rationale for deepening and extending the European political 'project' via technical and scientific management (cf. Clark 2014). Indeed, a question can be raised in this sense as to whether the concept of globality underpinning the Copernicus programme 'risks becoming but another tool in the hands of those who wish to relocate political authority to institutions beyond the purview of popular sovereignty' (Bartelson 2010: 219).

'Virtual globes', 'slippy maps' and 'keyhole' views of security

Whereas GMES/Copernicus is envisaged to be primarily at the disposal of governmental and administrative elites (as well as potential commercial applications), the development of systems such as Google Earth has, for some at least, created the prospect of a more 'participatory', more 'democratic' public engagement with space technologies and images of Earth from space. In Google Earth (and comparable systems such as NASA's World Wind), readily available to those with a computer and access to the internet, 'data are displayed "naturistically" as if on a planet seen from space' (Crampton 2009: 92): Google Earth begins as an Earth-from-space view (a view in turn collated from satellite images of Earth), and users of the system can then 'spin' the Earth. The system incorporates layers of satellite and aerial images, allowing the users to zoom 'downwards' from the level of the planetary scale to, say, a

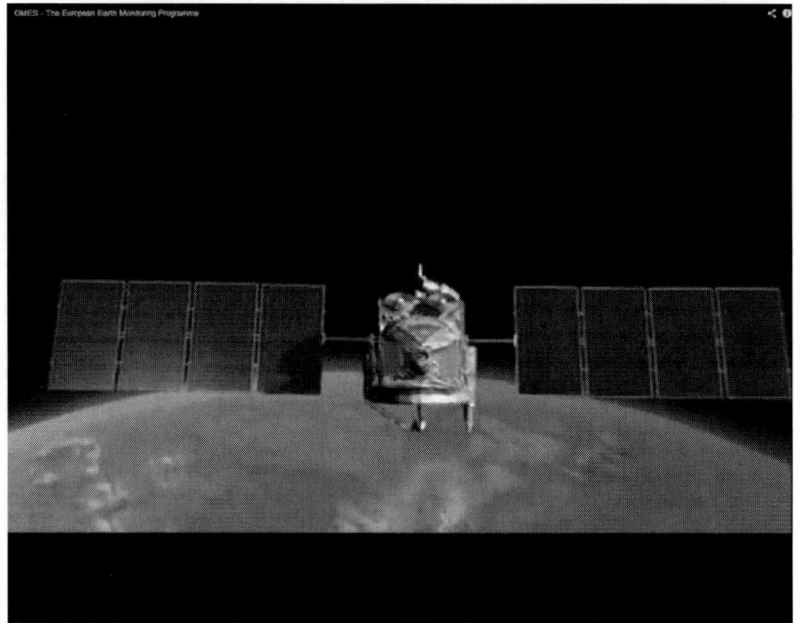

Figure 8.5.1 GMES [Copernicus] The European Earth Monitoring Programme, still #1 (Satellite overview of Earth)

Figure 8.5.2 GMES [Copernicus] The European Earth Monitoring Programme, still #2 (Water glass)

Figure 8.5.3 GMES [Copernicus] The European Earth Monitoring Programme, still #3 (Lab flask)

Figure 8.5.4 GMES [Copernicus] The European Earth Monitoring Programme, still #4 (Orbiting satellite over virtual globe)

Figure 8.5.5 GMES [Copernicus] The European Earth Monitoring Programme, still #5 (Virtual globe – climatic data overlayed)

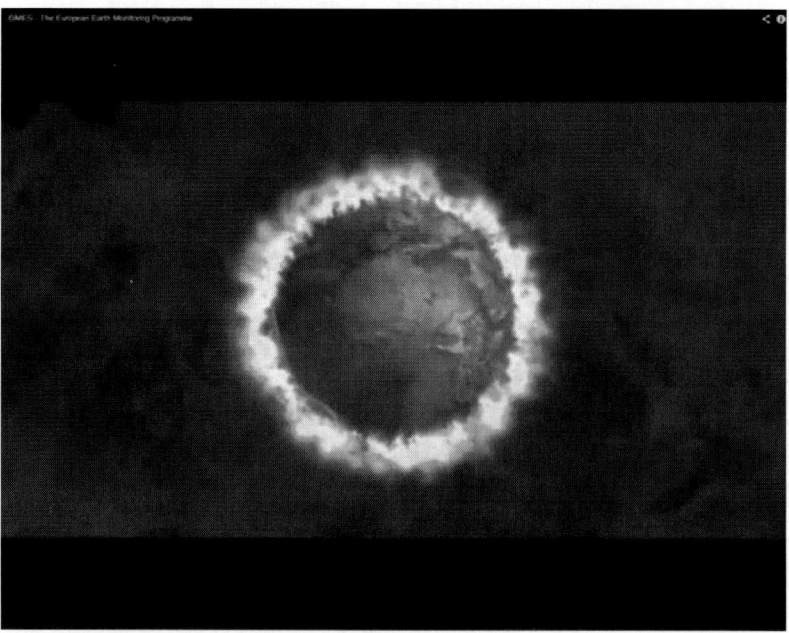

Figure 8.5.6 GMES [Copernicus] The European Earth Monitoring Programme, still #6 ('World on fire')

specific feature of the Grand Canyon, the Great Wall of China, or the user's own backyard. Overviews of the Earth from space thus morph into 'slippy maps', where users can 'slide' across the map on their screen and zoom in on an area of particular interest. Additionally, 'data from different sources can be integrated and easily layered' (Crampton 2009: 92) such that Google Earth and comparable systems can be used to create a 'virtual globe' or '3D Earth' onto which particular data can be projected. A prominent example in this respect is the US National Oceanic and Atmospheric Administration's 'Science on a Sphere Project',

> a room-sized, global display system that uses computers and video pro-jectors to display planetary data onto a six-foot-diameter sphere, analo-gous to a giant animated globe [...]. Animated images of atmospheric storms, climate change, and ocean temperature can be shown on the sphere, which is used to explain what are sometimes complex environmental processes, in a way that is simultaneously intuitive and captivating.
>
> (Science on a Sphere 2014)

To contextualize the emergence of such programmes, it is worth noting the ways in which 'security' imperatives of a different sort both beget and impinge upon such 'public' views of Earth from space. In addition to the well-known provenance of civilian satellite navigation from military Global Posi-tioning Systems (GPS) (owing to which the highest resolution images are still usually strictly restricted for exclusive use by the US military and intelligence agencies), some go further in suggesting a more substantive relation between militarization and technologies and practices of visualizing the Earth even as they migrate beyond explicit military applications and into wider public usage. Roger Stahl (2010: 67), for example, notes that Google Earth 'began its life as the very picture of war. Specifically, the prototype platform that even-tually became Google Earth first gained exposure during the television war coverage of the 2003 invasion of Iraq'. Even leaving aside philosophical reflections on the extent to which views of Earth from space are inherently militarized (see also Harris 2006), the practical importance of military drivers in the historical development and continuing political economy of satellite imagery is undeniable. Cosgrove and Fox (2010: 77) note that Keyhole, Inc. – which Google purchased in 2004 and then used the Keyhole 'Earthviewer' as the foundation for Google Earth – relied on satellites 'funded in part with venture capital funds from the CIA'. Similarly, GeoEye, a high-resolution commercial imaging satellite launched in 2008 was 'part supported by Google' but over half of its $502 million cost was funded by the US military, and US military and intelligence agencies remain the largest users of images provided by systems such as DigitialGlobe and GeoEye (Dodge and Perkins 2009: 498).

In that sense, military imperatives remain a key part of the 'infrastructural globalism' (Edwards 2010: 23) of contemporary geosurveillance, and in regard to the development of 'slippy maps' US military and intelligence agencies in particular have likewise become particularly adept in developing and using layered, interactive satellite maps. The end product is, for military users, a kind of military slippy map in which the global overviews provided by satellite imagery are annotated and coded by captions and dropdown menus, with the additional technological capacity to zoom in on or 'fly' over specific locations for military reconnaissance, planning and targeting purposes (see National Geospatial-Intelligence Agency 2014c). Yet simultaneously, as Martin Dodge and Chris Perkins note (2009: 497), 'the social and spatial disposition of high resolution satellite imagery of the Earth is diffusing much more widely and freely' and is not solely limited to military prerogatives and applications, thanks in large part to public availability of systems such as Google Earth. 'Free', as they also note, with the caveat that large corporations such as Google and Microsoft heavily subsidise provision of high-resolution satellite imagery in order to dominate the market, and in other instances such provision is accompanied by targeted advertising (see also Brannon 2013). And breadth of availability too remains an issue. As but one example Lisa Parks (2009: 536, 543) notes that in the case of Google Earth's 'Crisis in Darfur' project, an effort to bring international attention to the conflict in Sudan via Google Earth's 'Global Awareness' layer, US export controls and economic sanctions meant that people in Sudan could not download software produced in the US – including Google Earth.

Yet the increased diffusion – even allowing for the limits of such diffusion as above – of satellite imagery is giving rise to an increasing range of non-governmental initiatives that seek to inform contemporary understandings of security (Litfin 2002). Among several instances, the efforts of the eponymous GlobalSecurity.org and its 'Public Eye' programme stand out as a self-conscious attempt to develop and enhance a particular sort of global security consciousness by employing satellite imagery. Founded by the US security policy analyst John E. Pike in 2000, GlobalSecurity.org positions itself as the leading non-governmental source of background information on 'defence, space, intelligence, WMD and homeland security' (GlobalSecurity.org 2014a). A key part of this is its 'Public Eye' initiative, which uses 'newly available [satellite] imagery to improve public understanding of nuclear weapons and missile programs around the world'. Moreover, Public Eye, the website asserts, 'is also evaluating the global security implications of the pervasive proliferation of high-resolution satellite imagery, and the general applicability of this novel information technology to enhance the potential of the non-governmental sector to impact public policy' (GlobalSecurity.org 2014b).

Public Eye uses satellite images in thumbnail form to accompany explanation of issues ranging from North Korea's construction of its Yongbyon nuclear facilities, the aftermath of Hurricane Katrina, the site where a US Black Hawk helicopter was shot down in Moghadishu in 1993 and missile test ranges in India to uranium enrichment facilities in Natanz, Iran. The images are drawn from a combination of sources including some declassified

military satellite images (such as from the US CORONA satellite programme), SPOT (the French Earth observation satellite system) and other
commercial image providers such as IKONOS, Space Imaging and Digital
Globe, and are a mix of publicly available and purchased (from commercial
providers) imagery. Clicking on the thumbnails, subscribers to the website (for
the website only allows a limited free preview) can then view the images
captioned or accompanied by explanatory text.

Public Eye offers its subscribers a 'keyhole' view on specific sites of security
and insecurity, defined and pre-identified as such. In doing so, it claims to
provide public insights that may challenge extant interpretations of current
security issues as well as allowing subscribers the chance to view otherwise
hidden sites. Thus the Public Eye Website claims that 'Already, we have demonstrated that North Korea's missile program is less extensive than previously
thought, and that India and Pakistan have laid a much more extensive foundation for an arms buildup than previously disclosed' (GlobalSecurity.org
2014b). And subscribers can, for example, view satellite images from 2002
(provided by ImageSat) of the US airbase on the island of Diego Garcia,
noting as the website does its distance from Baghdad and the island base's
subsequent supporting role in 'Operation enduring Freedom' in Iraq (see
Figure 8.6).

Among the multiple thumbnails of the Public Eye initiative, the choice of
Diego Garcia is significant, allowing as it does an overhead glimpse of one of
the previously 'secret' sites of US military power. Yet the exact purpose of the
illustration is more opaque, aside from increasing the public 'view' of a far-
flung cog in the US military machine. Elsewhere, updated colour versions of
the same images from 2004 are used to illustrate the fact that the island was
unaffected by the Andaman Tsunami – used, seemingly, by the website as an
effort to counter reports by 'Islamists' that the island was 'wiped off the map'
in an act of God in revenge for the base's use as a launch pad for B-52
bombing raids on Iraq and Afghanistan (GlobalSecurity.org 2014c). Among
the contextual explanation of the Diego Garcia images on the Public Eye site,
no mention or reference is made to the island's longer history of controversy,
most notably the mass expulsion of the island's native Chagossians in the
1970s by successive British governments in order to create an 'uninhabited'
island on which the military base could then be constructed (see Pilger 2006:
37–90). Drawing attention to that historical context would provide for a very
different framing of the satellite images of Diego Garcia in security terms (cf.
Salter and Mutlu 2013). But the overall effect of the Public Eye initiative,
taken as a whole, is that it self-consciously functions as a kind of non-
governmental geospatial intelligence agency for those seeking to influence
public policy in the US. In this sense it has been argued that Public Eye is
'very much part of the system that it documents, rather than serving as a
critical outsider' (Perkins and Dodge 2009: 553; cf. Litfin 2002).

As the work of Chris Perkins and Martin Dodge details, the Public Eye
initiative is but one among multiple attempts to deploy satellite imagery in

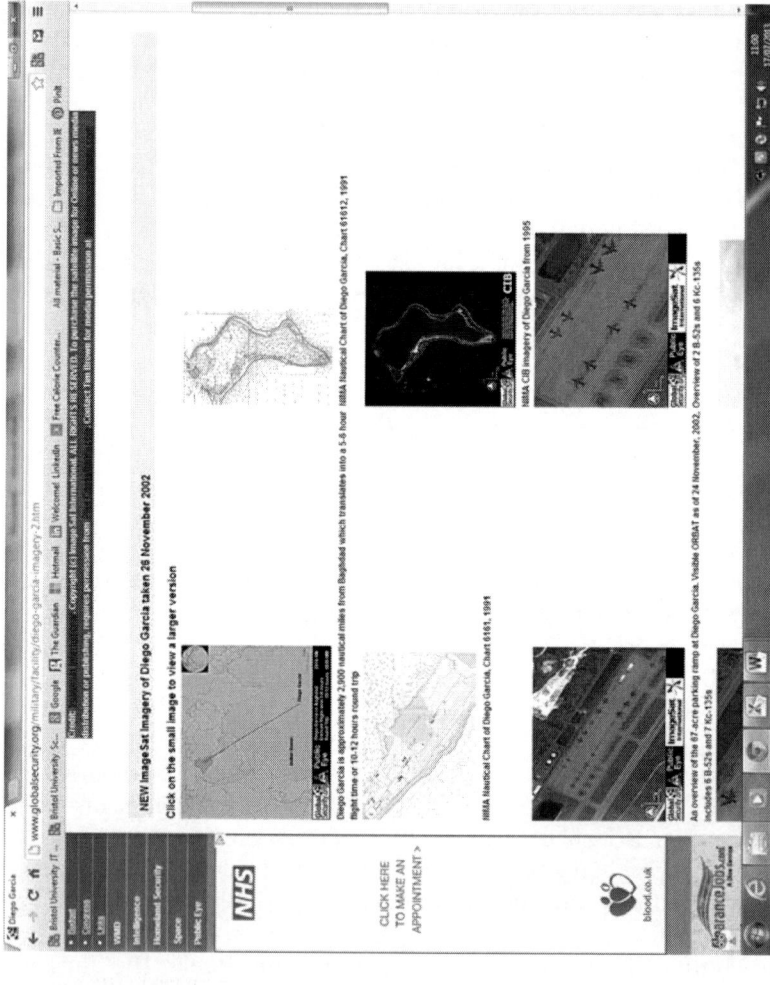

Figure 8.6 Screenshot: GlobalSecurity.org, Public Eye, captioned as 'NEW Image Sat Imagery of Diego Garcia taken 26 November 2002'. Source: ImageSat International.

ways that might run contrary to their military or 'official' uses. Others are, they argue, more explicitly subversive and 'anti-hegemonic' than Public Eye in their efforts to repurpose and reframe (Kurgan 2013: 13) such imagery. They note in particular the 'Eyeball Series', which serves as an 'anti-secrecy web-based archive' by documenting satellite images of sites otherwise enclosed within the literal and figurative ring-fences of national security: Guantanamo, air force and naval bases, nerve gas storage facilities, nuclear power plants, the Kennedy Space Centre. The Eyeball Series is part of the broader 'Cryptome' project, which self-consciously seeks to illustrate the 'reverse-panopticon and counter-deception potential' of imagery intelligence (IMINT) (Perkins and Dodge 2009: 551). Yet, despite their differences, both the Public Eye and the Eyeball Series might ultimately be regarded as providing 'keyhole views' of global security. Both employ the practice of 'zooming in' on select or pre-selected sites of security and insecurity. GlobalSecurity.org in particular stakes a claim, in its very title, of a concern with global security. But in its Public Eye initiative, this gives way to a more functional use of Earth imaging technologies (namely satellites) to illustrate specific, spatially delimited narratives of security and insecurity. With the advent of systems such as Google Earth, it is as if 'a keyhole view of the world predominates despite the apparent promise to browse at will across the whole (virtual) globe' (Dodge and Perkins 2009: 498).

Conclusion: seeing global security differently?

As well as such pertinent questions of mediation, framing and perspective, the tendency to treat views of Earth from space simply as backdrop or starting point from which to zoom in on terrestrial security concerns may also have wider significance in undercutting the potential for envisioning security and insecurity at the global or planetary scale. In some ways, this is the unifying theme of the otherwise distinctive uses of the Earth-viewed-from-space motif in the case studies examined here. Rather than being 'global' in dictionary definition of encompassing the 'whole', on closer examination each of the cases here indicates an ultimate concern with partial and particularistic understandings of security: as the extension of American power and national security; as the preservation of a bounded and economically prosperous European Union; as the ability of individuals to zoom in on pre-defined sites of security and insecurity.

An alternative and as yet only partially realized approach to the use of space technologies is in their potential for monitoring and envisioning security and insecurity at a truly global scale as the 'larger picture' and 'context in which security now needs to be rethought'. The scale of anthropogenic climate change and environmental degradation, Simon Dalby has argued, now requires a fundamentally different understanding of 'geopolitics' in order to adequately represent the effects of human civilization on the Earth itself and the radical insecurities this creates for the human species as a whole of Earth's future in/habitability (Dalby 2013: 2; see also Clark 2014). The development of Earth system science and associated projects such as the aforementioned 'Science on a Sphere' have already gone some way in depicting changes in the biosphere via virtual, layered globes. Such projects, where the Earth itself is the 'referent object' to be secured rather than simply the backdrop for pre-existing security issues and concerns, might hold the beginnings of a substantively different, 'whole Earth' view of security.

Of course, similar caveats still apply in this mode of viewing Earth: the 'virtual globe' that one wishes to see represented depends heavily on the 'data-sets' it is based upon. And there is a constant risk that, as with previous efforts at 'world modelling', in the enthusiasm to 'overcome, via computer-aided synthesis, the falsely partitioned understanding of global reality imposed by disciplinary divisions of scholarly labor and spatial, temporal, and sectoral divisions of social practice' (Ashley 1983: 497), such virtual globes simply come to underpin different sorts of 'totalizing discourses', encased by a veneer of scientific abstraction and 'inattentive to the specificity of their cultural and historical assumptions' (Cosgrove 1994: 287). In short, there is no reason to assume that such visions of 'planetary' insecurity are any less political than the views of Earth as envisioned in the other security discourses assessed above, nor should we as scholars shy away from critically engaging the conditions of their production and reception. But if the history of the Earth from space motif in security discourses tells us anything, it is that global security has been and is envisaged in different ways accompanying and emblematizing different political assumptions and projects. That observation at the very least reminds us to question the 'globality' of such visions of security; and, by politicizing the practice of viewing Earth from outer space, it opens up the scope for investigating how we might come to see global security differently.

References

Agnew, John (2003) *Geopolitics: Re-visioning World Politics*. London: Routledge.

Ashley, Richard K. (1983) 'The Eye of Power: The Politics of World Modelling', *International Organization*, 37(3): 495–535.

Bartelson, Jens (2010) 'The Social Construction of Globality', *International Political Sociology*, 4(3): 219–235.

Brand, Stewart (2009) *Whole-Earth Discipline: Why Dense Cities, Nuclear Power, Transgenic Crops, Restored Wildlands, Radical Science and Geoengineering are Necessary*. London: Atlantic Books.

Brannon, Monica M. (2013) 'Standardized Spaces: Satellite Imagery in the Age of Big Data', *Configurations*, 21(3): 271–299.

Buzan, Barry and Ole Wæver 2009. 'Macrosecuritization and security constellations: reconsidering scale in securitization theory', *Review of International Studies*, 35(2): 253–276.

Clark, Nigel (2014) 'Geo-politics and the disaster of the Anthropocene', *The Sociological Review*, 62(S1): 19–37.

Cloud, John (2001) 'Imaging the World in a Barrel: CORONA and the Clandestine Convergence of the Earth Sciences', *Social Studies of Science*, 31(3): 231–251.

Copernicus: The Earth Observation Programme (2011) 'Video on the Copernicus Programme'. Available at http://copernicus.eu/pages-principales/overview/videos/ (accessed 21 August 2014).

Copernicus: The Earth Observation Programme (2013) 'Copernicus in Brief'. Available at http://copernicus.eu/pages-principales/overview/copernicus-in-brief/ (accessed 9 July 2013).

Cosgrove, Denis (1994) 'Contested Global Visions: One-World, Whole-Earth and the Apollo Space Photographs', *Annals of the Association of American Geographers*, 84(2): 270–294.

Cosgrove, Denis (2001) *Apollo's Eye: A Cartographic Genealogy of the Earth in Western Imagination*. Baltimore, MD: Johns Hopkins University Press.

Cosgrove, Denis (2006) *Geographical Imagination and the Authority of Images*. Munich: Franz Steiner Verlag.

Cosgrove, Denis and William L. Fox (2010) *Photography and Flight*. London: Reaktion Books.

Crampton, Jeremy W. (2009) 'Cartography: Maps 2.0', *Progress in Human Geography*, 33(1): 91–100.

Crampton, Jeremy W. (2010) *Mapping: A Critical Introduction to Cartography and GIS*. Oxford: Blackwell.

Dalby, Simon (2013) 'Globality and Climate Change: Geopolitics in the Twenty-first Century', paper presented to the International Studies Association annual convention, San Francisco, April.

Defence Intelligence Agency (2014) 'About the DIA Seal'. Available at www.dia.mil/About.aspx (accessed 15 September 2014).

Deibert, Ronald J. (2003) 'Unfettered Observation: The Politics of Earth Monitoring from Space', in W. Henry Lambright (ed.) *Space Policy in the Twenty-first Century*. Baltimore, MD: Johns Hopkins University Press.

Deudney, Daniel (1983) *Whole Earth Security: A Geopolitics of Peace*. Worldwatch Paper 55, July.

Dodge, Martin and Chris Perkins (2009) 'The "View from Nowhere?" Spatial Politics and Cultural Significance of High-resolution Satellite Imagery', *Geoforum*, 40(4): 497–501.

Edwards, Paul N. (1996) *The Closed World: Computers and the Politics of Discourse in Cold War America*. Cambridge, MA: MIT Press.

Edwards, Paul N. (2010) *A Vast Machine: Computer Models, Climate Data, and the Politics of Global Warming*. Cambridge MA: MIT Press.

European Commission (2012) 'Copernicus: New Name for European Earth Observation Programme'. Available at http://ec.europa.eu/enterprise/newsroom/cf/itemdetail. cfm?item_id=6321 (accessed 15 September 2014).

European Space Agency (2013) 'Green Light for GMES Copernicus'. Available from www.esa.int/Our_Activities/Observing_the_Earth/GMES/Green_light_for_GMES_Copernicus (accessed 15 September 2015).

GlobalSecurity.org (2014a) 'Overview'. Available at www.globalsecurity.org/org/over view/history.htm (accessed 15 September 2014).

GlobalSecurity.org (2014b) 'Public Eye – Introduction'. Available at www.globalsecur ity.org/eye/intro.htm (accessed 15 September 2014).

GlobalSecurity.org (2014c) 'Diego Garcia 7°20'S 72°25'E Post-Tsunami Imagery'. Available at www.globalsecurity.org/military/facility/diego-garcia-imagery-3.htm (accessed 15 September 2014).

Haraway, Donna (1980) 'Situated Knowledges: The Science Question in Feminism and the Privilege of Partial Perspective', *Feminist Studies*, 14(3): 575–599.

Harris, Chad (2006) 'The Omniscient Eye: Satellite Imagery, "Battlespace Awareness," and the Structures of the Imperial Gaze', *Surveillance & Society*, 4(1/2): 101–122.

Herz, John H. (1959) *International Politics in the Atomic Age*. New York: Columbia University Press.

Jasanoff, Sheila (2001) 'Image and Imagination: The Formation of Global Environmental Consciousness' in Clark A. Miller and Paul N. Edwards (eds) *Changing the Atmosphere: Expert Knowledge and Environmental Governance*. Cambridge, MA: MIT Press.

Kurgan, Laura (2013) *Close Up at a Distance: Mapping, Technology and Politics*. New York: Zone Books.

Lazier, Benjamin (2011) 'Earthrise; or, The Globalization of the World Picture', *American Historical Review*, 116(3): 602–630.

Lamy, Jérôme and Arnaud Saint-Martin (2014) 'The Politics of Earth Observation', in Cathy Dubois, Michael Avignon and Philippe Escudier (eds) *Observing the Earth from Space: Space Data – Social and Political Stakes*. Paris: Dunod.

Litfin, Karen T. (1998) 'Satellites and Sovereign Knowledge: Remote Sensing of the Global Environment', in Karen T. Litfin (ed.) *The Greening of Sovereignty in World Politics*. Cambridge, MA: MIT Press.

Litfin, Karen T. (1999) 'The Status of the Statistical State: Satellites and the Diffusion of Epistemic Sovereignty', *Global Society*, 13(1): 95–116.

Litfin, Karen T. (2002) 'Public Eyes: Satellite Imagery, the Globalization of Transparency, and New Networks of Surveillance', in James N. Rosenau and J. P. Singh (eds) *Information Technologies and Global Politics: The Changing Scope of Power and Governance*. Albany, NY: SUNY Press.

Lovelock, James (1989)*Gaia: A New Look at Life on Earth*. Oxford: Oxford University Press.

Masco, Joseph (2010) 'Bad Weather: On Planetary Crisis', *Social Studies of Science*, 40(1): 7–40.

Masco, Joseph (2012) 'The End of Ends', *Anthropological Quarterly*, 85(4): 1107–1124.

Malcolm, Andrew (2010) 'Sometimes a Pentagon Missile Logo is Just a Missile Logo', *Los Angeles Times* online, 26 February. Available at http://latimesblogs.latimes.com/washington/2010/02/logo-missile-defense-agency.html (accessed 15 September 2014).

National Geospatial-Intelligence Agency (2014a) 'Homepage'. Available at www1.nga.mil/Pages/default.aspx (accessed 15 September 2014).

National Geospatial-Intelligence Agency (2014b) 'Office of Geomatics: World Geodetic System 1984 (WGS 84)'. Available at http://Earth-info.nga.mil/GandG/wgs84/ (accessed 15 September 2014).

National Geospatial-Intelligence Agency (2014c) 'NGA Products and Services'. Available at www1.nga.mil/PRODUCTSSERVICES/GEOINTANALYSIS/Pages/default.aspx (accessed 15 September 2014).

Oikonomou, Iraklis (2012) 'The European Defence Agency and EU Military Space Policy: Whose space odyssey?', *Space Policy*, 28(2): 102–109.

Parks, Lisa (2009) 'Digging into Google Earth: An Analysis of "Crisis in Darfur"', *Geoforum*, 40(4): 535–545.

Peoples, Columba (2010) *Justifying Ballistic Missile Defence: Technology, Security and Culture*. Cambridge: Cambridge University Press.

Perkins, Chris and Martin Dodge (2009) 'Satellite Imagery and the Spectacle of Secret Spaces', 40(2): 546–560.

Pilger, John (2006) *Freedom Next Time*. London: Transworld Publishers.

Poole, Robert (2008) *Earthrise: How man first saw the Earth*. New Haven, CT: Yale University Press.

Salter, Mark B. and Can E. Mutlu (2013) 'Securitisation and Diego Garcia', *Review of International Studies*, 39(4): 815–834.

Science on a Sphere (2014) 'What is Science on a Sphere?' Available at http://sos.noaa.gov/What_is_SOS/index.html (accessed 15 September 2014).

Sheehan, Michael (2007) *The International Politics of Space*. Abingdon: Routledge.

Slijper, Frank (2009) 'The EU Should Freeze its Military Ambitions in Space', *Space Policy*, 25(2): 70–74.

Smith, Neil (1992) 'History and Philosophy of Geography: Real Wars, theory Wars', *Progress in Human Geography*, 16(2): 257–271.

Stahl, Roger (2010) 'Becoming Bombs: 3D Animated Satellite Imagery and the Weaponization of the Civic Eye', *MediaTropes*, 2(2): 65–93.

United States Strategic Command (2014) 'Command Emblem'. Available at www.stratcom.mil/emblem/ (accessed 15 September 2014).

Walker, R. B. J. (2010) *After the Globe, Before the World*. New York: Routledge.

Whole Earth Catalog (2014) Available at www.wholeEarth.com/history-whole-Earth-catalog.php (accessed 15 September 2014).

Afterworld

Paul N. Edwards

Before we scale up, let's scale down – way down. Consider: over 90 percent of the cells in 'your' body aren't you. They're microbes in your gut, in your mouth, on your skin, elsewhere too. They eat first, then you eat their waste products; without them, you can't digest much. They surround your body, in a detectable bacterial cloud (Meadow et al. 2015: 305). They even control your mind. (Well, that might be an exaggeration, but they do make neuro-chemicals that can affect your mood.) Viewed this way, you're a 'human supra-organism' (Turnbaugh et al. 2007). Your meta-genome – yours plus that of all your (very) little symbionts – contains at least a hundred times as many genes as the DNA in your own chromosomes, enabling you to benefit from many genetic capabilities that human bodies, alone, do not possess (Yang et al. 2009).

If we extend this idea to everything involved in eating, as Annemarie Mol has been urging, we rapidly arrive at a radically decentred understanding of actors and action. For Mol, as for Bruno Latour, in Western traditions the archetypal 'actor' has always been an isolated individual who thinks and chooses, while the archetypal 'action' is, in the first instance, the motion of an individual muscular body: walking, grasping, fighting. Reconceived as an eater, however, an actor is never alone or independent. Eating implicates soil bacteria, manure, plants, carbon dioxide, oxygen, animals, farmers, water, food safety organizations, shipping, trucking, refrigerators, cooks, more water, gut bacteria, compost, more animals, more bacteria, excrement, toilets, even more water, sewers, methane, sludge. And so on.

For eaters, accounts of action become accounts of 'integration, spreading out, and letting go' (e.g. releasing excrement – about half of which, on any given day, consists of dead gut bacteria). Only a little of what eaters do involves individual thought, consciousness, or choice. A lot more involves socio-technical systems and infrastructures of widely varying sizes: farming, shipping, kitchens, waste disposal, sewer systems. Even more of the things eaters do, really the great majority, are wrapped up with other organisms, nutrients, water, air and soil.[1] Mol's 'actor as eater' takes us beyond indivi-dualism, beyond social constructivism, beyond societies and actor networks to a humbling yet potentially inspiring eco-logical view. Human eaters, she might say, belong to socio-techno-ecologies comprised of entities both much larger and much smaller than human beings. In staggering numbers, many of these entities are also alive. *Entia non sunt multiplicanda praeter necessitatem,* Ockham's razor tells us, yet when we take eaters as actors, necessary entities multiply all by themselves.

***

A similar shift of perspective lies mostly latent in this book. Most writers here are concerned (as I have been) with how globalities are created, asserted and deconstructed by means of concepts, language, ideas and ideologies. They ask after the many uses of the term 'global', the actors who invoke it, the context of assembly and the stakes involved. As they so vigorously reveal, globality has a complex, conflicted history, and it can mean a lot of things. For many, globalism has been a call to unity, whether individual (thinking globally), social (spaceship Earth), political (world government), or environmental (global climate change, the Anthropocene). Yet as usual in human affairs, unity competes perpetually with discord (Hardin's commons vs. multiple life-boats; areas belonging to 'mankind' vs. territorial sovereignty). 'Common' global futures formed, proliferated, morphed and disintegrated (the World Futures Institute). 'Solutions' to putatively global problems have figured multiple, often competing views of agency and power at many scales: carbon accounting for self-monitoring individuals; carbon trading in national and international markets; carbon taxes imposed by governments on corporations and consumers; or military concern with climate change as a threat to international security.

In these accounts the 'global' seems a human thing, something that must be 'assembled', in our title phrase, rather than simply found or encountered. Actors, action, actor networks *make* things global through language, discourse, law, organizations, economies and polities.[2] Global assemblages have material elements and do material work, but those who do the assembly are always human actors or groups. From this perspective, globality comes across as an idea, a concept and/or a classic boundary object: a singular term with multiple meanings which somehow remains useful and usable for different people and groups with varying, even opposing stakes. You and Donald Trump can discuss the 'global economy' even though your 'global' and his are only remotely related.

This is so largely because the topologies of many globalities are not themselves globe-shaped, in the sense of smooth, evenly distributed spherical surfaces. In terms of human life and experience, most 'global' things – the economy, international law, common futures, the Framework Convention on Climate Change – are in fact lumpy, disjointed, full of holes and dropouts, much more network-y than spherical. To take just one example, Manuel Castells (along with many others) has emphasized the weird placelessness of the 'space of flows' inhabited by the most global citizens (such as Trump), those who travel the circuits among 'global cities' like New York, Singapore, Tokyo, London, and Hong Kong. Hopping across Rio, Shanghai and Bangalore in their helicopters, gazing down serenely on the festering slums below, they dwell in the premium spaces of airports, hotels, Trump Towers and tax havens whose very predictability and sameness facilitates the steady flow of premium people and their money (Castells 2000; Augé 1992; Graham and Marvin 2001). That's a globality very few of us inhabit. More glimpse it on business trips or wallet-sucking vacations; most see it only on television, if at all. Yet it's also one of the globalities where the greatest power resides.

At the same time, and for the same reasons, much of the planet remains imperceptible to such citizens; it appears to them, if at all, only as the assets and liabilities of corporate balance sheets, as pure Heideggerian 'standing reserve'. The billions living in poverty also remain invisible to certain 'global' perspectives. Among them are the many millions of migrants who traverse, in intimate, often perilous modes, the lands and seas claimed as resources – but rarely seen, much less experienced – by the supra-national super-rich. These immigrants too are global citizens, but they inhabit an entirely different world.

Globalities, then, turn out to be a tangled set of messy, contradictory, often failed or incomplete projects that look very different depending on who you are and where you stand. Many of our chapters wrestle with these projects and their meanings, interests and stakes, teasing apart globality's complexities and contradictions. One imagines a set of spherical Russian dolls, each globe containing another one, all similar yet also different. And all essentially human. The time scales are human, too; mostly here we're talking about the last 75 years or so. Sometimes a few centuries, never more. Much of our discussion takes place on the standard terms of academic airport security: intercepting passengers checked in on Global Airways, inspecting their ideological baggage and interrogating them about their social relations – especially should they be so unfortunate as to drop the word 'we' in an insufficiently specific way.

If you're seeking a less misshapen sphere, one that expands the 'we' in ways that might intrigue Mol or Latour, look past the global to the planetary. Used most often in this book to designate what scientists call 'the Earth system', the planetary seems larger, grander, and more multi-scalar than the global. Climates differ from place to place, nations clash over scraps from the economic pie – but at the planetary spatial scale, the atmosphere and oceans circulate unrestricted. Climate remains a unified physical system, driven by solar radiation and orbital cycles. On geological time scales, gigantic tectonic plates slosh around on Earth's semi-liquid mantle, colliding, raising mountain ranges and volcanoes. The Earth rotates and revolves around the Sun, ice ages come and go, sea levels rise and fall by hundreds of metres. Bacteria come into this planetary story too, and in a very big way. Somewhere between three and 2.3 billion years ago, when early cyanobacteria learned to photosynthesize, they generated so much oxygen (as a waste product) that they poisoned themselves out of existence in the Great Oxygen Extinction – not a bad simile for what human beings are doing today. This newly liberated oxygen reacted with and destroyed the vast quantities of methane that made up much of Earth's atmosphere at the time. This process reduced greenhouse gas concentrations so much that it triggered the Huronian glaciation, a 'snowball Earth' phase lasting at least 300 million years.

As evolution continued, oxygen-breathing microbes, animals and sea creatures became symbiotic, *on the planetary scale,* with the photosynthesizing, CO_2-breathing plants and plankton, each using the other as a source for its metabolism and a sink for its chemical waste (Canfield 2005; Crowe et al. 2013). In this way the atmosphere became the 'circulatory system of the biosphere', in Margulis and Lovelock's striking phrase (1975). Ecosystems thus came to strongly influence – if not exactly to control, as Gaia purists would have it – the composition of Earth's atmosphere, maintaining a planet fit for both CO_2-breathing plants and oxygen-breathing animals and microbes (Lovelock 2000; Schneider and Boston 1991).

On these larger scales of space, force and time, the human species is merely a ridiculous speck. Or rather it *was* a ridiculous speck, until July 16, 1945 at 05:29:21 Mountain War Time, plus or minus two seconds. At that moment, near Alamagordo, New Mexico, Manhattan Project scientists detonated the first atomic bomb, thus inaugurating what Masco (this volume) might call the Age of Fallout. The subsequent hundreds of above-ground atomic weapons tests left a signature that is, and will remain, 'easily identifiable in the chemostratigraphic record' over much of the world. As a result, a working group of the International Commission on Stratigraphy now recommends designating that moment as the start of the Anthropocene epoch (Zalasiewicz et al. 2015). That stratum also happens to align rather neatly with what scientists name the 'Great Acceleration' that began around 1950, a period of exponential growth in ... well, basically everything: population, industrial production, energy consumption, agriculture, natural resource extraction, domesticated animals, dams, waste, cars, pollution (Hibbard et al. 2006).

The Anthropocene marker designates humanity's graduation to the status of a geological force (a dubious distinction if ever there was one). Taken on its own terms, the Anthropocene joins human history to planetary geology in what Bruno Latour calls 'geostory' (Latour 2013b: 73). Peter Haff has argued that the current period of geostory has witnessed the rise of an autonomous planetary *'technosphere',* analogous to the biosphere, lithosphere, hydrosphere, and atmosphere.[3] For him, the technosphere is:

> the interlinked set of communication, transportation, bureaucratic and other systems that act to metabolize fossil fuels and other energy resources ... The technosphere is of global extent, exhibits large-scale appropriation of mass and energy resources, shows a tendency to co-opt for its own use information produced by the environment, and is autonomous. Unlike the [biosphere], the technosphere has not yet evolved the ability to recycle its own waste stream ... . Humans are 'parts' of the technosphere – subcomponents

essential for system function. Viewed from the inside by its human parts, the technosphere is perceived as a derived and controlled construct. *Viewed from outside as a geological phenomenon, the technosphere appears as a quasi-autonomous system whose dynamics constrain the behaviour of its human parts.*

(Haff 2014: 301, emphasis added)

This description of a quasi-organic, self-perpetuating, autonomous socio-technological globality will no doubt induce immediate heartburn in committed constructivists, for whom human choice is always possible and paramount. After all, science and technology studies has spent decades debunking theories of autonomous technology and billiard-ball notions of 'social impact' (Bijker et al. 1987; Winner 1977; Winner 1980).

And yet Haff's point is that the view of choice depends on where you stand. Every element of the technosphere indeed resulted at some point from contingent human choices, thus appearing to us as 'a derived and controlled construct' (Haff 2014: 301) Yet major infrastructures such as roads, railways, sewers, pipelines, power grids and the internet inhabit a temporal mesoscale of decades to centuries, enduring longer than most institutions, corporations and governments. As a result, each new generation encounters and experiences the infrastructures chosen, designed and built by its ancestors as quasi-natural background (Edwards 2002). To paraphrase Margulis and Lovelock, the technosphere has become the circulatory system of the sociosphere, conveying food, materials, information, knowledge, money, energy and waste. And, of course, people. New generations elaborate, improve and occasionally replace elements of this infrastructural second nature, but normally they can neither dispense with nor reject the whole of it, or even any of its major elements. In providing these infrastructures with materials, energy and maintenance, it is we who serve the technosphere.

The technosphere metabolizes not only fossil and nuclear fuels but also solar energy, through processes including photosynthesis (agriculture), wind and hydroelectric power. The technosphere's metabolites – its waste products – are in turn transforming both the biosphere and the geosphere. Microplastics, artificial chemicals and human-made radioactive materials can be detected in the cells of organisms all over the world, including in the deep oceans. Anthropogenic greenhouse gases and aerosols are transforming the planetary climate. Paraphrasing Foucault, we might thus say that the geostory that bears and determines us has the form of a metabolism (relations of consumption and waste), rather than that of a war (relations of power) or a language (relations of meaning).[4] As with the cyanobacteria before us, human beings' inability to take into account the *geological* effects of our activity is altering the very planetary parameters that enabled our evolutionary and societal success.

Nigel Clark's analysis (this volume) strikes me as apposite here. Post-World War II one-world projects to 'align human globality with the space-time of Earth' – the conceptual targets of much of this volume – are coming undone 'not simply because humankind is shot through with inequality and differ-ence, ... but because Earth in its very physicality convulses with differential and other-worlding forces'. With Clark, I believe it is a mistake to view phe-nomena such as global climate change – or concepts such as the Anthro-pocene, planetary boundaries, and the technosphere – as always or only manifestations of that old impulse to unify and align. Instead, they are har-bingers of a geostory that integrates, shapes and counterweights not only human history but also the geo-human future: the Anthropocene epoch.

***

Globe, planet ... world. Whatever we may think or say about it, we all inhabit and experience Earth as not only a meaning-bearing assemblage and physico-ecological support but also the very substrate of our species' inbuilt experi-ences of struggle, pain, beauty, love and death. For lack of a better word – or because there can be no better word – let us call this Earth-as-dwelling-place 'the world'. This brings us back to ancient structures of thought, found neither in concepts nor in data, but instead in archetypal narrative forms.

In *The Closed World* (1996), I described how one such archetypal narrative shaped the American view of the Cold War. Cold warriors represented the entire planet as a single, inescapable scene of superpower struggle, a theatre of total war where ideology, culture and politics all responded to a technological imaginary of panoptic surveillance and computerized control. This narrative became much more than a story; it became a central, framing discourse of Cold War strategy and policy. The containment policy inaugurated by Pre-sident Truman was much more than an abstract intention or aspirational statement. 'What I advocate is that *we defend every place, and I say we have the capacity to do it*. If you say we haven't, you admit defeat,' blustered General Douglas MacArthur to the US Senate in 1951.[5] Containment moti-vated, and then created, a globe-spanning infrastructure of C^3I: command, control, communications and intelligence. Cold War visionaries such as Jay Forrester and John von Neumann held that then-new digital computers would underpin this infrastructure, as indeed they have. In the 1950s, it was seen as the solution to the Soviet nuclear threat. Today, 'the C-cubed' (as geekier Cold Warriors liked to call it) has hypertrophied into C^4I^2 (Command, Control, Communications, Computers, Intelligence and Interoperability) and other, similar military mega-acronyms. The Bush-Obama drone assassination pro-grammes make the success of this infrastructure abundantly, sickeningly clear.

As the metaphors of scene, theatre and imaginary should convey, the closed-world concept descends from neither politics nor history, but instead from literary theory. The closed world's archetype is the siege, with the *Iliad* as originary model. War, either literal or figurative, is its driving force. Closed-world drama is marked by a unity of place, such as a walled city (Troy) or a castle (Elsinore, Dunsinane). The conflict that drives action in closed worlds occurs within its characters as well. Faced with relentless antagonists, including inner demons (Hamlet, Macbeth), they struggle to gain the upper hand, or at least to maintain control. Ultimately they duel with death. Offering no escape, closed-world dramas end in tragedy (Hawkins 1967). These are narratives of apocalypse, whether personal or collective.

The alternative to the closed world, in literary theory, is neither a boundless nor an open world. Instead, it is a *green world,* where action moves from town to forest, meadow or sea, from human-built to natural settings. Here magical, spiritual and natural forces are at play, in every sense (Frye 1957: 187ff). The green world's archetypal form is the quest. Its model is the *Odyssey*, an epic voyage across seas and lands filled with wonders, enchantments, terrors and strange beings, some benign, others malevolent. Green-world characters struggle not only to overcome but also to integrate the world's complexity and multiplicity. They journey toward fulfillment and renewal, enduring, like Odysseus, much suffering and many setbacks along the way.

Green-world drama thematizes the restoration of community and cosmic order through the transcendence of rationality, authority, convention and technology. Such narratives celebrate the power of love; they often end in marriage. Thus, the green world is indeed a space where the limits of law and rationality are surpassed. Yet it is no formless anarchy. Rather, it expresses the life-affirming opening of human-centred, inner, psychological logic into a magical, natural, transcendent one – an impulse that also underlies the 'deep ecology' movement and the natural religions (Abram 2011).

As archetypal narratives, both the closed world and the green world reflect vital aspects of human experience: conflict, loss and the inevitability of death, on the one hand; the bodily and spiritual sustenance of nature and the redemptive power of love, on the other. Today, they may be equally important as descriptions of realities we actually inhabit.

We live now in the age of the managed planet, of the 'rather fantastic effects' upon the climate that von Neumann (1955) imagined. We read daily of deadly serious explorations of 'geoengineering', of 'solar radiation management', the deliberate control of incoming sunlight to stop the planet from overheating. Schemes are afoot for orbiting Mylar mirrors the size of India; for fleets of robot ships spraying fine seawater mist to whiten the air and reflect heat; for rockets to blast the stratosphere with sulphate particles, artificial volcanic dust (Fleming 2010). Computer models are being put to work to test their effects and to compare the risks of their unintended consequences with the possibly even more terrible risks of doing nothing (Kravitz et al. 2013). Perhaps this is the ultimate version of the closed world: taming the green world as complex system, with feedbacks we can (try to) control and interacting systems we can (try to) master, and technologies so powerful they can regulate the sunlight reaching Earth.

Perhaps. But sometimes, instead, I still prefer to think the green world as Gaia, the mysterious, magical, sometimes terrifying superorganism to whom we belong and to whom we will return, and with whom we, the Earthbound (Latour 2013), must now negotiate our place. And sometimes, in my darker moments, I prefer to see the managed Earth we now inherit under another colour: blue, the Blue Marble of the famed Apollo photographs, the 'Whole Earth', the lonely planet lost in space. Blue, as in the sky we have altered beyond repair. And blue as in 'blues', the ineffable, insurmountable grief of a lost love, a ruined life, a world with no future – at least not for us.

The bacteria will, no doubt, survive.

Notes

1 Annemarie Mol, 'What if the actor were an eater?', oral presentation, Science, Technology & Society Program, University of Michigan, 13 April 2015.
2 See the discussions of 'making global data' and 'making data global' in (Edwards 2010).
3 If Google search results are to be believed, the Canadian control engineer J.H. Milsum (1968) coined the term 'technosphere' in the late 1960s, but the idea seems to have found few if any adherents prior to Haff's apparently independent conception.
4 'The history that bears and determines us has the form of a war rather than that of a language: relations of power, not relations of meaning' (Foucault 1980: 114).
5 General Douglas MacArthur in *Hearings Before the Committee on Armed Services and the Committee on Foreign Relations of the United States Senate*, 82nd Congress, 1st session to 'Conduct an Inquiry into the Military Situation in the Far East and the Facts Surrounding the Relief of General of the Army Douglas MacArthur from his Assignments in the Area' (1951), 68, 81–83. Emphasis added.

References

Abram, David (2011) *Becoming Animal: An Earthly Cosmology*. New York: Vintage.
Augé, Marc (1992) *Non-Lieux: introduction à une anthropologie de la surmodernité*. Paris: Le Seuil.
Bijker, Wiebe, Thomas P. Hughes and Trevor Pinch (1987) *The Social Construction of Technological Systems*. Cambridge, MA: MIT Press.
Canfield, D.E. (2005) 'The Early History of Atmospheric Oxygen: Homage to Robert M. Garrels', *Annual Review of Earth and Planetary Sciences*, 33: 1–36.
Castells, Manuel (2000) *The Rise of the Network Society*. Cambridge, MA: Blackwell Publishers.
Crowe, Sean A., Lasse N. Døssing, Nicolas J. Beukes, Michael Bau, Stephanus J. Kruger, Robert Frei and Donald E. Canfield (2013) 'Atmospheric Oxygenation Three Billion Years Ago', *Nature*, 501(7468): 535–538.
Edwards, Paul N. (1996) *The Closed World: Computers and the Politics of Discourse in Cold War America*. Cambridge, MA: MIT Press.
Edwards, Paul N. (2002) 'Infrastructure and Modernity: Scales of Force, Time, and Social Organization in the History of Sociotechnical Systems', in Thomas J. Misa, Philip Brey and Andrew Feenberg (eds) *Modernity and Technology*. Cambridge, MA: MIT Press, pp. 185–225.
Edwards, Paul N. (2010) *A Vast Machine: Computer Models, Climate Data, and the Politics of Global Warming*. Cambridge, MA: MIT Press.
Fleming, James R. (2010) *Fixing the Sky: The Checkered History of Weather and Climate Control*. New York: Columbia University Press.

Foucault, Michel (1980) *Power/Knowledge: Selected Writings and Other Interviews 1972–1977*. New York: Pantheon.

Frye, Northrop (1957) *Anatomy of Criticism*. Princeton, NJ: Princeton University Press.

Graham, Stephen and Simon Marvin (2001) *Splintering Urbanism: Networked Infrastructures, Technological Mobilities and the Urban Condition*. New York: Routledge.

Haff, P. K. (2014) 'Technology as a Geological Phenomenon: Implications for Human Well-Being', *Geological Society, London, Special Publications*, 395(1): 301–309.

Hawkins, Sherman (1967) 'The Two Worlds of Shakespearean Comedy', *Shakespeare Studies*, 3: 62–80.

Hibbard, K. A., P. J. Crutzen, E.F. Lambin, D. Liverman, N. J. Mantua, J. R. McNeill, B. Messerli and W. Steffen (2006) 'Decadal Interactions of Humans and the Environment', in R. Costanza, L. Graumlich and W. Steffen (eds) *Integrated History and Future of People on Earth*. Cambridge, MA: MIT Press, pp. 341–375.

Kravitz, Ben, Alan Robock, Piers M. Forster, James M. Haywood, Mark G. Lawrence and Hauke Schmidt (2013) 'An Overview of the Geoengineering Model Intercomparison Project (GeoMIP)', *Journal of Geophysical Research: Atmospheres*, 118(23): 13, 103–113, 107.

Latour, Bruno (2013) 'Facing Gaia: Six Lectures on the Political Theology of Nature', The Gifford Lectures on Natural Religion, Edinburgh, 18–28 February (draft version).

Lovelock, James (2000) *The Ages of Gaia: A Biography of Our Living Earth*. Second edition. Oxford: Oxford University Press.

Margulis, Lynn and James E. Lovelock (1975) 'The Atmosphere as Circulatory System of the Biosphere – the Gaia Hypothesis', *CoEvolution Quarterly*, 6: 30–41.

Meadow, James F., Adam E. Altrichter, Ashley C. Bateman, Jason Stenson, G.Z. Brown, Jessica L. Green and Brendan J. M. Bohannan (2015) 'Humans Differ in Their Personal Microbial Cloud', *PeerJ*, 3:e1258. Available at https://dx.doi.org/10.7717/peerj.1258.

Milsum, J. H. (1968) 'The Technosphere, the Biosphere, the Sociosphere: Their Systems Modeling and Optimization', *IEEE Spectrum*, 5(6): 76–82.

von Neumann, John (1955) 'Can We Survive Technology?' *Fortune*, 51: 106–108 and 151–152.

Schneider, Stephen H. and Penelope Boston (eds) (1991) *Scientists on Gaia*. Cambridge, MA: MIT Press.

Turnbaugh, Peter J., Ruth E. Ley, Micah Hamady, Claire Fraser-Liggett, Rob Knight and Jeffrey I. Gordon (2007) 'The Human Microbiome Project: Exploring the Microbial Part of Ourselves in a Changing World', *Nature*, 449(7164), 804.

Winner, Langdon (1977) *Autonomous Technology: Technics-Out-of-Control as a Theme in Political Thought*. Cambridge, MA: MIT Press.

Winner, Langdon (1980) 'Do Artifacts Have Politics?', *Daedalus*, 109(1): 121–136.

Yang, Xing, Lu Xie, Yixue Li and Chaochun Wei (2009) 'More than 9,000,000 Unique Genes in Human Gut Bacterial Community: Estimating Gene Numbers inside a Human Body', *PLoS One*, 4(6), e6074.

Zalasiewicz, Jan, Colin N. Waters, Mark Williams, Anthony D. Barnosky, Alejandro Cearreta, Paul Crutzen, Erle Ellis, Michael A. Ellis, Ian J. Fairchild, Jacques Grinevald, Peter K. Haff, Irka Hajdas, Reinhold Leinfelder, John McNeill, Eric O. Odada, Clément Poirier, Daniel Richter, Will Steffen, Colin Summerhayes, James P. M. Syvitski, Davor Vidas, Michael Wagreich, Scott L. Wing, Alexander P. Wolfe, Zhisheng An and Naomi Oreskes (2015) 'When Did the Anthropocene Begin? A Mid-twentieth Century Boundary Level is Stratigraphically Optimal', *Quaternary International*, 385 (October).

Index

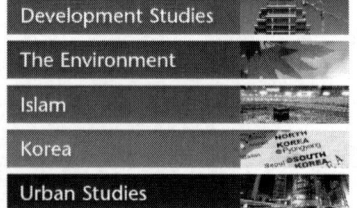